Flooring
1-2-3®

Meredith® BOOKS

Flooring 1-2-3®
Editor: Larry Johnston
Copy Chief: Terri Fredrickson
Publishing Operations Manager: Karen Schirm
Senior Editor, Asset and Information Manager: Phillip Morgan
Edit and Design Coordinator: Mary Lee Gavin
Editorial and Design Assistant: Renee E. McAtee
Book Production Managers: Pam Kvitne, Marjorie J. Schenkelberg,
    Rick von Holdt, Mark Weaver
Contributing Copy Editor: Don Gulbrandsen
Contributing Proofreaders: Becky Danley, Joel Marvin, Barbara Simpson
Contributing Indexer: Donald Glassman

**Additional Editorial and Design contributions from
    Abramowitz Creative Studios**
Publishing Director/Designer: Tim Abramowitz
Graphic Designers: Kelly Bailey, Joel Wires
Photography: Image Studios
    Account Executive: Lisa Egan
    Photographers: Bill Rein, John von Dorn
    Assistants: Rob Resnick, Scott Verber
    Technical Advisor: Rick Nadke
Additional Photography: Doug Hetherington
Illustration: Jim Swanson, Performance Marketing

Meredith® **Books**
Executive Director, Editorial: Gregory H. Kayko
Executive Director, Design: Matt Strelecki
Managing Editor: Amy Tincher-Durik
Executive Editor/Group Manager: Benjamin W. Allen
Senior Associate Design Director: Tom Wegner
Marketing Product Manager: Brent Wiersma
National Marketing Manager—Home Depot: Suzy Johnston

Publisher and Editor in Chief: James D. Blume
Editorial Director: Linda Raglan Cunningham
Executive Director, Marketing: Steve Malone
Executive Director, New Business Development: Todd M. Davis
Director, Sales—Home Depot: Robb Morris
Executive Director, Sales: Ken Zagor
Director, Operations: George A. Susral
Director, Production: Douglas M. Johnston
Director, Marketing: Amy Nichols
Business Director: Jim Leonard
Vice President and General Manager: Douglas J. Guendel

Meredith Publishing Group
President: Jack Griffin
Senior Vice President: Bob Mate

Meredith Corporation
Chairman and Chief Executive Officer: William T. Kerr
President and Chief Operating Officer: Stephen M. Lacy
In Memoriam: E.T. Meredith III (1933–2003)

The Home Depot®
Marketing Manager: Tom Sattler
© Copyright 2006 by Homer TLC, Inc.
All rights reserved.
Second Edition.
Printed in the United States of America.
Library of Congress Control Number: 2006921272
ISBN-13: 978-0-696-22857-5
ISBN-10: 0-696-22857-2
The Home Depot® and **1-2-3**® are registered trademarks of
Homer TLC, Inc.

Distributed by Meredith Corporation.
Meredith Corporation is not affiliated with The Home Depot®.

Note to the Reader: Due to differing conditions, tools, and individual skills, Meredith Corporation and The Home Depot® assume no responsibility for any damages, injuries suffered, or losses incurred as a result of following the information published in this book. Before beginning any project, review the instructions carefully, and if any doubts or questions remain, consult local experts or authorities. Because codes and regulations vary greatly, you always should check with authorities to ensure that your project complies with all applicable local codes and regulations. Always read and observe all of the safety precautions provided by any tool or equipment manufacturer, and follow all accepted safety procedures.

We are dedicated to providing accurate and helpful do-it-yourself information. We welcome your comments about improving this book and ideas for other books we might offer to home improvement enthusiasts. Contact us by any of these methods:
Leave a voice message at: 800/678-2093
Write to:
    Meredith Books, Home Depot Books
    1716 Locust St.
    Des Moines, IA 50309–3023
Send e-mail to: hi123@mdp.com.

How to use this book

P eople work on their homes for many reasons: to save money; to improve the home's beauty, value, or safety; to enjoy the satisfaction of a job well done; or, sometimes, simply because they enjoy the work. Whatever the reasons, success with a home improvement project depends on four factors:

- Mastering unfamiliar skills
- Using the right tools and materials
- Working safely
- Doing the job right the first time

Most homeowners need a little help balancing these components, so a home improvement resource—like *Flooring 1-2-3*—that's accessible, easy to use, and full of the right information can become one of the most valuable additions to a do-it-yourselfer's bookshelf. Here's how to get the most out of *Flooring 1-2-3*.

The wisdom of the aisles

Associates at The Home Depot have a genuine desire to help people say, "I can do that!" That's why these flooring experts from around the country have contributed their knowledge from years of on-the-job experience and the wisdom of the aisles to *Flooring 1-2-3*. Their contributions have helped create a hardworking, accurate, and easy-to-follow guide for every aspect of flooring, including design and planning, installation, maintenance, and repair.

The organizing principle

Flooring 1-2-3 consists of nine sections that provide detailed coverage of design and planning; preparing for installation; wood flooring; laminate flooring; vinyl flooring; ceramic and stone flooring; carpet; concrete; and trim, as well as an overview of all the tools you'll need for any job.

Doing the job step-by-step

All the projects include complete instructions along with detailed, step-by-step photography to make successful completion easy.

You have everything you need to do the job right the first time, following standards set by manufacturers and the trades—just like the pros.

Tips, tricks, and timesavers

Each page includes more than just instructions for completing the job. To help plan your project and schedule your time, each job is rated for difficulty and how long it might take you.

Project Details fills you in on the skills you'll need, time involved, and variables that might complicate the job.

Stuff You'll Need provides a materials list, along with commonly used tools.

Other features provide added information: *Buyer's Guide, Closer Look, Design Tip, Good Idea, Old vs. New, Safety Alert, Timesaver, Tool Tip,* and *Work Smarter* are bonus sidebars designed to help you work efficiently and economically. *Real World* sidebars describe difficulties do-it-yourselfers have encountered, and how to avoid them. Whenever a project involves something special—whether it's safety tips or getting the right tool—you'll be prepared for whatever comes up.

To make the best use of what's inside, read through each project carefully before you begin. Walk yourself through each step until you're comfortable with the process. Understanding the scope of the job will limit mistakes and prevent you from spending the money to redo a job.

Helping hands

Tips, insights, tricks, shortcuts, and even the benefit of 20/20 hindsight from the pros at The Home Depot help make any do-it-yourself project a snap. Years of experience translate into instant expertise for you. As you use this book look for these special icons, which signal detailed information on a specific topic.

BUYER'S GUIDE

Helps you select the best materials for the right price.

CLOSER LOOK

Provides you with detailed information about a task.

OLD VS. NEW

Points out new ways to work with old stuff.

WORK SMARTER

Tells about work practices that will save you time.

DESIGN TIP

Shows design options you can consider for your home.

TIMESAVER

Reveals shortcuts pros use to make a job go faster or easier.

TOOL TIP

Explains how to use tools for special situations.

GOOD IDEA

Offers tips and tricks that will get you the results you want.

SAFETY ALERT

Gives information that will keep you safe on the job.

Flooring 1-2-3®
Table of contents

Chapter 1
DESIGNING YOUR FLOOR 6

Chapter 2
TOOLS AND TECHNIQUES 46

Chapter 3
PREPARATION 68

Chapter 4
WOOD FLOORING 92

Chapter 5
LAMINATE FLOORING 126

Designing your floor

nterior designers often call the floor a room's "fifth wall." The floor is a major element in the room design that is frequently overlooked. It sets the tone for everything else in the room, so it deserves the same level of attention you pay to choosing paint colors, fabrics, window treatments, lighting, and furnishings.

When choosing flooring materials, consider how the room is used, who uses it, where traffic passes, and other design choices you have made for furnishings, lighting, and decorative elements. It may sound like a formidable job, but it can also be an enjoyable part of a room makeover. When you change your flooring, the effect is both immediate and dramatic.

This chapter will help you make big decisions by first exploring a series of smaller ones. You'll consider both aesthetic matters, such as style, scale, color, pattern, and texture, and practical issues, such as comfort, maintenance, safety, wear, noise control, and cost. Along the way, you will learn which skills are needed so you can decide whether you want to do all the work yourself or contract some of it out to a pro. And because the first flooring decisions concern materials, this chapter includes a survey of the available options.

Chapter 1 highlights

8 FLOOR-PLANNING ESSENTIALS
Getting organized is the first step in developing a good plan.

10 ELEMENTS OF DESIGN
Color, texture, pattern, and scale are important considerations when you select flooring.

14 PRACTICAL PLANNING
Study the functional aspects of different flooring choices as part of your planning.

18 WOOD FLOORING
A variety of wood products have long been popular for new flooring.

22 LAMINATE FLOORING
Laminates are synthetic products that wear like iron and look like other more costly materials.

24 RESILIENT FLOORING
Resilients are soft underfoot and include vinyl, linoleum, and other products.

28 CERAMIC TILE
Ceramic tile is the king of design possibilities with a wide range of colors, sizes, and styles.

32 STONE TILE
Stone tile has innumerable expressive powers and installs as easily as ceramic tile.

34 MOSAICS
Those tiny tiles that used to be set piece by piece are now bound together in a mesh-backed unit.

34 CEMENT-BODY TILE
Made of cement rather than clay, this durable material can give any room a rustic feel.

35 CONCRETE
Once just gray, concrete now comes in colors and designs you might not have thought possible.

36 CARPET
Carpet is more difficult to maintain, but nothing beats it where comfort is required.

39 AREA RUGS
Area rugs are a nice compromise between hard floors and carpet.

40 UNDERLAYMENTS AND MEMBRANES
Your planning is not complete until you have listed everything that goes under your new floor too.

41 ADHESIVES, GROUTS, AND SEALERS
These hold your floor in place, fill the seams between the pieces, and protect the surface.

42 TRIM AND TRANSITIONS
Baseboards, trim, and places where different flooring materials meet are design elements too.

Floor-planning essentials

t's easy and quick to change the appearance of a room with a new coat of paint or a few rolls of wallpaper. Those materials are relatively affordable and planning is relatively easy: You can make design decisions with a few color chips or paper samples. Planning a new floor, on the other hand, represents a larger expense and more involved installation, so you need to make sure your decisions are right the first time. Once the floor is down it's much harder and more expensive to pick it up and start over.

Making the right flooring choices starts your project on solid ground. Good decisions will result from spending time researching possibilities and examining your taste and personal style, consulting with professionals as necessary, and deciding how much of the installation you're willing to do yourself.

Basic questions

Your goal in planning and design is to choose flooring that will contribute both aesthetically and practically to the overall scheme—in a way you can afford. To begin, act as your own designer by answering some of the same basic questions a designer would ask you when starting a project.

Where will the new floor go? It sounds like an obvious question, but the answer is important because the physical characteristics of the flooring you choose must be appropriate for its location. If you're planning a basement room, solid hardwood flooring is not a good choice. Carpet might work if the slab isn't damp. Vinyl sheet goods might be perfect, especially if the area is wide open, which makes the job easy.

How will the room be used? Entryways get hard use and plenty of traffic. An entry floor has to be tough—ceramic tile or stone is both long wearing and attractive. Carpet might wear quickly and stain. A floor in a family room should be comfortable enough to stretch out on, especially for children. Kitchen floors might get dirty faster than any other floor—vinyl hides dirt and wears well. Make a family list of the uses of the room—let your lifestyle help define your flooring.

Is the floor part of a complete makeover or is it the only element you're changing? If the walls and furnishings will stay the same, take into account existing colors, window treatments, and furnishing style. If you're starting from scratch, pick the floor first and decorate the room around it.

What is the style of the room? The answer to this can be elusive, but your goal is to create an integrated environment that makes a unified style statement. If you're not sure what your personal style is or what style ideas you'd like to explore, take a look at "Discovering Your Own Style," on page 10.

How will the new flooring relate to the rest of the house? No room exists in total isolation. The kitchen floor moves into the dining room and that into the living room or family room. Even though the flooring in each room should relate to the particular room's purpose

and design, it also creates a visual relationship with adjacent rooms. That transition should be smooth and complementary, both visually and physically.

Plan the project in phases

Planning a flooring installation is easier if you break the process into phases. It may seem obvious, but it's important to make your decisions about design before you move forward with installation plans. Problems, sometimes expensive ones, can arise if you start spending time and money before you're sure about what you want. It's easy to change your mind on paper or while poring over samples in the store. It's much harder when you're halfway through an installation and are unhappy with the result you're seeing.

Need design help?

At this point you may want to seek advice from a professional designer. Home centers and flooring stores usually have a staff of consultants who can advise and guide you through the process. Many also offer the same design and installation packages provided by interior decorating firms.

Planning and installation from A to Z

Once you've decided on your design, you're ready to make a plan and put it into action. Here are the steps to follow when planning the installation of a new floor:

1. Make sure the subfloor can accommodate the new flooring. Tile and stone, for instance, are heavy and require a rigid, flat subfloor to support the weight.

2. Draw a scaled layout of the room on graph paper. Include all obstructions, such as pipes or heating units.

3. Calculate the square footage by multiplying the length and width, and shop around before you select a supplier.

4. Order the materials. Order 10 to 20 percent more than your estimate to account for mistakes, broken or warped pieces, color variations, or complex patterns. Store unused pieces for later repairs.

5. Allow plenty of time to complete the project. Don't expect to have a new floor in place by Thanksgiving if you start the planning on November 10.

6. Remove the old flooring. Before doing so, wait until you have the new flooring on-site so you can examine it to make sure it is what you ordered and is in good condition. Most manufacturers recommend that homeowners store flooring materials such as tile, laminates, and wood in the room for up to 72 hours to adjust to temperature and humidity levels.

7. Have a plan for disposing of the old flooring. Order a trash container, if necessary.

8. Prepare the subfloor. It's essential to have a subfloor that's in good condition, and meets the specifications given by the flooring manufacturer. Proper preparation is the most important

factor in a successful flooring installation—so critical that the warranty is often voided if a floor is installed over the wrong subfloor.

9. Install the flooring. Carefully read and follow the step-by-step instructions for the project you choose. Consult with experts if you need advice, and be sure to read and understand the manufacturer's instructions for installation. They take precedence over any other advice. Take your time: If the adhesive requires a certain amount of time to set up before installing the tile, wait patiently. Follow all the steps recommended for finishing the floor carefully. Make sure the job is done properly before you move furniture and family back into the room.

Building codes and common sense

Building codes enforce consistent methods of installation to ensure safety, but they can be confusing and sometimes seem unreasonable. If your flooring project involves electrical work or altering plumbing, new construction building codes may apply and must be followed. The procedures discussed in this book meet relevant national codes, but local codes can sometimes be more stringent. If you have concerns about your project, check with a local building inspector.

Common sense is more difficult to impart because it comes from instinct and experience. Practices that are common sense to a seasoned pro aren't always perfectly obvious to a do-it-yourselfer. Glazed tile on a bathroom floor or entry stairway, for instance, will be slippery when wet—somebody could get hurt. You also must consider important factors in relation to industry standards, good construction practices, and manufacturer's requirements for honoring warranties. Planning carefully and asking questions will help balance a lack of experience.

Elements of design

Style

Deciding on a particular style for a room is an important step in determining the right kind of flooring for that room. Because style can be difficult to define, it's sometimes helpful to start with the big picture and work toward specifics. Two generalized categories—formal and informal—will help you define your style.

Formal styles tend toward symmetry, using repetitive patterns and precise geometric relationships to create a sense of logic and order. Examples of more formal styles are traditional, colonial, and Victorian.

Informal styles incorporate asymmetry and natural patterns, shapes, and elements. Their geometries are often less precise and less ordered. Logic is subtle, derived from mixing and highlighting elements. Examples of informal styles include contemporary, Arts and Crafts, and country.

▲ Contemporary styles often rely on a simple and symmetrical arrangement of elements. The focus is uncluttered and basic and features a natural color palette. Hardwoods tend toward exotics such as bamboo, mahogany, and teak. Tiles are natural stone, such as marble, and may include inlay and mosaic. Polished concrete is often layered with area rugs of natural woven materials, such as hemp and sisal.

▲ A taste of the Southwest is created from Spanish and Native American influences. You'll see a strong desert inspiration in the color palette, thick, naturally pigmented quarry tile, natural stone, primitive patterns, and mosaic inlays. Softwood, wide-plank flooring, or wall-to-wall carpet in neutral tones might complete the decor.

Discovering your own style

If you are unsure which style best suits you, here are a few things you can do: First study home decorating magazines and cut out photos of rooms that appeal to you. Never mind why they have an appeal, just cut them out and stash them in a manila folder. Look around rooms in the homes of friends and neighbors, and when you get home, jot down what you saw and liked. Continue this for a few weeks, and when you get ready to make the final decisions, spread out everything from the folder on a table. Go through your collection piece by piece and toss the items that don't have appeal. Study the remaining ideas and look for consistent elements in them. Jot these elements down and use them to form a basis for the style of your room.

- Strong colors dominate. To add color without weight, break up the strong hues with an infusion of mosaic inlays or borders.
- Generally colors have greater intensity in larger spaces, particularly where a great deal of reflection and natural light exist.
- Reds and oranges become focal points. Yellows and violets create a feeling of warmth. Greens and blues lend a sense of serenity and calm.
- Deeper tones and shades lean toward formality.
- Lighter tones and tints are more relaxed and informal.
- Darker colors make rooms seem smaller, while lighter colors add to the sense of space.
- Glossy sheens reflect light; flat sheens absorb light.

◀ **Blue as the focus in a color scheme usually suggests coolness and serenity. In this western-style living room, however, blue combines with the warmth of white stucco walls, the rich blonde trim, and cozy colors in the area rug, creating a warm atmosphere.**

Color

Choosing color is perhaps the single most important design decision you'll make when putting together a room design. The process is most obvious when you are deciding how to treat the walls, ceilings, window coverings, and furnishings, but the floor color plays a significant role in the decisionmaking process as well. Even though there are fewer rules in the design trade than a half century ago, here are some tried and true guidelines you can rely on:

- Today's design standards give you a great deal of freedom to mix and match colors. If you trust your instincts and give yourself time to test color choices before making a final decision, you will usually be pleased with the results. It helps to know the color basics, whether you choose to follow or ignore them.
- In the natural world, darker colors tend to be at the bottom (earth) and lighter colors at the top (sky). You can reflect this in your home. Darker flooring carries visual weight and anchors a room, while lighter colors evoke transcendency.
- The most simple and soothing schemes usually have a single dominant color combined with complementary and accent colors.

▲ **This red-and-blue country-style bedroom is about basics. Pine-plank flooring is painted bold red but does not overwhelm the decor because the overall space is broken up with other colors and patterns. Where there is a danger of one strong color dominating, use area rugs to break it up.**

Pattern and scale

Pattern and scale go hand in hand in enhancing the mood or feel of a room. "Pattern" for flooring refers primarily to how the individual flooring units are arranged in a room. For example, the pattern of solid wood strip and plank flooring is linear and somewhat limited. Both will accentuate the linear qualities of a room. The patterns available in ceramic tile, on the other hand, are endless.

"Scale" refers to the relationship of the size of the material (or pattern) to the overall size of the room. In general, small rooms look better with smaller-scale flooring (small tiles in a small bathroom, for example) and larger rooms can make use of larger flooring units. The size of the pattern, however, can also affect this relationship. If you arrange small tiles in a large pattern, the effect of the pattern might overwhelm a small room. Here are some of the effects of flooring pattern and scale:

- Using the same flooring pattern throughout your home produces a connected, expansive feeling.
- Strip flooring laid parallel to the longest wall moves the eye forward, while horizontal layouts, parquet, or inlaid patterns retain the focus within their space.
- Shiny surfaces reflect light and feel more spacious, while surfaces with little or no sheen, such as carpet, absorb light and confine scale.
- Large planks or tiles in a small room accentuate the sense of smallness; smaller planks or tiles fit the scale.
- Isolated and irregular shapes in an otherwise symmetrical tile installation draw attention to themselves, while a series of shapes inlaid in a uniform progression, such as a border around the edge of a hardwood floor, create a sense of motion. Mixing the two can create a dramatic effect.
- Color is an essential ingredient in the perception of scale. Darker floors draw attention, defining and confining space. Lighter floors let other elements in the room become prominent, making the room feel larger.
- None of the guidelines is steadfast. Ignoring them in some cases will give the look you want for a room. Experiment with alternatives while you're making design decisions.

▲ **The combination of patterns and forms makes for strong visual interest. The inlaid geometric tile border surrounding the flowing pattern of the area rug dynamically defines this formal dining space.**

▶ **Here's an example of pattern and scale working together to enhance a room. The small size of the mosaic tile by itself might have ended up looking busy in some areas of this bath. Arranging contrasting tiles in an area creates a nice balance.**

Bold or subtle statements?

The more complex the pattern, the bolder the statement. Subtle patterns tend to meld into the overall concept of the room. Bigger and broader patterns become design statements in and of themselves. Bold choices, such as richly colored geometric area rugs, make the floor the focal point of the room.

In a small room with a large architectural detail—such as an extensive molding, for example—matching the scale of the flooring to the scale of the detail results in a strong and pleasing effect.

◀ **Mixing patterns produces bold accents. Large offset painted squares contrast sharply with the linear plank flooring, providing a dramatic accent to the room and making the floor something more than just a neutral background.**

Texture

Texture provides both a visual and a physical element in floor design. It affects not only the comfort and look of a room, but also its maintenance requirements and safety. Texture is best understood in opposites—soft/hard, thick/thin, rough/smooth.

For example, roughly textured natural stone can impart a rustic look underfoot—an excellent visual choice for a backdoor mudroom or sunroom. The mudroom choice, however, might be tempered by the fact that even though the rough textures are warm, friendly, and slip-resistant, they are more difficult to clean. For a stone floor that's easier to clean, choose etched marble or machine-made pavers—but be careful of polished surfaces. They clean easily, but are dangerously slippery when wet.

Plush carpet feels comfortable underfoot in a bedroom or living room where there's not much traffic or clean-up problems. The same carpet with a low pile works better in a child's room.

Textural juxtapositions add drama to a design while defining spaces. For example, a marble foyer easing into a living room floor covered with maple strips imparts a strong visual contrast while physically and visually separating the two areas. A flagstone floor on its own might be unsuitable for a family room, but combined with a lush area rug, it could be the perfect marriage of practicality and design. Use texture not only to help define a room's style but to define its purpose as well.

◀ **Bold color and texture on the floor add up to a visually stimulating, comfortable space. The area rug is a thick weave of colors that create an island of warmth on the wood floor.**

Practical planning

Comfort

When it comes to comfort, flooring materials generally fall into two categories—hard and soft. Hard floors—which also tend to feel cold—include wood, stone, ceramic, and concrete. Soft floors—which are more likely to feel warm—include carpet, resilient flooring, rubber, vinyl, and cork. Within these two basic categories are variations. Tile and concrete are harder than wood and, therefore, they're less forgiving. Resilient flooring is considered a soft material, but it is not as soft as carpet. Then, too, not all carpets offer the same comfort. Some are softer than others, depending on their thickness, material, and pile.

Comfort is primarily about how a floor feels underfoot, but there is also an emotional component. A solid wood floor is a hard material, but it may evoke pleasant memories in a living room. When you consider comfort, think not only about the physical properties of a material but how it supports the ambience you want for the room.

Form and function

The right floor for a room almost always depends on how it will be used. Extremely hard floors such as tile, hardwood, or concrete offer little or no resilience, which can make standing on them for long periods of time unpleasant or even painful. Ease of maintenance, however, makes these solid-surface materials natural choices for bathrooms and kitchens.

A combination of materials can provide livability and easy clean-up to virtually any room. Combining materials adds comfort without sacrificing aesthetic or practical concerns. A series of area rugs, for instance, provides comfort underfoot in the working areas of a kitchen.

Technology can also add warmth to flooring. A hard, natural stone floor offers a chilly reception on a winter morning, especially after stepping out of a warm bed or shower. But if natural stone is the way you want to go, consider installing radiant heating under it to warm the floor and make it more comfortable. Almost any flooring material can be warmed up with one of the many styles of radiant heating currently available.

▲ Ceramic tile has long been a favorite choice for bathroom floors. Add comfort to this otherwise cold material with electric or hydronic radiant heating.

▲ Hardwood floors came with this home, but when the owners wanted more comfort for their Georgian revival bedroom, the choice was easy. An area rug provides a softer surface than the wood flooring and blends perfectly with the design of the room.

▲ Tile is the perfect choice for this laundry room. It is durable, impervious to water, and easy to clean and maintain. Flooring choices for high-traffic, heavy-use areas such as this can be both beautiful and functional.

▲ Rough stone or textured ceramic tile provide good traction in slip-prone areas.

Maintenance

Flooring material needs cleaning and maintenance on a regular basis. Regular care lengthens the life of your floor, guarantees that the warranty will be honored, and keeps the surface looking its best. Once the floor is in use, dirt, stains, scratches, and tears are inevitable. The longer the time between cleanings and repair, the worse it becomes.

How much are you willing to do?

The amount of care a floor needs after installation and the amount of time you are willing to spend taking care of it are important planning considerations.

■ Choose flooring materials that are appropriate for how the room will be used. High-traffic and heavy-use areas such as entrances, staircases, landings, and kitchens might stand up to the wear and require less maintenance when covered in durable materials such as hardwoods, nonslippery tile, natural stone, vinyl, indoor/outdoor carpeting, or laminate. Softer coverings, such as plush carpet, work well in more lightly used areas, such as living rooms and bedrooms, where comfort is desired over durability. Keep in mind that wear varies from one area to another across the floor; edges tend to get less wear than major traffic areas, such as in front of a sofa or at an entrance.

■ Decide how much time you want to spend on care and maintenance. Pick your flooring to fit your lifestyle. Some materials are more maintenance-intensive than others. Avoid carpet if you loathe vacuuming. Choose flooring other than light-colored, wall-to-wall carpeting for a beach house, a second home, or a primary residence with children or pets.

Maintenance requirements vary even among similar materials. Ceramic tile requires less maintenance than natural stone, which must be resealed and polished occasionally. Cork and hardwoods also require reapplication of sealers and finishes as they wear.

Safety

Safety is a primary concern when choosing flooring. Falls are dangerous for everyone, but especially so for children, the elderly, and the physically challenged. The majority of slips and falls that occur inside households are due to improper installation and maintenance of materials, a buildup of grease and grime, extensive wear, or the properties of the flooring material itself. You can avoid many accidents if you put the right flooring materials in the right places and properly maintain them. Here are some common potentially slippery areas:

■ Hard surfaces, especially those that are polished or glazed.
■ Grease or liquid spills in a kitchen or water puddled on a bathroom floor.
■ Area rugs without a slip-resistant backing.
■ Carpet improperly secured on stairs.
■ Highly polished ceramic tile or plush carpet on a staircase or entry floor.
■ Loose tiles or floorboards, as well as protruding nails or staples.
■ Extensive carpet wear, such as holes or tangles of fiber.
■ Uneven transitions between rooms or types of flooring.
■ Flooring material that visually obscures transitions between levels.
■ Wood floors that are not properly sanded and sealed. (They present the risk of splinters for bare feet.)

The least slippery surfaces are rubber, textured surfaces, low-pile or indoor/outdoor carpet, surfaces with low-gloss or no-gloss finishes, and surfaces that absorb water.

▲ **A runner adds color and pattern while dampening sound on a hardwood staircase. Brass rods keep the carpet in place.**

Sound control

How a floor sounds when you walk on it is an important consideration that is often overlooked when designing a room. The look of quarry tile or inlaid hardwood might be perfect for your design, but if the click-clack of heels or the scratching of pet's claws on the surface drives you crazy, opt for flooring that diminishes sound rather than accentuates it.

The harder the material, the noisier it is, generally. Hardwoods, tile, natural stone, and concrete fall into the noisy category. Softer flooring materials, such as carpet, rubber, vinyl (sheet and tile), cork, and linoleum, all have noise-dampening qualities. These materials also reduce the transfer of noise from one level to another in multistory dwellings.

Laminate flooring is a hard material, but the foam underlayment required for its installation provides good sound insulation. Carpet provides the most complete acoustic control, but where wear and maintenance prohibit carpet, cork flooring, which is used extensively in public spaces, is an extremely effective sound dampener. Cork is also incorporated into some laminate flooring materials to make it more sound absorbent.

To further increase the separation of noise from one space to another, install soundproofing materials underneath the floors (hardwood frames only, of course). In some cases your soundproofing material can go between the finished surface and the subfloor. In others, like tile and natural stone, which require rigid subflooring, soundproofing means installing insulation under the subfloor.

Area rugs on wood or ceramic tile can help deaden the sound within a room and reduce its transference to other parts of the house. Laying a soft and more sound absorbent pathway, such as a carpet runner, through a room with hard flooring is another option for acoustical control.

Cost

There's a variation of the adage "You get what you pay for" that applies to flooring—"Buy the best you can afford." Then install and maintain it properly.

Higher-quality flooring stands up to wear and tear better, lasts longer, may require less maintenance, and is sometimes easier to install. (Some materials, however, require removal of the existing floor and installation of a new subfloor and you should treat these costs as part of the cost of the new material itself.) Manufacturers of premium flooring usually offer better warranties, more complete product information, and better service.

Wood flooring is a special case when it comes to the questions of cost and longevity. Although all woods will eventually show wear and suffer dings and dents from dropped objects and traffic, wood floors can be considered cost-effective in the long run because you can refinish them, often more than once. Even do-it-yourself refinishing is not inexpensive, but it is less than the cost of replacing with new materials.

When pricing materials, factor contracted labor, subfloor repair, and waste disposal expenses into the cost. Even the best installer wastes 10 to 20 percent of the flooring during installation. Trimming materials to meet out-of-square walls, encircle pipes, or fit snugly in corners makes a surprising amount of waste.

To get an overall view of your investment, consider the cost of your flooring in relation to the number of years you will use it. If you intend to remain in a house for only a few years, an inexpensive flooring may be more appropriate. Good-quality laminates and engineered wood flooring offer the look of wood and other materials without the high cost—and they won't decrease the resale value of your home.

▲ **Assess your flooring needs carefully and buy the best materials you can afford.**

Evaluate your skills

Good store associates will do their best to qualify customers for flooring projects by asking some basic questions to get a sense of their abilities and interests. These associates are more than curious—they want you to succeed.

These are some questions you should ask yourself before tackling a project:

- Do you enjoy working on your house? If the answer is yes, move on to the next question. If the answer is no, pass this book on to someone who does.
- Do you mind getting dirty? Flooring projects can be messy and require a lot of cleanup.
- How about heavy lifting? Cartons of tile and hardwood and bags of mortar are heavy. Physical labor is part of installing a floor.
- Do you like working with tools? Do you have any? Most flooring projects involve a variety of hand and power tools. You may need to add tool costs to the price of your investment.
- How are you at geometry? Abilities to visualize level and vertical surfaces and compute dimensions and areas (including fractions) are required for flooring installation.
- Are you willing to do research and make a plan? Understanding the process and scope of a project is essential. Learn the skills and understand safety issues before you begin.
- Do you know your limitations? It's OK to admit that a particular project is a little beyond your current skill level. It's better to pay a professional to do a job you're not comfortable with than to pay extra for someone to fix a mistake.

Ready for the mess?

You never know what's under your existing floor. Even the experts can't tell you what's under there without looking. If you live in a newer home, it may be a subfloor and it may be in good shape. If your home is older, it could be a couple of other floors, the last of which might be solid oak strip flooring. No matter what it is, in most cases it will either have to be removed or repaired in some way—and repair and replacement mean dust.

Home remodeling projects are not only time-consuming, they're messy. You'll save yourself a lot of frustration if you take steps to minimize the infiltration of the mess into the rest of your home.

First find out if and when your trash service takes remodeling debris. Then plan your job so you do the rip-it-up work in warm weather. That way you can open a window to toss out the debris. For first-floor jobs you can either bag or tie up the trash indoors or pile it outdoors and dispose of it later. For second-story projects build a plywood chute and hang it on the window. If you're tearing up a large area, let the chute empty into a trash container.

Keep another window open and put a window fan in it to exhaust the dust. Even if you can close the workspace off with a door, hang a plastic sheet on the work side to keep the dust from being sucked out when you open and close the door. Put a rug or carpet sample just outside the work area to take the dust off the bottom of your boots when you leave. And leave the boots on the rug at the end of each workday.

Wood flooring

f you're looking for flooring with warmth and classic, timeless beauty, then wood might be the best choice. Wood floors provide an ideal backdrop for almost any decorating style. Even when stained to a dark tone, they provide a neutral yet distinctive presence that anchors a room without calling attention to itself. Properly installed, wood floors can outlast the house they're in, and the patina they acquire with age increases their beauty.

Browse through the aisles of your home center and you'll find several species of wood flooring, generally in any of three styles: solid wood flooring, engineered flooring, and parquet.

Solid wood flooring

"Solid" exactly describes this kind of flooring; it's wood clear through. Wood flooring is manufactured from several species and three styles: strips (2¼–3 inches wide × ¾ inches thick), planks (more than 3 inches wide × ¾ inches thick) or random-width planks. All come in random lengths. Strips are milled with tongues on one side and grooves on the other. When you install this flooring, you drive nails diagonally through the tongues, anchoring the material solidly to the subfloor. Some plank flooring comes with tongues and grooves, but most have square edges.

You can purchase solid wood flooring either unfinished or prefinished. Unfinished flooring requires sanding and roughly two weeks of work, but allows you to choose the stain that's just right for your room. Prefinished flooring has a tough synthetic varnish. Prefinished flooring is ready to walk on the minute you install it. Many prefinished brands have a chamfered or rounded edge, which hides unevenness in the installation by creating a small valley between boards.

What species you choose will depend largely on the style of your room and the size of your budget. You will hear the terms "hardwood" and "softwood" when you're shopping for flooring, but don't let them mislead you. They are not so much an indicator of the durability of the wood as what kind of tree it comes from. Hardwoods come from trees that lose their leaves. Softwoods come from evergreens.

Pine, hemlock, and fir

Pine tends to dent more easily than most hardwoods, but fir is a hard flooring. Older softwoods were much tougher, and many homes from the 1930s, '40s, and '50s have strip floors made of long-leaf Southern yellow pine, which is worth refinishing if it's basically in good shape. Pine, hemlock, and fir are perfect for creating a country look but might seem a little too casual in a formal dining room. In many retail outlets, softwoods are special-order flooring.

Maple and birch

Maple and birch are look-alike species. Each displays a whitish color with light brown grain lines. The pores are closed, and the wood is very

▲ Wood floors tend to exhibit a consistent tone. If your floor needs a lot of variety, consider mixing two species, a dark walnut with a lighter birch or oak. The contrasting tones can be startling and bring drama to the room.

▲ Strip flooring, a favorite choice for the better part of a century, works well in contemporary settings. Choose a light wood with grain sections that will darken with stain. Quartersawn oak has a wonderful array of design applications.

▲ **Plank flooring creates a country or traditional look because it was the flooring commonly used by early home builders. You can achieve the same effect today by using wide planks with plugged screw holes along the edges.**

◀ **An inlaid border can help divide large areas into smaller spaces and add variety to wide expanses of solid wood flooring.**

smooth as a result. (They are used for bowling alleys.) Both woods are usually given a clear finish and no stain. The surface burns easily during sanding, so leave finishing to a professional. Both are good for creating a clean, modern look or a light floor when you need to brighten up a dark room.

Oak

Oak is a light brown wood with dark grain lines and open pores. It comes in two types: red oak and white oak. Red oak has a pinkish tinge. The grain in white oak is more subtle than in red, and white oak is somewhat browner than red oak. Oak is easy to finish and is usually stained to make it somewhat darker. It's good for creating a traditional-looking floor.

Ash

Ash is the wood baseball bats are made of. It's whiter than oak, looks a lot like it, and wears about as well. It's difficult to finish and is usually a custom-order floor.

Walnut and cherry

Both woods are favorites of furniture makers because they are attractive, stable, and work well. They are tough but softer than oak. Walnut is brown with open pores and finishes easily. Cherry is a lighter reddish brown with closed pores, and the surface tends to burn when sanding. The color of walnut usually lightens with age, while cherry's red color deepens as the years go by. Both are special-order woods and expensive.

Low-grade lumber— for the right floor

Lumber grading includes a careful assessment of the appearance of boards. In one way it is an indication of quality, but it's one you may not necessarily need to include in your consideration of flooring. Select lumber (one of the best grades) exhibits a uniform color from board to board and has no knots. Common lumber contains small knots and variations in coloration from board to board. Both grades will wear about the same, so when it comes to longevity, you may not need a high-grade lumber. For a rustic design theme, the appearance of a lower grade of flooring may in fact be just what you're looking for—and it's a lot cheaper. (It may be a special order, however, and probably won't be available prefinished.)

Engineered hardwood

Engineered hardwood flooring is made of wood, but it's not solid. Instead it is a laminated product like plywood, with a thin but tough veneer of real wood on top laminated to three to five layers of less expensive wood (or medium-density fiberboard) and bonded under pressure with strong glues. The grain of every other sublayer runs at right angles to the others, resulting in a remarkably strong (but less expensive) product. The cost is less because there is less hardwood used (generally a layer ⁵⁄₁₆ inches thick). Its thinner profile weighs less and costs less to ship.

This innovative product helps conserve forests by using less hardwood. It is sold in strips, planks, or planks composed of several strips joined. Multistrip planks are the most common choice because installation goes more quickly. You can cover a lot more floor faster with a three-strip, 7-inch plank—in a third less time and effort than with three individual strips.

Engineered advantages

Because of its construction, engineered hardwood brings with it a number of advantages over solid wood flooring.

- Its laminated layers make it more dimensionally stable than other flooring and therefore less subject to the effects of moisture. You can use it above grade, at grade, or below grade.
- Installation is easier—some brands simply snap together, others require staples, adhesive, or glue. Wider planks allow you to cover more floor area faster.
- Engineered floors come prefinished with a tough varnish coat. You can install it in the morning and use it that evening.
- Its thin profile (generally ⅜-inch thick) might allow installation in a kitchen without having to remove the old floor to get undercounter appliances in and out.

On the other hand . . .

There are some drawbacks, of course. Because the hardwood top layer is only ⁵⁄₁₆ inches thick, it will withstand only one sanding and refinishing. (Solid wood can be refinished three times.) Assuming a refinish job every 12 years, an engineered floor will last 24 years, while a solid floor will be good for 48 years. (The thin veneer does not leave much room for error—sanding is a job for the pros.)

Engineered flooring is manufactured with chamfered edges, which you might find somewhat more difficult to clean.

But what does it look like?

In general, you'll find the same hardwood species available in engineered floor as in solid wood stock—but with several (and increasingly more) additions. Manufacturers are adding exotic woods to their inventories because these woods offer dramatic design opportunities. The thin veneer makes the costly woods affordable and forests are not rapidly depleted. These woods offer design possibilities that are simply not available in domestic woods.

▲ Engineered flooring is assembled with tongues and grooves like solid wood flooring, but is thinner than solid wood. The tongue-and-groove edges keep the top surface of each plank level with the rest.

▲ Even at close range, you might find it impossible to tell an engineered wood floor from solid wood. Engineered products offer the same design flexibility at a lower cost.

◀ Planks are also a mainstay of engineered flooring. You'll find them in two forms—as single and multiple boards. But like other engineered products, you can't tell them from solid wood.

Affordable exotics

If you're in the market for a new floor, look for affordable engineered exotic wood products. Brazilian cherry, bamboo (actually a grass as shown above), and teak are showing up on an increasing number of residential floors.

Parquet tile

Parquet tile is one of the most subtle flooring materials. It brings an understated variety and pattern to a floor, providing interest without becoming overwhelming. It was a choice available only to the wealthy in times past because each strip (or fillet) of wood was laid separately—a job requiring a skilled craftsman and a big budget. Today parquet is available as ready-made tiles that can be adhered to the floor.

Fillets for the tiles can be cut from a wide range of wood species and in several configurations—in wide parallel strips and narrower angled patterns. The beauty of parquet is enhanced by its changing geometries as well as the spread of slightly different wood tones across each tile. What's more, it's easy to install using an adhesive made specifically for this purpose. In higher grade parquet, the tongues and grooves are milled to give each corner a perfect fit. Don't scrimp on the cost of this flooring. Inexpensive parquet may have a thinner veneer layer, which won't wear well, and its glues may deteriorate over time, leaving you with loose or curled fillets.

▶ Parquet is a tile made of individual pieces of wood. It installs like a vinyl tile but gives you the opportunity to create visual effects impossible with other tiles.

Laminate flooring

L aminate flooring has been popular in Europe for more than 25 years but is a relatively new product in the U.S. It's completely synthetic, with a tough melamine wearcoat over a kraft-paper (or medium-density fiberboard) core. The beauty of laminate flooring is that it can be made to look like any material—stone, ceramic tile, wood, and more—at a fraction of the cost of the real thing. The effect is achieved in the second layer, which contains a photographic representation of the real flooring material. In its early days, laminate was faulted for looking unrealistic, but today's technology gives the surface of laminate planks the texture as well as the look of wood, tile, or stone. What's more, the construction of laminate flooring results in a stable product that can be installed below grade.

Laminate flooring goes down easily—most products simply snap together and the planks float on a layer of plastic foam underlayment. You can use it where you can't use wood. You can install it without spreading the adhesives you'd need for vinyl or installing sheets of cement backerboard as you would for ceramic tile. The underlayment provides some resilience as you walk on it, which makes a more comfortable surface than stone,

wood, or tile. The underlayment also helps deaden sound in the floor.

In its early generations, laminate floors were available as pieces that glued together along the edges. Some manufacturers recommend glued laminate for kitchens or bathrooms, where watertight joints are required, or for hard-use areas like recreation rooms. Installations that snap together create a floor that's one large piece, held down around the edges by a baseboard or shoe molding. Because the pieces do not need to be nailed or screwed

■ **By far, the most popular installations are of laminates that imitate wood. In the photo on the left, the laminate resembles a wide plank floor, right down to the faux saw marks. In the photo above, the laminate is made to look like oak.**

to the subfloor, laminates make a great floor covering for concrete.

Laminate wear layers are tough and durable—made from the same polymer as laminate countertops, but thicker. They stand up extremely well to dents, but not as well to scratches, and scratches in laminate can't be rubbed out or repaired. That makes them a less-than-ideal floor for backdoor mudrooms and other rooms that are likely to receive rough abrasive treatment and get scuffed up from shoes coming indoors. The melamine finish is hard, resists dirt, and requires only periodic damp mopping.

◀ **Durability is one advantage of laminate flooring. Another plus is that it can look like many different materials. You can buy planks that look like wood, wood inlay, or ceramic tile, as shown here. Some patterns are available as planks or square tiles, although the patterns available in tile may be fewer in some areas.**

Grain patterns more versatile than Mother Nature's

Some laminate products are available with a wood-grain look that minimizes the possibility that you'll repeat the same pattern across the floor. The grain pattern is configured so pairing pieces creates the illusion of one continuous plank, no matter which combination of the planks you use. The photos show plank 1 paired with plank 2 and again with plank 3, both continuing the grain.

Quality is invisible

Two pieces of laminate flooring can look identical but vary widely in quality. That's because of the thickness of the melamine wearcoat. The thicker the layer, the longer the floor is likely to last. But since the wear layer is virtually invisible, you have no way to tell how thick it is.

Warranties give you a clue: The planks with the thickest wear layer will also have the longest warranty—as much as 25 years or more. They will also be the most expensive, but at least you know why.

Resilient flooring

Resilient flooring materials are designed to bounce back when compressed (or dented). Vinyl sheet goods and vinyl tile are the most commonly used resilient flooring materials, but the category also includes cork, rubber, leather, and certain soft plastic interlocking materials used chiefly as garage floor coverings.

Resilients have many advantages: easy installation, low maintenance, a profusion of design patterns, and moderate cost. Though they're not as soft as foam rubber, they are pliable enough to give some comfort underfoot and some small insurance that dropped dinnerware might not break. Spread over the surface of the floor, they weigh very little so they don't require reinforcement underneath. They do, however, require a surface that's absolutely smooth. Because resilient flooring is thin and flexible, any imperfections in the subfloor will be visible in the floor surface and could damage the flooring.

Vinyl sheet goods and vinyl tile are manufactured in two compositions—printed and inlaid. Printed vinyl is actually a photograph of a pattern, which can include stone, ceramic tile, and woods. As such, the pattern lies on top and is subject to wear. Inlaid vinyl carries its pattern into the body of the material so it's more wear resistant. It's also more expensive.

Vinyl sheet flooring

Vinyl sheet flooring comes in a variety of patterns in 12-foot-wide rolls. That width will fit many rooms with a minimal need for seaming. When seaming is necessary, consider locating the seam in the least conspicuous part of the room.

Vinyl is popular in kitchens, laundry rooms, and bathrooms. It's easy to clean, requires little maintenance, and is waterproof. You do need to be careful, however, because the adhesive that holds it in place is water soluble. Mopping with too much water will, over time, dissolve the adhesive, and the corners of the tile will start to lift.

The most common type of vinyl is felt-backed for strength. It is laid as a full-spread installation, which means you cover the entire floor with adhesive and unroll the vinyl back onto it. Another type, called modified loose lay, is extremely stable dimensionally and contains a fiberglass scrim. It's designed to be laid without general adhesive, using only strips of double-sided tape under appliances and at the door. The least commonly used sheet material is backed with vinyl and is designed to be glued to the floor around the edges only.

■ Not long ago, vinyl flooring was a bit drab. With today's manufacturing methods it can bring the look of more expensive materials—even marble and porcelain tile—into your home at a fraction of their cost, as shown in these floors.

Choose a sheet vinyl pattern to suit the room and help you create the right ambience. Some sheet vinyl is traditional and monochromatic. Some patterns imitate other materials, stone and parquet in these cases. Still others resemble no other surface you've ever seen, creating a whole new dimension of interest.

Vinyl tile

For ease of installation vinyl tile is less intimidating than vinyl sheet goods. Whether you lay the tiles in adhesive or use self-stick tiles, they go into place one piece at a time. It's easy to trim, and if you make a mistake, you've wasted only a single tile. Tile is also extremely versatile when you want to exercise creativity and develop patterns of your own. You can also use tile to generate a wide variety of effects. You can mix and match tiles to create patterns, or you can buy tiles with patterns that are almost identical to those found on sheet vinyl.

Underlayments

Vinyl must be installed over a plywood underlayment designed specifically for that purpose. Unapproved plywoods with rough surfaces can cause trouble—the roughness will eventually show through the tile. Natural pigments contained in woods like lauan eventually bleed through some tile and become visible. Unstable or poorly manufactured plywood may warp and lift your floor.

If the underlayment ruins your floor, it's covered by the underlayment manufacturer's warranty, not the vinyl manufacturer's warranty. Purchase an underlayment that's approved by the Engineered Wood Association (formerly American Plywood Association) for vinyl use. Appropriate plywood sports an APA stamp that says it's certified as underlayment for vinyl flooring.

▲ Some tiles are as vivid as others are tame. The pattern on the tile above mimics patterns in sheet vinyl, and once the tiles are down, they are virtually indistinguishable from sheet goods.

Printed vinyl and inlaid vinyl

The patterns on vinyl flooring materials are either printed or inlaid. Printed vinyl, sometimes called rotovinyl because of the printing process used to produce the pattern, is protected by a wear layer. It is available in a wide range of patterns and colors. Inlaid vinyl is made of millions of tiny granules of vinyl that are deposited in precise patterns and fused into a solid sheet. The inlaid vinyl pattern and color go clear through the tile. Most inlaid tiles require periodic sealing to keep dirt from migrating deep into the tile where you can't remove it.

Peel-and-stick tiles are printed tiles, and their surfaces are usually embossed to help create a three-dimensional effect. The quality of these tiles varies widely from manufacturer to manufacturer. Avoid tiles that are so flexible you can bend them almost edge to edge. They won't hold up.

▲ To create a surface that functions as a backdrop for the rest of the room, choose a vinyl tile with a ceramic pattern in a light color.

Cork flooring

Once used only in the most expensive homes, cork tile is now finding wider use. It's soft, resilient, dampens noise more effectively than other materials, and looks classy. Cork comes from the bark of the cork oak. Stripping it does not damage the tree, which regenerates new bark at a regular cycle of several years. Once harvested, the cork is ground and mixed with resins and dyes to create different tones. Cork installation is similar to installation for vinyl tiles.

▲ Contrasting vinyl tiles make a distinctive style in a room. Alternating tiles with the same dominant color creates a unified look. Alternating contrasting colors can create a modern or retro look.

Linoleum

Linoleum is the original resilient material. An amalgam of linseed oil, cork, wood, and sometimes stone chips, it was once popular for floors, countertops, and other surfaces. Although it seemed to have dropped from sight for a number of years, this flooring is experiencing a resurgence of interest, in part because of the muted colors and tones associated with it, and because linoleum is naturally resistant to bacteria. It also possesses antistatic qualities that make cleaning easier because it repels dust.

Linoleum is installed in sheets using the same techniques as for vinyl sheet flooring. Linoleum seams can be heat-sealed. Unless you have some experience with linoleum, heat-sealing is a task better left to a professional flooring installer.

Ceramic tile

Ceramic tile is one of the oldest manufactured materials. Tiled floors in some Roman ruins are still intact and 4,000-year-old ceramics have been found in ancient Mesopotamia. Durability that can be measured in thousands of years makes tile a flooring worth considering.

Ceramic tiles are slices of clay fired at high temperatures—usually between 1,900 and 2,100 degrees. Color can be applied as a glaze that tints the surface, or it may be mixed with the clay. When glaze is applied directly to untreated clay, the tile is single-glazed. Double-glazed tiles are fired, coated with glaze, then refired. Single-glaze tiles are more vivid; double-glaze tiles show patterns better.

Tile comes in so many colors, shapes, and textures that deciding on a design for your tile floor can be a challenge. Your best bet is to look at a lot of decorating magazines and tear out pictures of tile layouts that appeal to you. You'll soon find you lean toward particular floor designs, such as large handmade saltillo tiles or intricate mosaics. Mosaics are small tiles, often mounted on mesh sheets so you can lay them quickly. You can also use individual tiles (anything under 2 inches) to create elaborate patterns.

As you plan remember two things about tile: First, ceramics last for a very long time. Avoid trendy colors or designs unless you're sure you'll like them 40 years from now. Second, think about how the floor interacts with the walls around it. Because of their shape and color, tiles have a stronger design presence than wood or carpet. Make sure the tile design complements the style of the room. A multicolor floor made from several different-size tiles, for example, might not work well in a room with busy wallpaper. Buy sample tiles and take them home so you can study them for a while to make sure the color, scale, and texture add up to something you want in your home.

Porcelain tile

Porcelain tiles are ceramic tiles made from highly refined white clay. They are fired at an extremely high temperature—around 2,500 degrees—for nearly twice as long as other ceramic tiles. The result is an extremely dense, waterproof tile with a glossy surface. Porcelain tile wears extremely well, even under heavy traffic or wet and freezing conditions. Porcelain is sold as surface-colored or through-bodied tiles. Surface color can wear or chip off. The color of through-bodied tiles won't. Which one should you buy? Make your decision according to what you can afford and how much traffic the floor will get.

▲ Porcelain floor tiles and walls can work together to create a muted ambience that perfectly suits this country-style kitchen. Notice how the understated border, using the same muted tones as the rest of the floor, adds variety to the design and defines the dining area specifically.

Design choices

From a design standpoint, you can do almost anything with porcelain tile. Because its clay is white to begin with, it can take on almost any color. The tiles are extruded (pressed in a mold), so they can be given a texture that closely resembles stone tiles, tumbled marble, terra-cotta, polished marble, travertine, or other surfaces.

Maintenance

Large-scale porcelain tiles were once difficult to make so they are a recent addition to tile catalogs. Porcelain tile fits into modern homes because it takes almost no effort to maintain it. Its density makes it extremely stain resistant, and it needs only periodic light cleaning to keep it looking fresh. That density also means that porcelain tiles don't need mass for strength. They are thinner than other ceramic tiles and therefore can be installed where thicker tiles would raise the floor level too much.

▲ When you need stone, but want something a little less expensive, think porcelain. There's virtually nothing it can't do. Here the various shades, shapes, and textures of the tile create interest and an old-world rhythm.

▦ Variety of color and shape means you can create an endless array of designs, from a diagonal checkerboard (above) to an elaborate pattern (right).

Terra-cotta and saltillo

Terra-cotta tiles are made of unrefined natural clay that has been baked (not fired) at low temperatures or dried in the sun. These tiles are comparatively low in cost and high in rustic charm. Because they are low-density and absorb water, however, you'll need to seal them often.

Saltillo tile is a terra-cotta tile named for the area in Mexico from which it originates. It is a large, colorful tile, handmade and dried in the sun. Because it is handmade, the tile colors and sizes aren't entirely uniform. This lack of uniformity produces a rustic look and requires grout lines of about ¼-inch to accommodate the irregularity. As demand for saltillo has grown, factories have begun to produce machine-made look-alikes. While not a true saltillo, the new tile retains much of the charm of the original.

These tiles are extremely porous and soak up water, which means they'll soak up stains too. A sealer should be applied (usually every year) to keep them from getting grimy. They will not withstand freezing temperatures and should not be used outdoors except in climates where they won't freeze.

▲ Saltillo tiles have a universal rough-and-ready appeal, and from a design standpoint are well suited to any room, especially when you want to create a rustic or Southwestern theme.

▲ The rough texture of terra-cotta tiles makes them an ideal choice on floors where safety is a factor. No material is completely slip-proof, but these tiles are more slip-resistant than many others.

Quarry tile

Today's quarry tile is a misnomer—these tile have nothing to do with stone quarries. The name originally applied to stone tiles cut from quarries, but because these high-fired tiles resembled stone, they were given the same name.

Quarry tile is a thick tile made from natural clays and shales. It's usually an earth color, from brick red to various shades of tan, off white, and gray. Some quarry tiles are fired at high temperatures, which makes them vitreous, so they are more water-resistant than their semi-vitreous counterparts. The semi-vitreous tiles are considered highly slip resistant—spilled water soaks in and doesn't remain on the surface. Stains will soak in also, a characteristic that you can remedy with the application of a penetrating sealer. Penetrating sealers soak into the body of a tile and do not form a coating on the surface. Thus they allow the tile to retain its original character.

▲ **Because quarry tiles are slip resistant, they are often found in areas like kitchens.**

Deciphering the label

Cartons of tile now have labels with a series of pictures that tell you important facts about the tile you're buying. Consider this chart your translator.

▪ **Grade:** Grade 1 is suitable for walls or floors. Grade 2 is similar but has slight imperfections. Grade 3 is thinner tile designed for walls. You can use floor tiles on walls, but do not put wall tiles on floors; they'll crack.

▪ **PEI (Porcelain Enamel Institute) Wear Rating:** This is the tile's resistance to abrasion. I and II—not suitable for floors (walls only); III—all residential; IV—residential and light commercial; IV+—commercial and heavy traffic.

▪ **Water absorption:** Measured as proportion by weight. Nonvitreous, more than 7 percent; semivitreous, 3 to 7 percent; vitreous, 0.5 to 3 percent; impervious, less than 0.5 percent. Only vitreous and impervious tiles should be used outdoors or in bathrooms.

▪ **Coefficient of friction:** Resistance to slip, measured by the force required to move an object across the tile divided by its weight. The lower the number, the more slippery the floor.

▪ **Tone:** A multishaded grid indicates variations in tone from tile to tile. This is true of most tiles, except for pure colors, such as black and white.

▪ **Frost resistance:** An indication whether tile directly exposed to the elements will crack because of freeze thaw cycles. If a tile is frost resistant, you'll find a snowflake on the label.

What should you get?

▪ Purchase only Grade 1 or 2 tiles for a floor.

▪ Look for a PEI, or wear rating, of 3 or more.

▪ Water absorption standards vary. Tiles should have a water absorption rate of less than 7 percent in areas that are occasionally wet, such as a bathroom or kitchen. Areas that are constantly wet, such as showers, should have a water absorption rate of less than 3 percent. Elsewhere, water absorption is unimportant.

▪ Make sure the coefficient of friction is 0.6 or more.

▪ Variations in tone affect the appearance of the finished floor.

▪ Tile installed outdoors in freezing climates should be frost resistant.

Stone tile

Stone tile includes natural materials such as granite, marble, slate, sandstone, limestone, and quartzite. Stone tile generally falls into one of three categories, depending on how it is surfaced—polished, tumbled, or cleft (rough). No matter what its finish, stone absorbs stains, which are then impossible to remove. Sealing helps reduce staining, but because nothing beats the unrivaled natural beauty of stone, you may find its use worth the risk. Be sure to use white thinset mortar on lighter colored translucent stones; gray thinset will show through.

Polished stone

Not too long ago, the predominant polished stone varieties were granite and marble. Recently onyx, quartzite, and travertine have become increasingly popular. All these materials display an unmatched individuality: marble with its hazy veins or creamy colors; granite with its mottled colors; onyx, its shades of light and dark spread throughout; the pebbly visual texture of quartzite; and the fine veins and pebbly colors of travertine. Stone is expensive (especially quartzite), but properly cared for will last a lifetime. In general stone tile looks best with very thin, almost nonexistent grout lines.

Tumbled stone

Tumbled stone tiles, with their characteristic rounded edges and rough-hewn qualities, present an elegant option for a tiled installation. The tiles, usually marble or granite, are tumbled in abrasives and sometimes bathed in acid to round the edges, accentuate the natural veining, and leave a porous surface.

▲ **Combining field tiles, which are usually 4≥4-inch squares, with borders, listellos, or predesigned and mesh-backed medallions, as shown, offers classic focal points on this marble floor.**

Each tile is unique. Flaws such as open veins, chips, and depressions are part of the charm of these materials. Colors are natural, ranging from neutral tans to reds, browns, greens, and blacks. Tumbling imparts a soft texture to this otherwise hard material, giving an already-aged look that is reminiscent of old Mediterranean villas. Tumbled tiles must be sealed before grouting to prevent the grout from staining the body of the tile.

▲ **Stone tile brings a touch of old-world charm to a tiled room. There's something that says "authentic" in a stone tile installation, perhaps because it is reminiscent of a time when craftsmanship was paramount.**

Rough stone

Rough stone tile includes both stone split (cleft) from larger deposits or cut away with saws (sandstone, for example, is not easily cleft). Slate and bluestone (a regional stone specific to the Northeast) are among the most common varieties. Limestone and sandstone are two of the softest materials.

Because they are soft, limestone and sandstone will wear quickly and should be installed in light traffic areas. Slate comes in both hard and soft varieties in a surprising array of greens, grays, and blues. Plan your installation to form a patchwork of these colors. The surface of slate is naturally ridged, which makes it a good choice for floors where safety is paramount. Bluestone has a very distinctive deep blue-gray hue, with hints of green, yellow, and other colors throughout its surface. Its fine-grained surface wears extremely well.

▶ Slate is an excellent floor for entryways because it is classic in appearance, durable, and extremely slip-resistant. Hard varieties are easy to maintain. Softer varieties, called Indian slates, need to be sealed.

▲ By combining different colors of polished stones in a carefully planned layout, you can achieve stunning formal effects as shown in this entry hall.

Mosaics

Any tile less than 2 inches wide is a mosaic. Although you can still find installers who will lay mosaics the traditional way—one tile at a time—most mosaic installations now are done with mesh-backed sheets of tile.

You'll find sheets of mosaic tile in an unbelievable array of colors, designs, shapes, sizes, and materials—glass, porcelain, clay, and even metal. Some mosaic patterns are regular—they do not vary from sheet to sheet. Other patterns are random, which can create an unusual floor design. You have to be careful with random patterns not to bunch similar sections of the pattern together, creating unsightly splotches of color or shape. Whatever the pattern, mosaics can create a stunning display of variety and form. This is not a material for a neutral backdrop. Designing with mosaics may take a little more forethought than planning a floor with a neutral porcelain tile. With mosaic tile, everything—wall colors and decorations, lighting and furnishings— must work together so that one element is not competing for attention with the others.

Cement-bodied tile

Cement-bodied tiles are made of cement (a sand-and-mortar composition) instead of clay and are cured, not fired. The result is a hard, durable flooring material that is excellent for adding a rustic touch to your room. They are made to resemble brick, glazed tile, or stone, but because they're made of concrete, you get the look of a fancier material at a considerable cost saving.

You'll find more variety in this product than you might expect from a concrete composition. Surfaces can be smooth or porous, dull or shiny, and come in a number of colors and tints. That's because concrete can take any color—even the appearance of veined marble. The color runs all the way through the tiles, so wear spots or chips are less noticeable.

These tiles are an economical choice, and although they have certain design limitations (you'll never get them to look like highly polished marble, for instance), they're tough and long lasting. Many porous tiles will crack in freezing climates. Check with your distributor if you're considering using these for a patio.

▲ **Cement-bodied tile offers a low-cost alternative to tile, and is especially useful in room designs with a rustic flavor. It is also the perfect companion for Southwestern themes, with fireplaces or woodstoves, or in rooms such as covered porches and sunrooms that provide a transition to the outdoors.**

Concrete

oncrete is a hot material in contemporary design schemes. Essentially the same gray stuff as your driveway or the front walk, designer concrete is versatile and can be used throughout the house. Its initial liquid state allows you to color it or embed things in it and make it any shape. You can stamp or cut designs into it to resemble brick or stone. And, of course, you can combine any or all of these techniques into a single floor. It may seem ironic that this old material, commonly considered unattractive, is experiencing a renaissance and in some ways offers the most creative design potential of any flooring product.

Concrete is most often thought of as a material most suited to basements or the outdoors, for patios, enclosed porches, and outdoor cooking areas. Although these applications are the most common, concrete is making slow and steady inroads into the realms of interior design. Poured concrete-polymer overlays,

from $\frac{1}{4}$ to $\frac{3}{4}$ inch thick, provide a stable surface that can be acid stained and cut into specific design sections. The technology also extends itself to existing concrete floors, so you can turn your utilitarian basement into a rec room with an appealing style. Properly cleaned and acid stained, your old floor can soon look like travertine or marble. You can even apply the stain in stenciled patterns.

■ Invented as a structural building material and for most of its history considered a mostly utilitarian product, concrete is now seen as a medium for creative expressions, resulting in wonderful—and affordable—design effects.

Carpet

On a cold day, there's nothing like getting out of bed and stepping onto a warm carpet. Tile may be durable. Wood may be traditional. Vinyl may be colorful and low maintenance. But carpet is the flooring that invites you to walk barefoot or stretch out in front of the fire.

Although most carpet is stretched over tack strips that grab and hold it, some carpet installs exactly like vinyl tile and other carpet installs like sheet vinyl. Most methods, however, begin with an oversize piece of carpet that's trimmed after it's installed. Rental shops carry the tools for installation. If this is your first installation, stick with a plain carpet rather than one that's patterned, and don't buy berber—it requires extra skill to install.

Look for the carpet that looks and works best on your floor. Because you'll encounter countless options, this is a somewhat difficult task. Your three basic concerns when you buy

carpet should be the type of fiber, the type of pattern, and the method of installation. Virtually all residential carpets require stretch-in installation and have a saxony pattern and nylon fiber.

Several national retailers have devised rating systems to help you choose the carpet that best meets your needs. Usually the higher the rating, the more durable the carpet. Unfortunately these ratings (stamped on the back of the carpet) are not standardized and may be different from store to store. But they're a good place to start when making carpet choices.

If you want a carpet pattern different from the ones you see at the carpet store, create your own. Carpet retailers can sew pieces together to create almost any custom carpet design you can imagine. A common approach is to choose a carpet and create a border of contrasting color. It makes the room appear smaller and more intimate. Design possibilities are limitless and include geometric patterns, abstract shapes, a profile of your prized poodle, or whatever strikes your fancy. If you're interested, shop by phone first. Then take along a carefully measured drawing of the floor and the design you'd like.

◀ **Patterned carpet can dominate a room, but if chosen carefully, functions as a design element in its own right. An unpatterned carpet would have left this bedroom feeling plain and visually uneventful.**

Carpet patterns

Tufted carpet accounts for more than 90 percent of all carpet sold. Other patterns include woven, which is made on a loom, and needle punch, used in making commercial-grade carpets. The two broad types of tufted carpet are cut and looped. Each comes in several varieties.

Cut carpet

SAXONY (TEXTURED)
Dense with tightly twisted fibers. Feels soft, disguises tracks, the best-selling carpet.

SAXONY (PLUSH)
Lightly twisted, longer fibers. Less dense than saxony—a luxurious feel. Readily shows footprints.

FRIEZE (FREE´-ZAY)
Dense, twisted fibers curl in different directions. Hides footprints, good in high-traffic areas.

Looped carpet

LEVEL LOOP
Tightly packed loops all the same height. Resists dirt. When made with long loops, it's luxurious to the touch.

BERBER
A level loop with thick yarn. Tight loops limit footprints. Usually flecked or multitoned. Can retain dirt and snag, especially if you have pets.

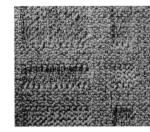

MULTILEVEL LOOP
Loops at different heights create a pattern. Random texture. Good for high-traffic areas. Smaller loops may hold dirt.

CUT AND LOOP
Combination of cut and looped fibers creates a pattern. Hides dirt and footprints.

▲ Patterns in carpet are not limited to prints and geometrics. Here the regularity of the pattern woven into the body of the carpet brings a quiet stability to the room design.

BUYER'S GUIDE

CARPET PADDING

Padding increases the durability and comfort of carpet. The best pad is neither the thickest nor the most expensive. In fact, thin and dense are generally better qualities—they provide the best combination of firmness, support, and cushioning.

The Carpet and Rug Institute recommends a maximum pad of $7/16$ inch. In no case should the pad exceed $1/2$ inch. Thicker padding lets the carpet flex, breaking down the backing. In most cases a pad with a 6- to 8-pound density is best—less may void the carpet warranty. Check with your retailer to make sure the pad you choose meets all warranty requirements.

Carpet padding is made from a variety of materials:

- **Rebonded urethane.** Accounts for 80 percent of the pad market. Good performance and resilience. Install mesh up.
- **Prime urethane.** Less resilient than rebonded urethane. Substantially more expensive.
- **Waffle-patterned rubber.** Heavy. Same performance as rebonded urethane at about twice the price.
- **Synthetic fiber pad.** Firm, good for level loops, required for berber. (Berber should be installed over a $3/8$- or $5/16$-inch pad with 24-ounce density.) Synthetic fiber pads prevent bounce and prevent flex at the seams. Good for home office and physically challenged users.

◀ A large expanse of carpet with a single tone can tend to overwhelm a room. The best way to preserve the integrity of your original plan is to use slightly contrasting colors on the walls and furnishings.

▶ Stains are the biggest problem with carpeted floors. Some manufacturers produce carpet with materials they boast as absolutely stainproof.

▲ Carpet tile is a less expensive but durable alternative to rolled carpet. Recent improvements in the design of carpet tile has made this material more attractive than the purely practical product it was originally.

Types of carpet fibers

■ **Nylon:** Ninety percent of all residential carpet is made of nylon. It's affordable, durable, resilient, colorfast, and resists dirt, abrasion, and mildew. Available in many colors.

■ **Olefin:** Trade name for polypropylene. Eighty percent of all commercial carpet, and all outdoor carpet, is made of olefin. It's affordable, resists fading, is moisture and mildew-resistant, and wears well. While the fibers will crush, it's a popular sports turf.

■ **Polyester:** It has a luxurious feel, is easy to clean, and wears well, but the fibers crush more easily than other fibers. Known for its color clarity, it's also colorfast and resistant to water-based stains.

■ **Wool:** A natural fiber, it's durable, maintains its fiber height, hides dirt well, and has a luxurious feel. One of the most expensive fibers, it is not moisture resistant and will fray.

■ **Acrylic:** It has the look and feel of wool— for less money. It resists fading, crushing, staining, moisture, and mildew but will wear quickly in high-traffic areas.

Area rugs

Area rugs have been essential to home furnishings for millennia. The first were rough reed rugs and animal hides for sitting and sleeping. Today an area rug is the fastest way to make over or breathe new life into a room.

You can treat the rug as the foundation of the design, then select furniture, coverings, and paint to match. That works well when you're planning to start from scratch. If, however, you have (or are planning) a room with a busy decor, a rug with a delicate pattern and subtle color will work well as a backdrop for the rest of the design.

Make your choice practical as well as pretty. The rug probably has a bigger job to do than just look good. Take into account where the rug will go. For example, darker colors (and durable fabrics) are best in high-traffic areas. Light colors help a room feel open and airy. Deeper hues make everything seem cozy.

The right rug in the right spot can help define areas of the room, providing, for example, a place to round up the chairs for conversation or marking out where the kids can play comfortably on a harder floor.

Some suppliers of carpets offer premade area rugs, often in standard sizes. You can have a carpet cut to size and have the edges bound to make a custom rug.

■ **Area rugs can add as much flair to a room as any other flooring material. Consider them as an attractive and less-expensive alternative to other kinds of flooring if your budget doesn't permit a complete new floor at this time.**

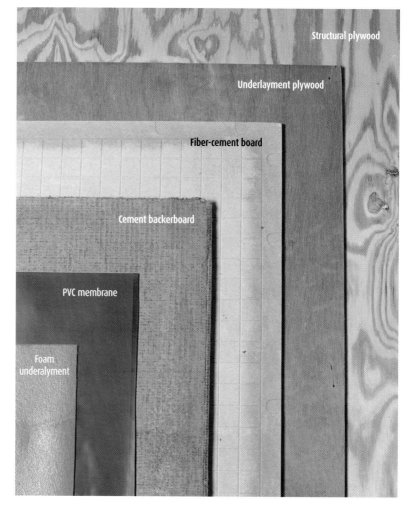

Underlayments and membranes

What goes under your flooring can make the difference between a successful installation and a troublesome one. Specific requirements for underlayment vary with the kind of flooring and how and where it is being installed.

An **isolation membrane** covers cracks in a concrete slab and keeps them from cracking the flooring material.

Cement backerboard or **fiber-cement board** provides a sturdy, inflexible surface for ceramic tile and stone.

Underlayment plywood is smooth and ensures that there won't be defects showing in resilient materials.

Structural plywood is a sturdy subfloor suitable for all flooring materials.

A **waterproofing membrane** (either troweled or sheet formed) keeps moisture from wicking through a slab and into the finished floor. For waterproofing material used in wet locations, such as bathrooms and showers, use 15 lb. felt paper.

PVC membrane waterproofs the floor of a custom shower, protecting both the subfloor and the framing from water damage.

Foam underlayment acts as a cushion under laminate flooring and helps deaden the sound in floating floors.

Fiberglass reinforcing tape reinforces the joints between backerboards.

Backerboard screws attach the board to the framing.

Embossing leveler smooths out the embossed pattern in vinyl tile and sheet goods so they can be covered.

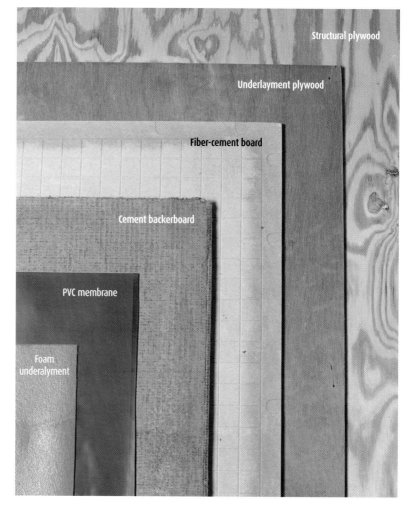

Structural plywood

Underlayment plywood

Fiber-cement board

Cement backerboard

PVC membrane

Foam underalyment

Waterproofing membrane

Trowel

Embossing leveler

Fiberglass reinforcing tape

Backerboard screws

DESIGNING YOUR FLOOR

1

Adhesives, grouts, and sealers

Adhesives hold a tile installation together and firmly attach the tiles to the subfloor. Grouts keep moisture from working its way into the adhesive, and they also have a decorative function, adding color and definition to a tiled surface. Sealers keep dirt and moisture from getting into and under the tile and grout.

Almost all tile requires a specialized type of adhesive, grout, and sealer. Consult with your retailer for information. Don't buy blindly off the shelf.

Thinset mortar is the adhesive of choice for most ceramic tile and stone.

Organic mastics are basically glue for wall tiles up to 6×6 inches. They come premixed in a can and cure by drying. Mastics are fine for wall tile, but should not be used for floors.

Latex additives increase the adhesion, flexibility, and moisture resistance of thinset.

Sanded grout is designed to fill joints from 1/8 to 1/2-inch wide.

Unsanded grout is used for thin joints, less than 1/8-inch wide, chiefly in stone tile.

Sealer, either penetrating or topical, helps protect tile from water and stains.

Floor tile adhesive is formulated for vinyl tile, sheet goods, and parquet.

Carpet adhesive holds down carpet in glue-down installations.

Seam sealer prevents carpet from fraying where two pieces meet.

Hotmelt seaming tape is a heat-sensitive tape placed across the back of carpet at the seams. It comes in different widths for different applications.

Carpet edgings, or binder bars, are metal strips placed at exposed edges of the carpet to protect it and act as transitions.

Tack strips hold the edges of carpet in stretch-in installations.

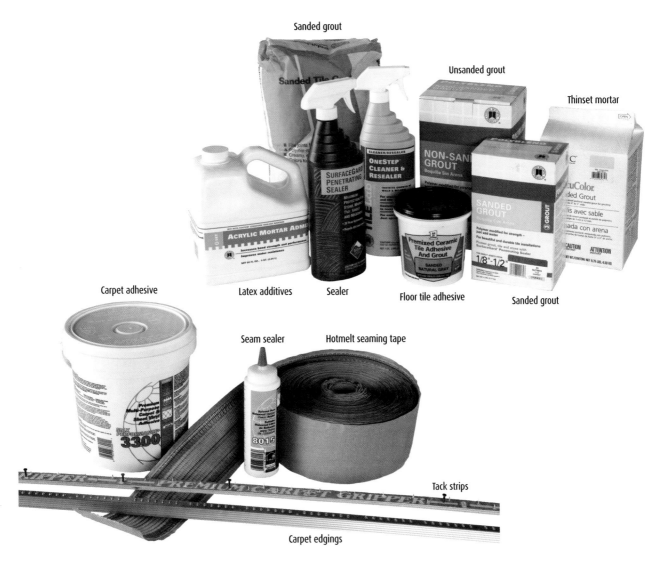

Sanded grout

Unsanded grout

Thinset mortar

Carpet adhesive

Latex additives

Sealer

Floor tile adhesive

Sanded grout

Seam sealer

Hotmelt seaming tape

Tack strips

Carpet edgings

Trim and transitions

Door moldings, window moldings, and baseboard—collectively known as trim—are more than aesthetically pleasing objects: They hide gaps. Consider a few such applications:

The framing that supports windows is larger than the windows themselves, allowing room to install them but leaving a gap between the window and the framing. Trim hides it.

The raw edge of drywall or plaster is exposed at doorways and windows. Trim hides it.

Walls crack. They crack at doorways, windows, and sometimes in the corner where the wall meets the ceiling. Trim hides it.

Some floors expand and contract with changes in temperature and humidity. This can lead to damage if there is not room for expansion along the edge. Once again, trim hides this space.

Trim and moldings come in a variety of styles and materials (see "Buyer's Guide," opposite). When shopping for trim choose the style that enhances the overall design theme of your room and new floor.

Baseboard

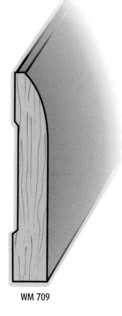

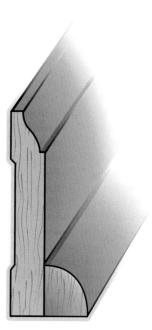
WM 709

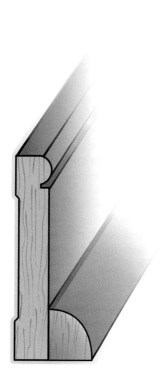
WM 750

WM 618

Casing

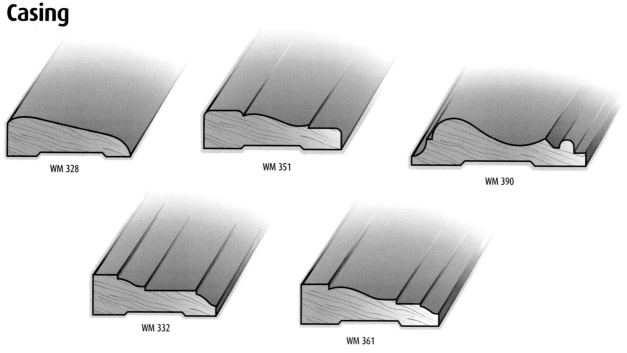

WM 328

WM 351

WM 390

WM 332

WM 361

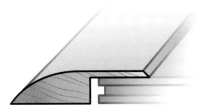

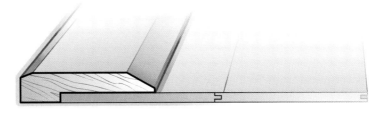

REDUCER STRIP

Use this as a transition from a wood floor to a thinner floor, such as vinyl flooring. It also works to trim the edge of a fireplace hearth or camouflage a sliding door track. Apply it as a threshold where floors end in a doorway.

THRESHOLD

Use this style where floors end in doorways. Fasten to the subfloor with adhesive or nails. If nailing, drill pilot holes to prevent the threshold from splitting.

💲 BUYER'S GUIDE

CHOOSING TRIM

Molding is available in the same shapes and sizes across the country, with few regional variations. The Wood Molding & Millwork Products Association (WMMPA) has standardized the shapes and dimensions for all types, from crown molding to closet poles. The shapes most typically used in baseboard and door trim are shown on the opposite page. The numbers below the illustrations correspond to WMMPA numbers, which you can use to order trim at any home center.

You can buy two basic grades of trim: stainable and paintable. You'll find the widest variety of stainable trim available in solid pine. In hardwoods, oak and birch or maple are often stocked in limited variety, and other hardwoods may be special-ordered.

Paintable trim comes in pine and medium-density fiberboard (MDF). Paintable pine is made of short pieces whose ends have been finger-jointed together. This allows the mill to make the best use of lumber and creates stock that's less likely to warp. Paint hides the joints.

MDF is essentially made of compressed sawdust and glue, and the surface is exceptionally smooth. Because of this, it holds paint well but is less durable than solid wood.

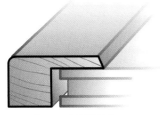

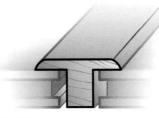

UNIVERSAL THRESHOLD

Sometimes called a square nosing, this is used when wood flooring meets carpeting. Install the stepped edge over the floor. Butt the carpet against the other edge, as if it were a wall.

T-MOLDING

This molding is a transition between floors of different types. One side covers the wood floor, the other covers ceramic tile, laminate, wood, or other flooring.

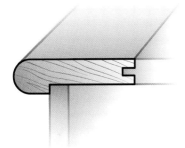

STAIR NOSING

Used primarily on stairs, though not necessary with prefabricated treads. Good for trimming the edges of a floor that sits slightly above another floor.

Transitions for laminates

Most manufacturers of laminate flooring produce trim that matches the style and color of their products. Many of these pieces, like the T-molding shown here, are anchored with a molding track. You install the track first by screwing it to the floor. Then you snap the T-molding in place. Corrugated recesses in the track hold the molding in place and make the fasteners invisible.

Tile transitions

As you choose your tile, decide how you want to bridge the junctions where it meets different kinds of flooring. Because tile has hard, straight edges, you could simply butt it against almost any other kind of flooring. However, even if your new floor ends up at the same height as the existing floor, it's difficult to avoid a gap between the two. And rarely will neighboring floors of different materials end up at the same height. With ceramic tile, especially, the combined thickness of the tile and backerboard can create a step between surfaces. For that you need a transition.

Ceramic floor transitions come in wood and metal. You also can buy ready-made marble thresholds that can be cut to length on a wet saw. Metal strips are versatile, but wood is best for making a good transition from one level to another. Buy the necessary transitions before you start tiling.

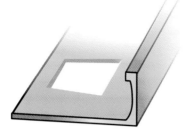

CARPET-TO-TILE DIVIDER
This metal trim works with glue-down or stretched carpet. It works best in circumstances where the carpet subfloor is level with the top of the backerboard.

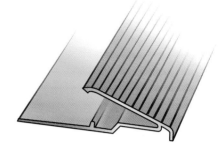

T-MOLDING
This metal or wood molding bridges the gap between two types of flooring and can be installed after the floor has been laid.

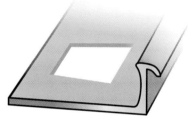

TILE REDUCER
This metal trim provides a transition from the edge of the tile to the top of a somewhat lower floor.

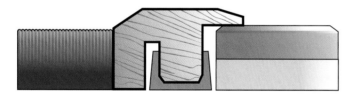

TILE-TO-CARPET TRANSITION
Made of wood, this trim is the most versatile of the transitions. One edge is recessed to fit over the tile. The other edge is square, and you can bring it right up against the edge of the carpet. A channel that screws or glues to the floor holds the trim in place.

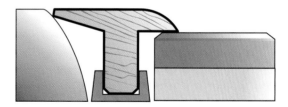

THRESHOLD MOLDING
If you'd rather hide the gap than caulk or mortar between the threshold and floor, use a threshold molding. Held in place by a PVC channel, it bridges the gap and provides a smooth transition between floors that are slightly lower than the threshold.

Carpet transitions

Transitions between carpet and other floors can be metal, vinyl, wood, or even a seam between different pieces of carpet. There are countless shapes and profiles. Typical solutions are shown here. Ask your retailer about others. If you can imagine it, someone probably makes it.

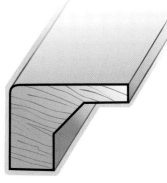

CARPET EDGING

This transition joins carpet to an existing floor. Nail the edging to floor and stretch the carpet over the barbs. Tap down the curved edge for a snug fit.

ZEE TRIM

Use this between tile or other hard surface and carpet. Snug the transition against the tile and nail to floor. Stretch carpet over barbs and tap down top edge.

SQUARE NOSE REDUCER

This wood molding covers carpet and butts against a wood floor to provide transition between the two. Nail it to the subfloor.

CLOSER LOOK

STAIN OR PAINT

There are two broad categories of trim molding: Paintable (or paint grade) and stainable (or stain grade). Stainable molding is defect-free with uniform grain so it will look best when stained. Stainable trim is commonly available in pine, but you can custom order several hardwoods as well. Paintable molding costs less and is often made of short pieces joined together with finger joints. The joints are not visible after painting. Some moldings are made of medium-density fiberboard (MDF), which is preprimed and provides a smooth surface for paint.

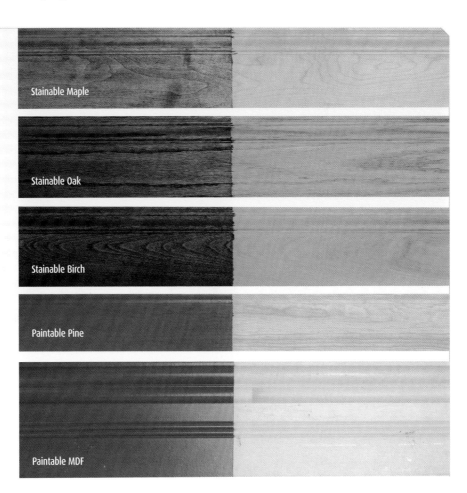

Stainable Maple

Stainable Oak

Stainable Birch

Paintable Pine

Paintable MDF

Tools and techniques

 f you've done a few home improvement projects, you probably have a pretty well-stocked toolbox and can get right to work. But if you haven't checked your tools in a while, you may want to get them out and make sure they're in good repair. A new project always provides an incentive—and a great excuse—for replacing a marginal tool or adding a new one to your set.

If you're new to home improvement projects, this chapter shows some of the tools you might need. Now is the time to gather the right ones to make your work proceed efficiently.

Whether old-timer or newcomer, make a list of any tools you need to round out your set so you won't have to make extra trips to the home center to buy the tools you forgot—especially once the work is under way. Nothing is more frustrating than having to stop work to go buy a tool.

The following pages show the tools you'll need, divided into some broad categories. Those in the basic home repair toolbox have multiple applications. They're the ones you'll need for almost any home improvement project, whether you're installing floors or making major renovations to your home. A carpenter's level, for example, is indispensable when it comes to evaluating a floor for high and low spots, so you'll definitely need it for your flooring project. And if you're adding a wall or changing one in a room, you'll need a level to make sure that new wall framing is plumb.

Chapter 2 highlights

A cordless drill/driver is an essential tool for most projects. The versatile tool not only drills holes, it is the fastest gun in the West—or anywhere else—when it comes to driving screws. A circular saw has so many applications in any project that you'll also want to have one of them handy.

You'll use some skills and techniques in a number of ways for your flooring project too. You'll rely on basic skills like marking and measuring repeatedly. Laying out a floor is a good example. The methods used for laying out most wood floors are the same, whether you're putting down solid wood or engineered flooring. Those principles will generally be applicable to laminate flooring too. The same goes for laying out a tiled installation. The procedures for snapping layout lines won't vary much whether you install ceramic, vinyl, or parquet tiles. Cutting corners and dealing with obstructions such as piping that comes through the floor likewise call for the same techniques, no matter what kind of flooring you're laying.

Basic home repair toolbox

Tool quality, durability, and price cover a broad range. Professional tools can last a lifetime if properly cared for—but they're expensive. Many home centers carry different grades of most tools for different needs. Good-quality tools are for small jobs and infrequent use. Better-quality tools are generally more durable and may be better finished. The best tools are the ones the pros use. They'll last a lifetime if you care for them properly. Follow this rule: Buy the best tools you can afford.

Buy or rent?

For some tools, renting instead of buying makes more sense. Renting a hammer, for example, doesn't make good economic sense; it's a tool you'll use often. On the other hand, buying a floor scraper or a tile wet saw isn't necessary or economical, unless you're going into the business. Whatever you rent, order it only when you're ready to use it. That way you're not paying for the tool while it sits idle.

ADJUSTABLE WRENCH
Use an adjustable wrench to remove nuts and bolts or loosen plumbing fittings.

CARPENTER'S LEVEL
Use a carpenter's level to level and plumb long sections of framing and for evaluating the condition of subfloors.

CAULKING GUN
You'll need a caulking gun for caulking joints and for applying construction adhesive.

CHALKLINE
A chalkline makes long, straight lines—essential when laying out a job.

CIRCULAR SAW
Use a circular saw to cut lumber and sheet goods as well as old flooring and underlayment when you need to remove them.

COMBINATION SQUARE
A combination square allows you to mark boards for crosscutting.

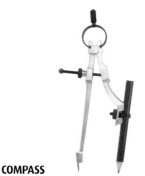

COMPASS
You'll find a compass useful when scribing the cut line for the flooring you lay next to the wall. The scribed line will follow any irregularities in the wall surface.

COPING SAW
A coping saw is necessary to correctly cut moldings at inside corners. Equipped with a carbide blade, it can cut curves in tile.

CORDLESS 18-VOLT DRILL/DRIVER
A cordless 18-volt drill/driver keeps the workplace free of extension cords. Use it for drilling holes and for driving screws.

DIAGONAL CUTTERS
You'll need diagonal cutters to cut electrical wiring when necessary. Always make sure the power to the circuit is turned off.

FRAMING SQUARE
Use a framing square to square large framing members.

GROOVE-JOINT PLIERS
This tool can grip pipes and fittings or loosen connections when removing fixtures.

HACKSAW
A full-size hacksaw cuts pipes and helps in removing rusted fittings and old sections of pipe.

HACKSAW—MINI
Use a close-work hacksaw in tight areas. Most use full-size hacksaw blades as well as shorter metal-cutting blades.

HOLE SAW
Use with a drill to bore big holes in wood and other materials.

JIGSAW
For cutting access panels, flooring, and holes for sinks, use a jigsaw.

LAYOUT SQUARE
A layout square does many of the same tasks as a framing square and can serve as a guide when crosscutting with a circular saw.

MAGNETIC SLEEVE AND SCREWDRIVER BITS
Use this with your cordless drill/driver. The magnetic tip holds the screw, and the sleeve slides down over it to hold it steady for driving.

MITER BOX
For cutting miters in trim, you'll need either a miter box or a power mitersaw.

NAIL SET
You'll find a nail set handy for driving finishing nails below the surface of moldings.

PLUMB BOB
A plumb bob hangs at the end of a line and provides a vertical reference.

QUICK CLAMP
Quick clamps tighten with one hand—a real advantage. You'll need several sizes to hold flooring stock securely to a work surface when cutting it.

QUICK-CHANGE SLEEVE
The holder chucks into your drill or drill/driver. You can then switch quickly between twist drills and screwdriver bits.

SPADE BITS
These bits bore rough holes through framing or subflooring for pipes and cables.

T-BEVEL
Set a T-bevel to transfer angles from one surface to another.

TAPE MEASURE
A tape measure is a compact ruler made for all measuring tasks. Get a 25-foot model with a 1-inch-wide blade.

TOOLBOX HANDSAW
A toolbox handsaw packs a lot of cutting power into a compact size and makes quick work of cutting things down to size.

TORPEDO LEVEL
Use a torpedo level where a carpenter's level won't fit.

UTILITY KNIFE
A utility knife does everything from sharpening pencils to cutting drywall.

16-OUNCE FRAMING HAMMER
A 16-ounce framing hammer is essential—heavy enough to drive framing nails yet light enough for trim work. Add a 22-ounce framing hammer for heavy work.

Demolition tools

CAT'S PAW
For pulling nails, nothing beats a cat's paw.

COLD CHISEL AND SMALL SLEDGE
To cut away a small section of concrete or to remove or replace ceramic tile, a small sledge and cold chisel may be all you need.

FLAT PRY BAR
A flat pry bar disassembles most framing joints and is also handy for prying off moldings.

FLOORING SCRAPER
Use a flooring scraper to scrape up residual adhesive after removing vinyl flooring.

PUTTY KNIFE
A wide-blade, stiff putty knife will come in handy for removing flooring adhesive.

RECIPROCATING SAW
A reciprocating saw cuts through studs and nails. It is useful for demolition work and floor removal.

RIPPING BAR
For heavy-duty demolition, you may need a long ripping bar.

STUD FINDER
A stud finder locates studs in walls. Get one that locates the stud by sensing its density, not the presence of nails.

Additional power tools

BRAD NAILER

A brad nailer typically drives 18-gauge fasteners ranging in length from about $5/8$ to $1 1/4$ inches. The compact nailer is ideal for trimwork.

COMPOUND MITERSAW

A compound mitersaw cuts angled pieces and makes crosscuts with precision. A mitersaw with a 10-inch blade has adequate cutting capacity for most jobs.

FINISH NAILER

A finish nailer is larger than a brad nailer and drives fasteners about $1 1/4$ to $2 1/2$ inches long. This range is suitable for trim jobs as well as installation of doorjambs. Less expensive nailers utilize 16-gauge fasteners, but the more robust 15-gauge nails in the better drivers won't bend as easily. You can get nailers with the magazine perpendicular to the head or angled. Many finish carpenters believe that the angled version is easier to maneuver into cramped corners.

ORBITAL FINISHING SANDER

Orbital finishing sanders use an oscillating motion to move sandpaper in tiny circles over the wood. The $1/4$-sheet size, called a palm sander, is popular. A detail sander allows you to smooth hard-to-reach areas, such as inside corners. A random-orbit sander uses a round abrasive disk that moves in a random pattern to remove stock faster than hand sanding and to minimize scratch marks. Most use 5- to 12-inch-diameter disks that attach with adhesive or hook-and-loop fasteners. A good choice is a 5- or 6-inch-diameter model with a connection for dust collection.

POWDER-ACTUATED FASTENER

Powered by an explosive gunpowder charge, a powder-actuated fastener is especially useful for attaching framing to concrete, such as when fastening 2×4 sleepers to a slab.

ROUTER

A router and a variety of router bits are useful for shaping decorative moldings and cutting mortises for door hinges.

10-INCH TABLESAW

A 10-inch tablesaw (blade diameter) cuts more accurately and is more versatile than a portable circular saw. A contractor-style tablesaw (with open legs) is usually the first large power tool a woodworker purchases—and the one likely to be used most often.

Tools for tile

ABRASIVE STONE FILE
An abrasive stone file helps shape tiles to fit special configurations.

CARBIDE GLASS BIT
A carbide glass bit drills small holes in tile.

CARBIDE ROD SAW
A carbide rod saw makes intricate cuts in tile.

CARBIDE SCORING TOOL
A carbide scoring tool is made especially for scoring backerboard.

GROUT BAG
Use a grout bag for filling wide (more than 1/2 inch) joints and joints between rough tile.

GROUT FLOAT AND TROWELS
Different jobs require different trowels, and filling the joints properly calls for a grout float.

HEAVY-DUTY DRILL AND MIXING PADDLE
To mix thinset mortar, use a heavy-duty drill and a mixing paddle.

MARGIN TROWEL
A margin trowel gets mortar into tight spaces and is a handy tool for scooping mortar from a bucket.

MASONRY STONE
A masonry stone removes rough or sharp edges.

NONABRASIVE PAD
A nonabrasive pad removes stubborn grout residue.

RUBBER MALLET AND BEATER BLOCK
Use a rubber mallet and beater block to set tile in mortar.

SNAP CUTTER
A snap cutter scores and snaps tiles in straight lines.

SPONGE
You'll need a sponge to clean the grout off the surface of the tiles.

STRAIGHTEDGE
Use a metal straightedge to keep tile courses straight.

TILE NIPPERS
Use tile nippers to chip away small pieces of tile when cutting circular or unusual patterns.

WET SAW
A wet saw makes quick work when you have lots of cuts to make.

Carpet tool kit

CARPET KNIFE
A kind of utility knife, a carpet knife is designed especially for cutting and trimming carpet edges and seams.

DUCKBILL NAPPING SHEARS
Duckbill napping shears trims off stray fibers from carpet seams.

KNEE KICKER
Use a knee kicker to stretch carpet along the initial walls of a room and on short wall sections.

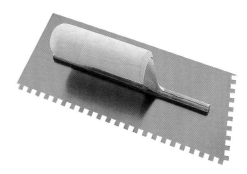

NOTCHED TROWEL
Use the appropriate notched trowel to spread adhesive for carpet, carpet tile, and parquet.

POWER STRETCHER
Use a power stretcher when you have long expanses of carpet to stretch across a room. Like many carpet tools, you can rent it instead of buying.

ROW CUTTER
Use a row cutter to cut carpet edges straight for seaming.

SEAM ROLLER

A seam roller helps press the back of a carpet into the seaming tape and smooth out irregularities in seams so they lie flat.

SEAMING IRON

A seaming iron melts the adhesive on seaming tape to hold both edges of a seam securely.

STAIR TOOL

A stair tool is designed to snug carpet in the gap between the floor and the wall.

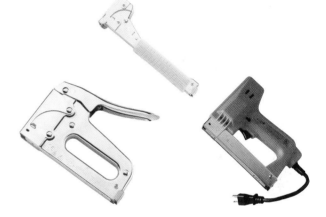

STAPLERS AND ELECTRIC STAPLE GUN

Staplers, electric staple guns, and hammer staplers are used to tack carpet pad to the subfloor.

WALL TRIMMER

Use a wall trimmer to make straight cuts in carpet along a wall.

75-LB. CARPET ROLLER

Rent a 75-pound carpet roller to smooth newly laid carpet.

Concrete tools

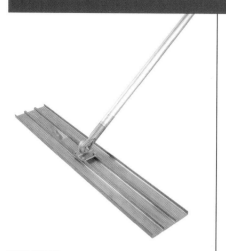

BULL FLOAT
With its long handle, a bull float can reach across larger areas than a darby or wooden float.

BROOM
Use a stiff-bristled broom to roughen the surface of a slab.

DARBY
A darby is a steel or magnesium float that imparts a smooth surface to concrete.

EDGER
An edger rounds off the edge of a concrete slab, making it less prone to chipping.

JOINTER
A jointer cuts control joints in fresh concrete to help minimize surface cracking.

MASON'S HOE
The holes in a mason's hoe are designed to let concrete flow through when mixing in a wheelbarrow.

MASON'S LINE
Mason's line is tightly woven nylon string used for laying out concrete projects.

MASON'S WHEELBARROW
A mason's wheelbarrow is made deep enough to mix concrete with minimal spillage.

MATTOCK
A mattock loosens clay and compacted soil, making excavation easier.

PORTABLE CEMENT MIXER
A portable cement mixer allows you to mix concrete closer to the site.

POINTED TROWELS
Various pointed trowels are used to smooth concrete, cut it away from forms, and place small amounts in low spots on the slab

POWER TAMPER
Rent a power tamper to compact soil and gravel in a slab bed.

ROUND-NOSE SHOVEL
A round-nose shovel is used to excavate patio sites and to move concrete from a wheelbarrow to the site.

SQUARE TROWEL
A square trowel is used to smooth concrete after using a darby.

WOODEN DARBY
A wooden darby is a tool used to carry out the initial smoothing of concrete after pouring.

Laying out a floor for tile

No matter what kind of tile you're installing, layout procedures will generally be the same. The keys to success in tiling are the guide lines (called layout lines). They show you where to start laying the tile and are arranged so the tile is evenly centered in the room. Centering the tile ensures that the tiled edges are the same width around the perimeter. A tile floor that isn't centered—or that is roughly centered—looks unbalanced because the tiles at opposite walls are different widths, and any irregularity in the walls is magnified.

Your onsite layout tasks will be more successful if you lay out the tile on graph paper first. That will give you an idea of where to start and how the finished installation will look.

1

FIND THE CENTER OF THE ROOM
Snap chalklines between the midpoints of opposite walls. The center of the room is where the chalklines cross.

CLOSER LOOK

AS EASY AS 3-4-5
When you're trying to lay out lines that are perfectly square, tools will ultimately fail you. A combination square is too small, and a framing square is never perfectly reliable. To determine whether two lines are square with each other, use a 3-4-5 triangle. Mark one of the lines 3 feet from the point where the lines cross. Mark the other line 4 feet from the crossing. Measure the diagonal distance between the two marks. The lines are square if the distance between the points is exactly 5 feet. This method works with multiples of 3, 4, and 5 (6, 8, and 10, for example, or 9, 12, and 15). It works whether you're measuring in feet, inches, yards, centimeters, or any other unit.

If the measurements tell you the lines aren't square, adjust one of the lines slightly and remeasure. Repeat as needed until you get a perfect 3-4-5 triangle.

5   3

4   90°

2

MEASURE FOR SQUARE
Measure and mark one layout line 3 feet from the intersection of the lines. Measure and mark the other layout line 4 feet from the intersection. If the layout lines are square, the distance between the marks will be exactly 5 feet. If they are not square, sketch the diagonal on the floor with a pencil for reference.

Original chalkline

3

ADJUST THE LINES IF NECESSARY
If the lines are not square (see "As Easy As 3-4-5," above), moving one end of either line will fix the problem. Whichever line you choose, move the end that's closest to the pencil line you sketched on the floor. If the diagonal measured more than 5 feet in Step 2, move the end toward the 90° angle. If the distance between points was less than 5 feet, move the end away from the angle.

4

TAKE A TRIAL RUN

Lay tiles along the chalklines in both directions without mortar but with spacers. Stop when the remaining space is smaller than a full tile.

5

READJUST THE LINES

If the space between the last full tile and the wall is less than half a tile width, move the line parallel to that wall until the tiles at both ends are of equal width, and if possible, more than half a tile wide. Repeat the process for the tiles on the other axis. Make sure the lines are still square.

6

MAKE A JURY STICK

When you actually lay the tiles in mortar, you will find it easier to set them in sections or grids. An easy way to lay out the sections with chalklines is to make a jury stick. Lay out a section of tiles with spacers and set a length of 1× stock along an edge. Mark the jury stick at the edges of the tile.

7

MARK THE LAYOUT

Set the jury stick along the wall and mark the floor at each mark on the jury stick. Repeat at each wall, then snap chalklines between the marks to lay out the grid.

Small rooms

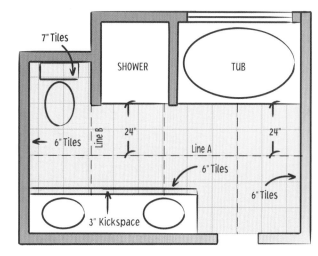

Bathrooms are generally too small to make use of the 3-4-5 triangle to establish reference lines. Lay out a single reference line on the center of the floor on its longest dimension. Dry-lay a row of tiles along this line and adjust the placement of the line so that tiles will be the same size at the edges on both sides of it. Snap lines to indicate the placement of the center tiles and the edge tiles. Repeat the process on the other dimension.

In this small bathroom, full tiles are used at the entrance and along the tub and shower. The layout was adjusted to avoid having a 2-inch strip of tile at the end of the vanity.

Multipurpose rooms

Kitchen/dining rooms and other multipurpose rooms may require special layout techniques.

If the rooms are joined by a doorway, separate the field tiles at the doorway with a threshold. Full tiles may be installed on both sides of the doorway without visually disturbing the pattern. The joints that carry through the doorway must, of course, line up.

In the kitchen and dining room shown here, the layout accounts for cut tiles along the peninsula counter, as well as the perimeter of the room. The width of the bay allows the installation of full tiles if the ½-inch to ¾-inch gaps along the walls are covered with baseboards.

Most of the cut tiles are obscured by the cabinet toe kick. The only place a design principle is violated is at the kitchen door, where there's a less-than-half-width tile.

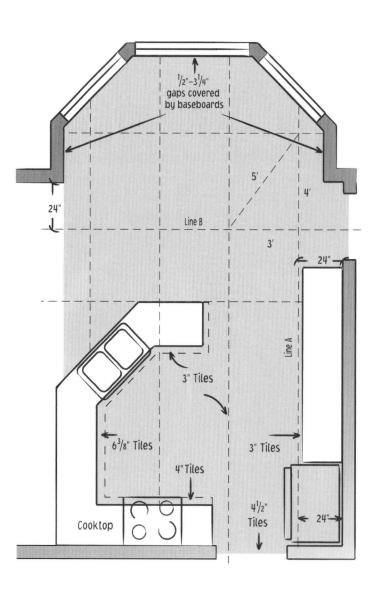

Connected rooms

Uninterrupted joint lines are the key to laying a tile design through multiple rooms. The method is simple: Run the primary reference lines through the doorways into the adjacent rooms.

In Option A, Line A runs vertically through the kitchen and the dining room. Using a 3-4-5 triangle, reference Line B runs horizontally through both the dining room and the utility room. A second 3-4-5 triangle establishes reference Line C vertically in the utility room. This allows full tiles to be set through the utility room doorway, which leaves 6-inch border tiles along both walls.

Option B shows a wood or marble threshold, the width of the wall, installed in the doorway, allowing full tiles to start in the utility room.

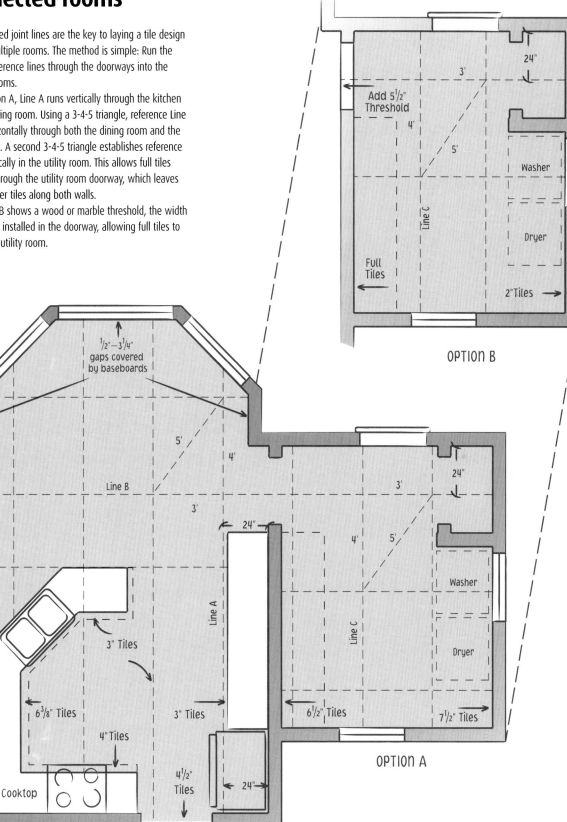

OPTION B

OPTION A

Obstructions and edges

1 f you're working in a room without obstructions or pipes, your floor installation can be a breeze. But obstructions, even piping coming through the floor, doesn't need to intimidate you. You can work around obstructions with a few simple techniques. The key to a successful installation is to center the pipe in the flooring material and make a smooth cutout that will place the flooring square at the location of the pipe.

Edges are similarly simple. In many cases, you will not have to worry about cutting the flooring at the wall to the same contour as the wall. If the gap between the flooring and the wall will not exceed ¼ inch anywhere along its length, you can cut the edge piece straight and let the shoe molding cover the gap. If, however, the gap along the wall will at any point exceed ¼ inch, shoe molding may not cover it. These situations call for cutting the flooring so it mirrors the contour of the wall.

Fitting strips and planks around pipes

1   **MEASURE TO THE WALL**

Cut the plank or strip so it would fit in the remaining space if the pipe weren't there. Then measure the distance from the wall (or spacer) to the center of the pipe. Mark the plank at this distance.

2   **CENTER THE WIDTH**

Measure the distance from the neighboring plank or strip to the center of the pipe, and mark the plank at this distance. The intersection of the lines will give you a center point for drilling.

Wear safety glasses when drilling.

Cut away this piece, then cut it to fit glued behind the pipe

3   **DRILL THE CUTOUT**

Where the lines cross, drill a hole ½ inch larger than the pipe diameter, drilling from the finished side of the flooring. Minimize the tearout on the reverse side by placing the flooring on a piece of scrap wood. Then finish the cutout with a coping saw and trim the cutout so you can glue it between the pipe and the wall.

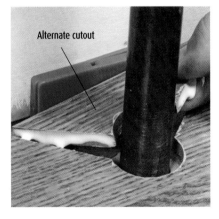

Alternate cutout

AN ALTERNATE CUTOUT

Instead of squaring the cutout, which often leaves a piece of flooring too small to work with, drill out the hole and then cut the flooring on the diagonal as shown above. This results in a larger cutout, one that's easier to work with. Glue the edges of the cutout to the flooring.

Cutting tile for pipes

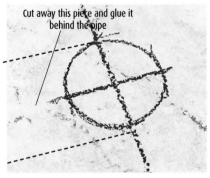

Cut away this piece and glue it behind the pipe

Measure the distances to the center of the pipe as shown for plank or strip flooring and where the lines cross, drill a hole ½ inch larger than the pipe diameter. This leaves room for the pipe to expand without buckling the flooring.

For vinyl tile, use a scissors to make the cutout. For ceramic tile and stone, make the cutout on a wet saw and fill in the gap behind the pipe with a piece cut from scrap tile. b

Scribing the contour of a wall

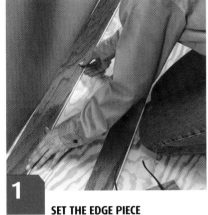

1
SET THE EDGE PIECE
Hold the edge piece parallel to a layout line or the edge of flooring already in place. Set the edge piece so it touches the wall at least at one point.

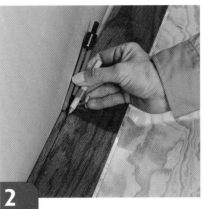

2
TRACE THE CONTOUR
Set a compass to the amount you want to remove—generally an amount equal to the largest gap between the flooring and the wall, plus about $1/4$ inch. (The extra $1/4$ inch makes the cut easier because it means there will always be stock on both sides of the blade.) If you're working with the last board in the room, adjust this amount if necessary so the trimmed piece will not be too narrow. Pull the compass along the wall, drawing a line on the flooring.

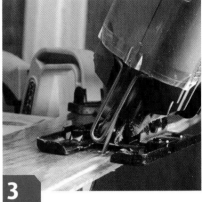

3
CUT THE CONTOUR
Cut along the line with the saw appropriate for your flooring. Bevel the cut so the blade trims more off the bottom than the top. Undercutting ensures that the bottom edge of the flooring won't touch the wall before the top does, resulting in what looks like a gap.

Marking tile edge rows

Tile to be cut

1
SET THE TRIM TILES
When you've reached the edge of the installation and need to cut tiles to fill the remaining space, set out the tiles to be cut exactly on the last row of tiles already in place.

Scribing tile

Tile to be cut

2
MARK THE CUT LINE
Set a full tile (a scribing tile) against the wall or against spacers if necessary (plywood or scrap tile as shown here). Taking care to not disturb the tile to be cut, draw a marker along the edge of the scribing tile. Move the scribing tile down the length of the wall and repeat the process until all the tiles are marked.

3
CUT THE EDGE TILES
Because the edge tiles may each be a different width, cut them one at a time and put them in place in the thinset mortar.

Cutting corners
Cutting outside corners

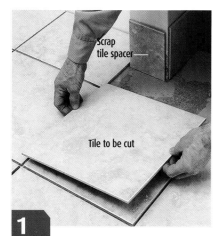

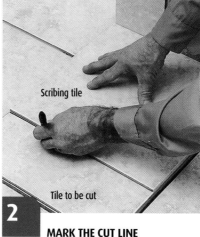

1 LINE UP THE EDGE TILE

Set the tile to be trimmed directly on top of the full tile opposite the outside corner. Set spacers (scrap tile or plywood) along the corners of the wall if necessary.

2 MARK THE CUT LINE

Put a full-size scribing tile against the scrap spacer and on top of the tile to be cut. Mark the cut line on the edge tile.

3 MARK THE CORNER

Once you've drawn the edge line, mark where the scribing tile meets the corner scrap, as shown.

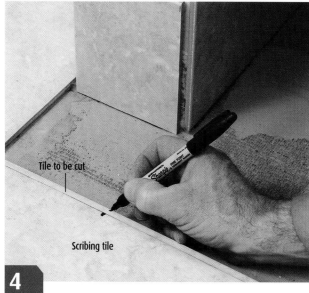

4 TRANSFER THE CORNER MARK

Slide the scribing tile slightly away from the edge and transfer the corner mark to the tile you will cut.

5 MARKING THE CORNER CUT

Using a square, draw a line from the corner mark to the edge line. Cut out the corner on a wet saw, positioning the fence so the blade just removes the line. Stop when the blade reaches the corner of the cutout and finish with a carbide rod saw if necessary.

Cutting inside corners

1 **SET THE SPACERS**
Set scrap tile in both sides of the corner to act as spacers. Then set the tile to be cut exactly on a tile already set in thinset.

2 **SET THE SCRIBING TILE**
Put a full-size scribing tile against the scrap on one wall and over the tile to be cut. Trace along the edge of the scribing tile to lay out a line on the tile that you will be cutting.

3 **MARK THE OPPOSITE WALL**
Put the scribing tile against the other wall and mark the second cut line. Cut the corner with a wet saw.

Installing flooring around doors

UNDERCUTTING THE DOOR TRIM
In places where the flooring meets door trim, the standard practice is to cut away the bottom of the trim and install the flooring under it. Once you've installed the underlayment—building felt, rosin paper, plywood, or foam—put a piece of flooring (wood, laminate, or tile) upside down next to the trim. Set a trim saw on the flooring and use it as a guide to cut away the trim. This will create a recess into which the new flooring will fit snugly when you install it.

Changing direction

Sometimes—at doorways, for example—a tongue-and-groove floor requires that two grooves face each other. Unsupported facing grooves are an invitation for loose boards, squeaks, expansion problems, and just about anything else that can go wrong with a floor.

To solve the problem, cut a spline (a piece of plywood) that fits into the grooves. To allow for expansion, cut the spline wide enough to bottom out in one groove and extend halfway into the other groove. Test-fit the pieces and make sure they form a tight seam when assembled. Glue the spline into one of the grooves, wipe off any excess glue, and let it dry. Nail the spline into the floor and install the groove of the next piece over it. If one of the boards is the last piece in the room and lies along the wall, you might have to trim the tongue from the opposite side to fit.

Preparation

 reparing to install new flooring is a part of the job people rarely think about, but it's the key to success. In some cases you have to remove the old flooring first. Old flooring comes off in different ways: Carpet lifts off, while vinyl tile scrapes off or comes up with the underlayment below it. Linoleum may be glued firmly in place or only around the edge. If you're lucky, it's not glued at all.

If you're really lucky, the new flooring can be installed over what is already there. For example, you can install almost any material over a sound wood floor. You can even lay ceramic tile over old ceramic tile. Laminate floors can be laid over almost any old flooring, including embossed vinyl.

New flooring won't fix structural problems. That's something you must do before the new material goes down. The repairs most often necessary call for driving a few nails or maybe pouring some leveling compound. Sometimes, but not often, floor repair calls for serious carpentry.

Preparation is the time to assess the strength of your subfloor if you're installing ceramic tile. You might need to reinforce the floor to support the considerable weight of backerboard, thinset mortar, and tile. This is also the time to install radiant heating if you want to have warm floors in the winter.

Keep your preparation work organized in sections. It always helps to ease into a job, especially if you're not familiar with its

Chapter 3 highlights

 70 REMOVING BASEBOARDS AND TRIM
This is the first task you'll need to do when you start your project.

 71 REMOVING TOILETS AND SINKS
Getting these fixtures out of the way will give you more working room.

 72 REMOVING CARPET
Removing carpet is easy when you start the job in a corner.

 73 REMOVING/REPAIRING WOOD FLOORS
Wood flooring must be free of damage and dents before you put new material on it.

 74 REMOVING VINYL SHEETS AND TILE
You can install some flooring right over old vinyl, but if you must remove it, here's how.

 76 USING CERAMIC TILE AS SUBSTRATE
Tile is one material you sometimes can leave in place.

 77 REMOVING CERAMIC FLOOR TILES
This laborious task requires hammers and chisels.

 78 REINFORCING A WOOD SUBFLOOR
Squeaks are not only annoying. They are a symptom that something's not quite right.

 82 PREPARING A CONCRETE FLOOR
A concrete floor must be flat and cracks must be treated before laying flooring on it.

 86 INSTALLING UNDERLAYMENT
Underlayment makes a smooth surface for new flooring materials.

 88 INSTALLING RADIANT HEAT
With some mats and staples, you can keep your new floor warm in cold weather.

 91 PREPARING VINYL FLOORS
Vinyl floors can be used as substrate if you treat them right.

details, so do the easy stuff first. Most flooring prep starts with the removal of the baseboard and shoe molding. Then remove fixtures and appliances that will be in the way. (Remember to turn off the electrical, gas, and water service to appliances you're moving.) Take your time and work carefully.

Removing baseboards and trim

1 f there are appliances or fixtures in the room, it's usually better to remove them before tackling the baseboards and trim. That way, you'll have clear access to the baseboard.

Take the shoe molding off carefully if you plan to reuse it. Shoe molding is not only relatively thin, it's probably brittle after being installed for years, and if you don't remove it by prying right at the nail locations, you'll almost certainly split it.

To make removal easier, drive the nails deeper into the wood with a nail set. That way they don't have as much wood holding them and the shoe molding will pop off the nail heads. If you plan to reuse the shoe, number the pieces as you take them off. In most cases, moldings will only fit in their original position without cutting.

REMOVE SHOE MOLDING AND BASEBOARD
Hold up a piece of scrap to protect the baseboard and insert a wide putty knife or flat pry bar behind the shoe molding at the nail locations. Gently pry the shoe loose—but not completely, to avoid splitting it. Then move to the next nails and pry again. Pull off the shoe and repeat the process for the baseboard.

REMOVE VINYL COVE MOLDING
Push the corner of a wide-blade putty knife behind the corner of the cove molding, and holding the putty knife as flat against the wall as possible, loosen the adhesive. Don't try to pry the molding off. Push the blade until you have enough molding loose to work with, then push the putty knife along the wall, breaking the adhesive bond.

Removing thresholds

 REAL WORLD

DON'T MEAN TO PRY
Removing baseboard isn't as easy as it seems. It's usually nailed top and bottom with the nails angled toward each other. More than one homeowner has had to buy a replacement baseboard after breaking the old one. Take your time. Do most of your work with a pry bar, and pry close to the nails that are creating the problem. If you still have trouble with the board, drive the nails through the molding and into the wall.

1 **CUT THE THRESHOLD**
If the threshold is screwed down, remove the screws and slide the threshold out from under the trim. If the threshold is nailed, use a handsaw or backsaw to cut through the threshold at about midway along its length. Cut all the way to the surface of the floor.

2 **PRY UP THE PIECES**
Insert the flat end of a pry bar under the pieces and pry them up. Be sure to work from the side of the room in which you'll be installing the new flooring to avoid damaging flooring you want to keep.

Removing toilets and sinks

I n one sense, removing toilets and sinks before a flooring job might seem optional. But removal is the most practical option in almost all cases. First, the absence of the fixtures will give you more clear working room. Second, with the toilet out of the way, you'll only have to cut the flooring for the drain hole. If you don't remove the toilet, you'll have to make many more cuts. In the long run, removing the fixtures will take less time than making all the cuts in the flooring.

Before you remove the toilet, pour a quart of bleach into the tank, flush it, and let it refill. Close the supply valve and flush again, holding the handle down until the tank empties. Push the water out of the trap with a plunger and stuff the bowl with rags.

3

PREPARATION

1

DISCONNECT THE SUPPLY LINES
Loosen the supply line nut with a wrench, unscrew the nut until it's completely loose from the threads, and pull the line from the valve seat.

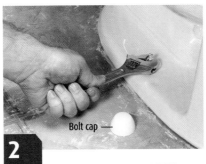

2

REMOVE THE FLANGE BOLTS
Pull off the bolt caps (or pry them loose with a screwdriver) and remove the bolts with a wrench or groove-joint pliers. Hacksaw the bolts if they spin.

Bolt cap —

3

REMOVE THE TOILET
The toilet trap fits snugly over a wax ring that seals it. You'll have to break the seal by gently rocking the toilet body as you lift it. Lift the toilet off the floor and carry it to another room. Get help carrying the toilet to avoid injuring your back.

Removing a sink

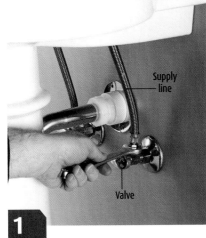

1

Supply line

Valve

DISCONNECT THE SUPPLY LINES
Shut off the hot and cold water valves, loosen the compression nuts with a wrench, and pull the supply line out of the valve.

2

REMOVE THE TRAP AND MOUNTING BOLTS
The trap will contain a small amount of water, so set a bucket under it. Loosen the fittings on both ends of the trap with groove-joint pliers and pull the trap off the tailpiece. Dump the water in the bucket and remove the mounting bolts.

3

REMOVE THE SINK
If your sink has a pedestal, remove the bolts attaching it. Grasp the sink near the wall and pull it up off the mounting bracket. Unbolt the pedestal from the floor and lift it off.

Removing carpet

Removing glue-down carpet

Carpets that are glued to the floor are harder to remove than those on tackless strips. Foam-backed carpets are especially difficult because pulling up the carpet leaves a layer of foam stuck to the floor. You have two options. One is a floor scraper—essentially a wide putty knife on a long handle. The other, a floor stripper with a vibrating blade that cuts through the carpet to the subfloor, is much quicker. First pull up whatever you can by hand. To use the floor stripper, start by cutting the carpet into long strips about 12 inches wide. Then cut a strip in the center of the carpet that is perpendicular to the long strips. Remove the center portion with the stripper, then remove the rest of the carpet piece by piece.

⊘ SAFETY ALERT

PROTECT YOUR HEARING
A floor stripper has a blade that vibrates up to 5,000 times per minute. Put on high-quality hearing protection while you're using the machine.

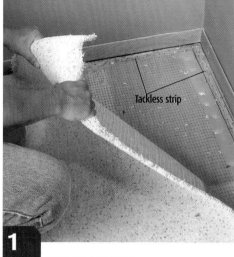

1
PULL UP A CORNER
Carpet is generally held in place by tackless strips, which are nailed to the floor around the edge of the room, as shown here. To remove the carpet, first pull the corner loose by grabbing it with a pair of pliers.

Tackless strip

2
PULL UP THE CARPET
Grab the loose corner of the carpet and pull. The carpet will begin to come loose from the rest of the tackless strips. Work your way around the wall, pulling on the carpet until it is completely free of the strips.

3
CUT AND ROLL
Once you have the carpet pulled away from the tackless strips—and if you're not going to resuse it elsewhere—cut it into strips 2 or 3 feet wide. Cut from the back of the carpet with a hook-bladed carpet knife, keeping your hands well away from the blade. Roll the strips one by one, tie them with cord, and haul them out of the room.

4
REMOVE THE PAD
Pull the padding loose from its staples. Remove the staples from the floor with a pair of pliers. To make sure you've removed them all, slide a wide putty knife or floor scraper across the floor. It will catch on any remaining staples. If the tackless strips are damaged or the new floor won't be carpet, remove the strips with a pry bar.

Removing/repairing wood floors

I f your existing floor is solid wood and it's in good condition, it's a good substrate for several flooring materials. The key question is whether the new floor level will be higher than the old level by more than ¾ inch. If the new floor will be thicker than that, it is usually better to remove the old one. Removing the old floor also reveals hidden faults you would otherwise not be able to see.

WORK SMARTER

INSTALLING OVER PREVIOUS FLOORING
Before you start tearing out old flooring, however, make sure that it's necessary. Sheet vinyl can often go over sheet vinyl; most floors, including ceramic tile, can be installed over existing ceramic tile. Almost anything can be installed over an old wood floor. To find out what's possible and what isn't, check the "At a Glance" sidebars at the beginning of each project. You can call the flooring manufacturer for advice too. The number is usually listed in the instructions.

Removing a hardwood floor

1

PLUNGE-CUT THE FLOOR
Set your circular saw so it cuts only through the thickness of the flooring and not into the subfloor. Starting in the center of the floor, rest the saw plate at an angle, start the saw, and lower the blade into the wood. Cut a section at least a foot wide.

2

PRY UP THE FLOORING
Tap a flat pry bar under the flooring at the nails and pry it up, working your way along each piece until you can pull it away. Be sure to push the pry bar under the board beyond the tongue or groove. Otherwise you'll simply snap off the tongue or groove and not remove the flooring.

Repairing a wood floor

INSTALL A PLYWOOD PATCH
Using the same techniques shown above for removing a wood floor, make a series of plunge cuts until you have a rectangle larger than the damaged area. Remove the flooring in this area and cut a plywood patch of the same thickness and dimensions as the rectangle. Fasten the patch to the subfloor with construction adhesive and screws.

Removing parquet

TAP AND PRY THE PARQUET LOOSE
Using a wide wood chisel (at least 1 inch) tap the blade under one edge of one parquet tile to lift it up. Work a pry bar under the tile and remove it. Then continue prying the remaining tiles loose with the pry bar.

Removing vinyl sheets and tile

I f you're certain your vinyl flooring is asbestos-free (see the "Safety Alert" below), removing it is straightforward. Usually the entire sheet is glued down to underlayment or a subfloor. Sometimes it's glued only around the edges. If you're lucky it lies flat on the floor with no adhesive at all. Whatever's there, you must keep removing layers until you have a solid surface for the new floor—subfloor, concrete, or old flooring. Underlayment applied over the subfloor is usually in bad shape by the time you remove whatever was over it—take this off as well.

Start by testing your luck in the middle of the floor. Remove a section with a utility knife to see if it's glued down. If so, rent a floor stripper. If the flooring pulls up freely until you reach the edge of the room, pull up what you can and scrape up the rest by hand or machine. If you lift up the sheet and don't run into any glue, cut the vinyl into manageable sections and toss it.

⊘ SAFETY ALERT

OLD RESILIENT FLOORING MAY CONTAIN ASBESTOS

To the naked eye, there's no difference between flooring that contains asbestos and flooring that doesn't. If a floor does contain asbestos, that doesn't mean you and your family are in danger with every step. Asbestos in old flooring is encapsulated in the material around it and isn't released into the air unless it's abused. Cutting through the flooring with a knife, for example, won't release asbestos fibers if done correctly. Sanding it, sawing it, scraping it, or removing it with a mechanical chipper, however, will. So the first rule of working with an old resilient floor is to assume it contains asbestos unless you know otherwise. If possible, lay the new floor right over it, which will further isolate the asbestos.

Several types of flooring, including wood, engineered wood, laminate, and vinyl flooring, can be installed over existing vinyl. Ceramic tile can be laid on backerboard set over old vinyl. You can also apply a ¼-inch plywood underlayment over the vinyl. Install carpet over the new underlayment using any of the techniques described in "Carpet," beginning on page 178.

Have suspect flooring removed only as a last resort—if it is damaged, flaking, or has been pulverized in spots, for example. Hire a flooring installer who has taken the 8-hour training seminar offered by the Resilient Floor Covering Institute. Make sure the installer uses the proper equipment, including a HEPA vacuum and a detergent that contains anionic, nonionic, and amphoteric surfactants.

If you plan to remove suspect flooring, contact the Resilient Floor Covering Institute, 401 E. Jefferson St., Suite 102, Rockville, MD 20850; 301/340-7283; www.rfci.com and ask for their booklet "Recommended Work Practices for Removal of Resilient Floor Coverings."

1

SEE WHAT'S UNDER THE FLOOR

This is where you'll find out if you have potential asbestos problems. Cut out a section in the floor with a utility knife or pry off the metal edge in a doorway. Examine the edge of the flooring to see what's under the vinyl. Starting from the bottom, this subfloor is covered with vinyl that may or may not contain asbestos; the suspect vinyl is covered with ¼-inch underlayment, which is, in turn, covered with the top layer of vinyl. If you suspect asbestos, hire a certified pro to remove the old flooring. If you are sure none of the layers contains asbestos, set the blade of your circular saw to the thickness of the layers and cut the flooring into 4×4-foot sections.

2

REMOVE VINYL AND UNDERLAYMENT

If the sheet vinyl is glued to an underlayment that is, in turn, nailed to the subfloor, remove the vinyl and underlayment at the same time. Put a pry bar underneath the corner of the underlayment and pry it loose. Move along both edges that form the corner, prying until you can lift off the underlayment and the vinyl on top of it. Pull up the underlayment one piece at a time. You'll encounter many nails; using a long-handled floor scraper as a pry bar may give you the leverage you need. If the underlayment was glued to the subfloor, remove both with a floor stripper.

3 **USE A FLOOR STRIPPER**

If the vinyl or underlayment is glued to a subfloor, try removing it with a hand scraper. First cut the floor with a utility knife into strips as wide as the scraper blade. If the floor won't come up, rent a floor stripper. With some strippers, you tilt the machine back; with others, you run the machine flat on the floor. Follow the manufacturer's directions, using a blade designed for the subfloor material. Push the stripper along between knife marks, scraping up the surface as you go.

4 **CLEAN THE SUBFLOOR**

Whatever is under the vinyl, whether it's adhesive or another layer of underlayment, remove it entirely. Unplug the machine and put in a new, sharp blade. Go over the entire floor again to remove the adhesive. Keep scraping until you have a clean floor. When you're finished, the floor may need some repair. If so, patch and level it as explained on page 80.

Removing vinyl tile

1 **SOFTEN THE ADHESIVE**

Vinyl tile will come up much more quickly if you soften the adhesive before you start scraping. Warm the adhesive with a heat gun or a hair dryer set on high heat. Start at a corner, insert a floor scraper or wide putty knife, and lift up the tile. Scrape the adhesive from the floor with a floor scraper.

2 **REMOVE THE TILE**

Continue softening the tiles, removing them one at a time until you have cleared the floor. If a lot of tiles tear as you remove them, keep the heat on the tile as you lift or scrape it.

3 **CLEAN UP THE ADHESIVE**

Once you have removed all the tile, clean the adhesive from the subfloor. Spray the floor in sections with an adhesive remover. Let the solution work according to the directions, then use a scraper to peel the residue from the floor.

Using ceramic tile as substrate

Before you tear out a ceramic tile floor for your new floor, remember that some flooring can be installed over existing ceramic tile as long as the increase in the height of the floor does not interfere with doors, appliances, and safety. In some cases, you can apply the new material directly over the tiles. In other cases, you'll have to do some prep work, but that work is not as hard or messy as removing the tile. If the new floor is to be nailed down, you'll have to provide a new nailing surface. If the new floor is resilient vinyl, you'll need to fill any irregularities (grout joints and surface texture) to which the new floor might conform. If the new floor is ceramic tile, laminate, or engineered wood, you can apply it over tile with a minimal amount of fuss.

Laminate and engineered: easy as pie

These rigid manufactured plank floors can be installed over ceramic tile quite easily. Laminate flooring can be installed directly over ceramic floors with no additional preparation. Engineered flooring can be glued directly to clean, dry, and sound ceramic floors. It cannot, however, be nailed in place.

SMOOTHING CERAMIC TILE FOR SUBSTRATE
The ceramic floor must be sound, clean, dry, and dust-free. Rough up the surface by belt-sanding with a 40-grit aluminum oxide belt. Vacuum and wipe with a damp rag. Patch holes with a fast-setting patch-and-underlayment compound. Spread the compound with a straight-edged trowel to create a smooth surface. Some compounds require application of a primer first.

INSTALLING WOOD FLOORING OVER CERAMIC TILE
It's impossible to nail into a ceramic floor, but you can adhere $3/4$-inch CDX plywood to the tile, and nail a wood floor to that (except on a concrete slab below grade). Cut the plywood into 4×4-foot sheets. Make $3/8$-inch-deep cuts on a 12-inch grid across the bottom of each piece; this allows the plywood to flex and follow the contour of the floor. Spread mastic across the floor with a trowel and put down the plywood sheets. Stagger the seams from row to row by cutting the first piece of every other row in half. If the ceramic tiles are on a concrete slab, apply two layers of construction felt before installing the plywood. Set each layer in mastic. Run the second layer parallel to the first, but stagger the seams.

INSTALLING CERAMIC TILE OVER CERAMIC TILE
Ceramic tile can be laid directly over an existing tile floor, as long as the existing floor is sound. Clean to remove soap scum and other residue. Rinse well and let the floor dry. Then spread thinset and lay the tile.

Removing ceramic floor tiles

Ceramic tile is difficult to remove. If you must remove the floor, remember that the edges of broken tiles are razor sharp. Protect yourself with long sleeves, safety glasses, and gloves. If the walls will stay as they are, protect them by leaning sheets of tempered hardboard against them.

If the tiles are set in mastic, they usually come up easily with a long-handled floor scraper. Older mastics might contain asbestos, however; unless you know otherwise, always assume asbestos is present. Removing asbestos-laden mastic requires special precautions and respirators and other equipment. For complete guidelines, contact the Resilient Floor Covering Institute, 401 E. Jefferson St., Suite 102, Rockville, MD, 20850.

Removing tiles set in thinset mortar is even harder work and will usually require removal of the subfloor also.

Removing tiles set in mastic

1 BREAK UP THE TILE
Break the grout loose between the tiles with a sledge hammer and cold chisel. Once the grout is loose, put the chisel against the edge of a tile and hit it with a sledge hammer to break it free. You may have to hit the tile in several places to break it loose. If the tile is especially stubborn, rent an electric chipping hammer.

2 SCRAPE OFF THE TILE
If you're certain the mastic is asbestos-free, scrape away the tile fragments and mastic with a long-handled floor scraper. If the floor is rough when you're finished, level it with a patching compound.

Removing tiles set in thinset or mortar

1 CHIP OFF THE TILE
Rent an electric chipping hammer and break the tile loose from the thinset or mortar bed. Start by chipping away a grout line, then break loose a tile. Once you've removed the first tile, work your way across the floor.

> ⊘ **SAFETY ALERT**
>
> **SHARP EDGE ALERT**
> Wear safety glasses, gloves, and long sleeves to protect yourself from the sharp edges of broken tile. Wear a dust mask when breaking up tile and mortar.

2 OPTION A: REMOVING BACKERBOARD
If the tiles were set on backerboard, cut through backerboard with a circular saw and a carbide blade. Set the saw just deep enough to cut through the backerboard (and not the subfloor) and cut it into sections. Remove the screws, pry up the backerboard, and break loose the thin layer of mortar underneath.

OPTION B: REMOVING A MORTAR BED
If the tiles were set in a thick bed of mortar, cut through the mortar bed and the subfloor. A mortar bed is thicker than a backerboard base, and the combined thickness of the floor may be more than an inch. It's a durable installation, and if the tile was set in mortar, you won't be able to salvage the subfloor. Put an old carbide blade in a circular saw and set it deep enough to cut through the mortar and subfloor but not into the joists. Pry up the sections with a pry bar. Install a new subfloor as recommended by the manufacturer.

Reinforcing a wood subfloor

Almost everything that goes wrong with a wooden subfloor shows up as a squeak. The sound you hear could be the floor flexing. It could be the floorboards or the sheets of the plywood subfloor rubbing against each other. It could be the sound of the bridging pieces rubbing against each other below the floor. It could even be water pipes or air ducts squeaking as they rub against floor joists or flooring.

Most often, the root of the problem is a loose board, and the solution is a few well-placed nails. When possible, fix squeaks from underneath the floor or staircase. If the bottom of the floor is covered by a finished ceiling, work on squeaks from above. On hardwood floors, drive finishing nails into the seams between planks to silence squeaking. Check pipe hangers, heating ducts, and bridging for rubbing problems. Loosen tight pipe hangers and remove and reinstall wooden bridging members, leaving a small space between them.

Fixing a squeak

1 **ONCE YOU'VE LOCATED A SQUEAK...**
Stand above it and shift your weight up and down to see if the squeak is caused by a loose seam or poor support underneath. If the boards flex along the seam, look for an area where one side is higher than the other. Drive 8d flooring nails into the high side to pull it down.

2 **IF THE SQUEAK IS IN THE INTERIOR OF A SHEET...**
The problem is either the subfloor or the joists that support it. Check the floor with a straightedge. If the straightedge rocks back and forth over the problem area, the subfloor has probably separated from the joists. Nail it into the nearest joists with 8d flooring or spiral-shank nails.

Water damage

The damage done by water leaking from sinks, bathtubs, and toilets is often unseen. Because leaks may continue for months or even years before they're discovered, the damage can be extensive, even if the leaks are small. Look for water damage before you install your floor. Obvious signs include stains and perhaps plaster or drywall damage. Look for warped, rotten, or damp floors and subfloors.

If you find damage, fix the leak before making other repairs. (The leak may be some distance from the damage.) Cut out blistered or damaged subflooring with a circular saw. Set the blade so it's just deep enough to cut through the subfloor. Make the cuts down the center of the joists so that the replacement piece can rest on them.

Once you have removed the subfloor, check the joists for damage by poking them with a screwdriver. If it penetrates rotten wood, put in a shorter version of the sister joists described on page 79. Cut a patch out of the same material as the subfloor, and nail it to the joists with 8d flooring nails, driving the nails every 3 inches.

3 **IF YOU SEE A GAP BETWEEN THE STRAIGHTEDGE AND THE FLOOR...**
Or if the floor is flat but still flexes downward, the floor joists have sagged. Shimming usually solves the problem. Wedge shims into the gaps between the joists and subfloor and tap them into place, driving them no further than is needed to close the gap. Driving them too far will lift the floor and cause more squeaking.

Cleating and bridging a floor

CLEATING A FLOOR

If the flexing in the floor is limited to a small area, a cleat may solve the problem. Cut a 2×4 cleat that is 3 or 4 feet longer than the springy area, and apply construction adhesive to one side. Put the side with the adhesive against the joist that supports the springy area, and wedge it against the subfloor with another 2×4. Nail the cleat to the joists with 8d common nails spaced every 16 inches.

BRIDGING THE FLOOR

If the floor flexes or squeaks over a large area, it's often because the joists beneath the floor are shifting slightly as people move around above. In turn, the joists are providing inadequate support to the subfloor. Nail steel bridging to the joists to stabilize the floor.

Installing sister joists

1 **MEASURE AND CUT**

If bracing fails to do the job, you may need to install a sister joist, a full-size joist of the same width and length as the problem joist. Remove any braces that are in the way, and cut the sister joist to length, guiding the cut with a layout square as shown.

2 **TEST-FIT THE SISTER JOIST**

Often pipes, ductwork, and the narrow space between existing joists make it difficult to get the sister joist in place. If so, you can take out a few extra inches by chamfering the sister joist's ends (see inset). If this fails, try cutting the board a little shorter, keeping it long enough to sit on whatever surface supports the joists. If this won't work, cut the joist in half and butt the two cut ends tightly against each other when you install them.

3 **APPLY CONSTRUCTION ADHESIVE AND NAIL**

Apply construction adhesive to the inner surface of the sister joist. Place the sister joist against the existing joist and nail through the sister with 8d common nails spaced every 16 inches. Drive two rows of nails, each about 1 inch from the edge of the joist. If you had to cut the sister joist to make it fit, apply a 4-foot-long cleat across the cut. Reinstall any braces you removed.

Leveling a subfloor

1

TEST FOR LEVEL

Working in 4-foot sections, set a 6-foot level on the floor, then measure any low spots to determine if they exceed the manufacturer's requirements.

2

MARK THE LOW SPOTS

Wherever the floor shows low spots that exceed the manufacturer's specifications, mark these areas with a carpenter's pencil.

3

PRIME THE LOW SPOTS

If the leveling compound requires it, you will need to prime the areas you intend to repair. Don't overapply the primer. Let it set according to the manufacturer's instructions.

4

SEAL OFF DOORWAYS

If you're leveling the entire floor, nail strips of wood across doorways to keep the compound from flowing into other rooms. The strips don't have to be particularly thick or high, but make sure they fit snugly in or across the doorway and that they are placed firmly against the floor. Close openings around pipes with self-adhering weather stripping.

5

MIX THE COMPOUND

If you're leveling the entire floor, find out whether the brand you're using requires you to staple sheets of metal lath to the floor first (inset). Mix the material in a 5-gallon bucket according to the directions on the bag. Have two or three buckets, and always clean them out and scrub them thoroughly before mixing more compound. Compound that has set up in the bucket can make the fresh compound dry almost immediately.

6

POUR THE COMPOUND

If you're filling a dip, pour some compound into it, spread it with a float, and let it seek its own level. If you're leveling an entire floor, start against a wall and pour the compound over an area near the corner. Have a helper spread it with a tool called a long-handled gauge spreader, shown here. The spreader has guides that keep it slightly above the floor so that you spread the compound instead of wiping it off. Work your way across the wall, then apply in rows parallel to the first.

Repairing problems on the second floor

Problems on the second floor, or those over a finished basement, can be harder to fix than those above an unfinished basement. You can still nail down uncooperative subflooring, and you can still level the floor if you must. Cleats and crossbracing are out of the question, however, because there's a ceiling in the way.

The standards for flooring are the same on the second floor as they are on the first. Ceramic tiles installed over a springy floor are still going to crack; the joints in unglued laminate floors may work loose; floating floors are likely to develop problems; and manufacturers won't guarantee any flooring installed over a floor that doesn't meet their standards. So what do you do?

You work from above by cutting away flooring. You'll need to install sister joists, and as you'll see, doing so can turn into a major job. If you have to install more than one sister joist, consider hiring a carpenter. If you have only one joist to sister, make sure it's worth doing. Tell your flooring dealer what the problem is, and ask whether it will affect installation and about any alternative solutions.

1 REMOVE THE SUBFLOOR

Walk over the floor and check it for problems as described on pages 78 and 79. If you find a problem joist, locate the joists on either side of it. Snap a chalk line down the center of these two joists and remove any nails along or within 1/4 inch of the line. Set your circular saw just deep enough to cut through the subfloor. (If you're not sure, start with a cut 1/2 inch deep and increase it by eighths until you've cut through.) Cut along the lines, guided by a straightedge you've nailed to the floor. When you reach the walls, make a crosscut between the lines, using the wall as a guide. Pry up the flooring between the cuts.

2 CUT A SISTER JOIST

Use a joist that's as thick, wide, and long as the existing joists. Once you've made the cut, drill two rows of 1/4-inch holes in the sister joist for bolts you will use to hold it in place. Space the holes 16 inches apart and 1 inch from each edge. If you drill the holes on the subfloor, protect it with pieces of scrap.

Measure the length of the problem joist and make sure you can get a 2× that long into the room.

3 DRILL THE BOLT HOLES

Put the joist in place and clamp it. Then drill holes through both joists. Remove the sister joist and apply construction adhesive to the face that adheres to the existing joist.

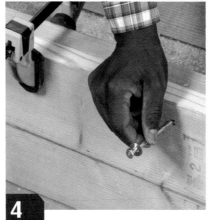

4 BOLT THE ASSEMBLY

Slip a washer over a 1/4-inch hex-head bolt and put the bolt in one of the holes. Slip another washer over the bolt, and hand-tighten the nut until it's snug. Further tighten with a wrench. Then install bolts in the remaining holes. Replace the subflooring you cut out, cutting new pieces if necessary, and nail them in place.

WORK SMARTER

SISTER ACT

Sister joists are used most often to shore up sagging joists; that is, joists that bend downward in the middle. Sometimes, however, a joist bows up instead of down. If this happens, start by asking a contractor to determine if it was caused by a structural problem. Find out what might have caused the problem, what can be done to fix it, and how much it will cost. Get opinions and estimates from at least three contractors before deciding what to do.

Preparing a concrete floor

PROJECT DETAILS

SKILLS: Mixing, measuring, and using a level
PROJECT: Preparing an 8'×10' floor

TIME TO COMPLETE

EXPERIENCED: Variable
HANDY: Variable
NOVICE: Variable
Prep time depends on the condition of the floor.

STUFF YOU'LL NEED

TOOLS: Duct tape, polyethylene sheeting, calcium chloride moisture test kit, floor scraper, chalk line and nail, level, gloves, safety glasses
MATERIALS: Self-leveling flooring compound for concrete

Preparation of a concrete subfloor requires steps similar to those required for a wood floor. Like a wood subfloor, a concrete slab must be clean, dry, flat, and free of oil. Any cracks should be repaired. In some cases, you might have to test the pH of the concrete to find out if the surface is compatible with the flooring that will cover it.

Is the slab clean?

Concrete that is oily, dirty, or waxy is unsuitable for a floor that requires any kind of adhesive, including mortar. The adhesives just won't stick to such a surface. To test the surface, first sweep the floor clean. Then dribble some water onto the floor. If the water beads up, you'll need to clean the floor. Ask your supplier for the appropriate cleanser. Some strippers leave behind residue that weakens the adhesive you put down. Rinse the floor thoroughly once you've cleaned it to remove all traces of stripper. Then, just to be on the safe side, test it again.

Most of the tests are simple. Work in sections with a carpenter's level and mark areas that are higher or lower than the main body of the floor. A glass of water is all you need to test for oil, and most moisture tests require nothing more than a piece of plastic.

By and large, repairs are simple too, but they can be messy. Wear gloves: The lime in concrete compounds causes extensive skin damage.

CLOSER LOOK

A SEALED DEAL
Concrete is often coated with a clear sealant to protect it and keep out moisture. Unfortunately, sealants will prevent mastics and mortars from sticking to the concrete. To test for sealer, dribble some water on the surface of the concrete. If it beads up, the surface is sealed. Depending on the sealer, you may or may not be able to remove it. Check with your flooring manufacturer for details.

Let a new concrete floor cure 3 to 4 months before installing flooring.

Testing and leveling the floor

1

TEST FOR MOISTURE

Water can wick up through concrete and damage or ruin your new floor. If you have a moisture problem, you'll need to fix it before leveling the floor. To test for moisture, tape several 2×2-foot pieces of polyethylene to the floor about 2 feet from each other. Put a light on the floor near the poly and turn it on to help create natural convection. If the concrete is dark after 72 hours or if the poly is cloudy or covered with condensation, the floor is too damp. Ask the manufacturer of the finished floor about possible solutions.

2

CHECK FOR SLOPE AND FLATNESS

Typically a floor should slope no more than about 1 inch in 4 feet, but again, check your manufacturer's specifications. Place a 6-foot level on the floor and lift one end until the bubble is centered in the vial. The gap between the floor and the level shows how far out of level the floor is: In this case, the floor slope is an acceptable $\frac{1}{2}$ inch out of level over a 6-foot span. Working in sections, rotate the level across the surface and mark high and low spots.

3 POUR LEVELER

If much of the floor is marked with high and low spots or is sloped more than 1 inch every 4 feet, you may have to pour leveler across its entire surface. Nail 2×4s between the door jambs to keep the leveler from flowing into adjacent rooms. Start in the corner that is farthest from the door, always pouring the next bucket so the material flows into wet leveler.

4 FILL LOW SPOTS

If you find low spots at random locations in the floor, repair them with spot applications of self-leveling compound. Mix up a small batch of compound according to the manufacturer's directions. Pour it into the low spot and spread it with a trowel or squeegee. The compound will flow out to a feathered edge. Let the patch dry for six days before applying the new floor.

Installing a waterproof or isolation membrane

ROLL ON THE ADHESIVE

Apply the adhesive with a roller, starting at a wall opposite the doorway. Work in sections. apply an even coat of adhesive on both sides of the crack. .

Water is the chief enemy of most building materials, including ceramic tile and other flooring materials. Water that penetrates a tile bed weakens the adhesive, promotes rot, and nourishes organisms destructive to the wood subfloor. Bathrooms, kitchens, and surfaces that require frequent cleaning are especially vulnerable. And even though many ceramic tiles and their mortars are waterproof, you can't be absolutely sure your installation is waterproof without a waterproofing membrane.

Waterproofing membranes come in several forms. There are fiber membranes and trowel-applied membranes. One of the easiest materials to install relies on an adhesive you spread with a roller.

An isolation membrane (also called a slip sheet) is a kind of bandage for cracks in concrete. It is designed to allow the concrete along a crack to expand and contract, without telegraphing those movements into the flooring.

TOOL TIP

TO BE PRECISE...

If there is a precise moisture requirement specified for your subfloor, you'll have to do a calcium chloride test. You'll need three kits (from your flooring distributor) for the first 1,000 square feet, and at least one for every additional 1,000 square feet. The kit contains a sealed container of calcium chloride and a protective plastic dome. Clean the floor of all adhesives and residue with a scraper and wire brush 24 hours prior to the test, and keep the heat and humidity at whatever levels the

directions indicate. To conduct the test, weigh the container of calcium chloride, remove the seal, and set it under the plastic dome for 60 to 72 hours. Then reweigh the calcium. Based on the results, you can calculate how much moisture is present.

You'll need a scale that measures to the tenth of a gram. If you don't have such a scale, you can find one at an electronics store, scientific supply store, or on the Internet for less than $50.

Testing the pH

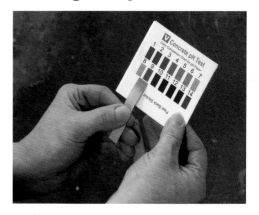

On some jobs—especially those that involve adhesives—the acidity or alkalinity of the floor is a concern. Check manufacturer's directions to determine whether you need to test the concrete's pH. If so, purchase a pH test kit from a flooring distributor. Pour a small amount of water on the floor as directed and let it sit for about a minute. Dab the litmus paper in the water. Compare the test strip to the color key to determine the pH of your floor.

Evaluating cracked concrete

Any concrete floor is almost certain to crack. Some cracks, called inactive cracks, do not become any wider and have stabilized themselves. They are almost always caused by shrinkage in the concrete and are of little concern. Active cracks—those which keep widening or cause the concrete to be higher on one side of the crack than the other—pose problems for flooring. Set a level across the crack. If the crack is active, you'll see a gap underneath one side of the bottom edge.

An active crack can indicate structural problems in the concrete. Such a crack defies most attempts to repair it and will crack or pull apart any flooring installed over it.

If you find active cracks in your concrete subfloor, you should consult a professional builder or flooring contractor.

AN INACTIVE CRACK
A harmless shrinkage crack is indicated if there is no vertical displacement across the crack. This crack probably occurred during the first year as the slab dried out.

AN ACTIVE CRACK
A troublesome active crack is indicated by vertical displacement—a difference in height—across the crack. The cause is movement of the soil beneath, which will continue and damage your flooring installation.

Repairing cracked concrete

Fixing large cracks

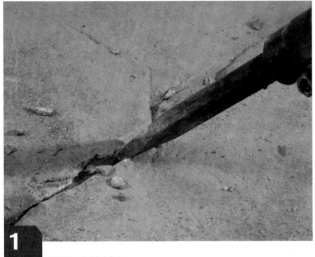

1 KEY THE CRACK

With a hammer drill or small sledge and masonry chisel, reshape the crack so the bottom is wider than the top (called "keying the crack"). Keying helps anchor the patching material. Chisel out any weak or crumbling spots too. If the crack is deeper than $1/2$ inch, paint it with a bonding adhesive made by the company that manufactures the patching compound you'll be using. Let it dry thoroughly before applying the patch.

2 PATCH THE CRACK

On cracks up to about $1/2$ inch deep, trowel in a vinyl concrete patch. Mix according to the directions on the bag or pail, and trowel a $1/4$-inch layer into the crack. If more layers are necessary, let the patch dry according to the manufacturer's recommendations before applying a new layer. Trowel the final layer smooth and flush.

3 FILLING DEEP CRACKS

On deeper cracks, prepare some sand mix according to the directions on the bag. Trowel it into the crack, filling it flush with the surface. When the sheen dries off the surface, work the patch so it matches the rest of the concrete. If the existing surface is slightly porous, smooth the surface with a wooden float. If the existing concrete is very smooth, even out the surface with a metal finishing trowel. If the surface is covered with swirls, pull a whisk broom across the patch.

Fixing a small crack

Blow dust from the crack with a shop vac. If the crack is deep, fill it partially with sand, leaving a space about $1/4$ to $1/2$ inch deep. Squeeze some crack sealer into the opening until it forms a layer $1/4$ inch deep. Let it dry overnight, then apply another layer. Repeat until the surface is flush with the floor. Be sure not to overfill.

Installing underlayment

Many floors require both a subfloor and some kind of underlayment. These terms are often used interchangeably, so make sure you are using the same definitions as your flooring retailer. To make it even more confusing, the word "substrate" is often a synonym for both underlayment and subflooring.

Essentially the subfloor is structural, usually made of $3/4$-inch plywood or oriented strand board (OSB) attached directly to the joists. It holds up the floor, and provides a solid base for the underlayment and the flooring material.

Underlayment (commonly some form of $1/4$-inch plywood, but also cement board for ceramic tile floors) performs several functions: It provides a puncture-resistant base for the floor, with a smooth surface that will expand and contract very little. Whatever you use as underlayment, leave small gaps in between sheets when you install it because plywood expands slightly as humidity rises. Some floorings require that you fill the gaps with an elastic filler; others don't.

You should be especially fussy about what is used underneath vinyl flooring. The vinyl conforms to underlayment defects over time, and you'll be able to see their outline in the vinyl. That's why it is extremely important to install smooth underlayment for vinyl. Some, but not all, lauan plywood has pigments that bleed through the vinyl, staining the floor. Be sure to ask the flooring dealer what kind of underlayment is recommended for your flooring.

Removing old underlayment

1 **CUT UNDERLAYMENT INTO SECTIONS**
Snap a grid of 2×2-foot chalklines (or any manageable size) on the underlayment. Set your circular saw so it cuts through the underlayment but not into the subfloor. Cut the underlayment on the lines.

2 **REMOVE THE UNDERLAYMENT**
If the underlayment is nailed to the subfloor, pry it up with a pry bar. If it's screwed down, you may be able to pop it loose with a pry bar, if the screws are not very long. Otherwise, you'll have to remove the fasteners before the underlayment sections.

Installing new underlayment

1 ACCLIMATE THE UNDERLAYMENT

Before installation, your underlayment needs to reach the same temperature and relative humidity as the subfloor. If it doesn't, it is liable to expand or contract once it's installed, resulting in gaps between sheets or even buckling. Bring the underlayment into the room at least three days before installing it. Stand the panels on edge and lean them against the wall.

2 INSTALL THE FIRST SHEET

Starting in a corner, set the underlayment so its length is perpendicular to the joists. Trim the panels, if necessary, so the edges are offset from the edges of the subfloor panels by at least 2 inches. Nail the panel in place with uncoated 4d ringshank or spiral-shank nails. Start about $\frac{3}{8}$ inch from the long edge and nail every 3 inches along it. Then work your way across the panel. Drive nails on a 6-inch grid across the face of the plywood and every 3 inches along the edges. If necessary, relocate individual nails to avoid nailing into the joists.

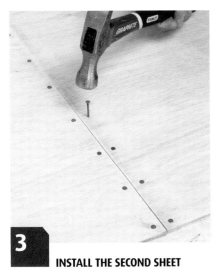

3 INSTALL THE SECOND SHEET

Put the next panel down, leaving a $\frac{1}{32}$-inch gap between the sheets to allow for the minor expansion that may occur. As before, drive the nails every 3 inches along edges and on a 6-inch grid across the rest of the surface. Continue laying sheets in the same row, trimming the last sheet as needed.

4 OFFSET THE JOINTS

Cut the first sheet of the next row in half so the end seam is offset from the end seam of the first row. (The allowable offset may be considerably less, depending on the floor that will go above it. Always follow the manufacturer's directions.) Nail it down as before, leaving $\frac{1}{32}$ inch between long edges of the sheets. Continue along the row, leaving $\frac{1}{32}$-inch gaps between sheets. Lay the rest of the underlayment the same way, alternating between full and half sheets at the beginning of each row.

5 FILL THE SEAMS

Some manufacturers require you to fill the gaps between sheets; others direct you to leave them open. If you need to fill the gaps, use a filler made especially for underlayment, applying it following the manufacturer's directions. Fill just the gaps—don't build up and feather out the surface the way you would mud a drywall seam. Make sure the trowel leaves a smooth surface without any ridges or gaps.

Installing radiant heat

3

PREPARATION

🔄 PROJECT DETAILS

SKILLS: Wiring, plumbing, masonry, and carpentry
PROJECT: Installing radiant heat in an 8'×10' floor

🕐 TIME TO COMPLETE

EXPERIENCED: Variable
HANDY: Variable
NOVICE: Variable

✓ STUFF YOU'LL NEED

TOOLS: Crimper, scissors, stapler, right-angle drill with ½-inch chuck and bit (Forstner or similar), hammer, safety mask, safety glasses, leather gloves, tubing cutter
MATERIALS: Low-voltage underfloor mats, 14-gauge tinned copper sleeves, staples, insulation, electrician's tape, PEX tubing, aluminum plates, nails

The principle behind radiant heat is simple: Instead of blowing hot air through a vent or pumping hot water to a baseboard radiator along the wall, radiant heat warms up the entire floor. No matter where you stand on a radiant floor, you're always directly above the heat source.

It's an energy-efficient system: In order for you to feel warm, the system only needs to heat the floor up to about 85 degrees. Studies show that, as a result, your energy costs may be 25 to 50 percent lower.

You can get heat into the floor two ways: through pipes carrying hot water embedded in or directly below the floor, or via electric mats, also in or below the floor.

Each has its advantages. Electric systems are thinner and, as a result, are good for retrofits. Some wires are designed to double as thermostats, simplifying installation. You needn't buy a separate furnace, so the initial cost is lower and no pipes will freeze or spring leaks.

Hot water is the standard for larger installations. It's generally more economical to operate and uses gas, propane, oil, solar energy, or geothermal energy (a heat pump) as a heat source. Because the flow can be minutely controlled, this system provides heat in the right amount exactly when and where you need it.

While there is a good deal of work you can do yourself, a hydronic floor is no less complicated than a zoned-baseboard heat system. It requires a boiler heated by gas, oil, or electricity. It requires valves and manifolds to distribute the water, as well as sophisticated thermostats to control the heat. While an electric system may be less complicated, certain systems involve heavy-duty wiring, and, in some cases, a new electrical panel.

If you're a hands-on person, find an installer who will work with you. Because running tubing or installing electrical elements is simple and time-consuming, it's the perfect job for a homeowner. If you're interested in saving a little money, let someone else design the system, then do the heavy lifting yourself.

🔍 CLOSER LOOK

ABOVE OR BELOW?
You can install radiant heat systems either above or below the subfloor. Ideally it's placed above the subfloor so the heat source is actually heating up the flooring material and not the subfloor. In a retrofit, however, this can raise the floor a couple of inches, creating problems with appliances and doors.

In an existing home, installation is usually below the floor—as long as the area beneath the floor is accessible. You can install the heating elements right against the floor. With a hydronic system, you'll attach aluminum plates beneath the floor to spread and store heat.

Whether the system is electric or hydronic, install insulation beneath it. If you don't, half of the heat you generate will seep away into the room below the one you're trying to heat.

Picking the right flooring

Radiant heating works great with some types of flooring, but not as well with others.

■ **Ceramic tile** has long been a favorite candidate for radiant heat flooring. You can lay the wires or tubes in a mortar bed underneath, and the tiles themselves conduct heat quickly. Wood has been considered a problem flooring in this arena because heat dries out wood, causing cracking and creating gaps between boards. Properly installed, wood does work over a radiant heat system.

■ **Vinyl** works well. It can be applied directly over a mortar, concrete, or gypsum base that covers the heating elements. Because it is thin, the floor heats quickly.

■ **Carpet** may or may not work, depending on the type. Thick carpets, or those with thick pads, won't work well because they act as insulation. Heat generated by the system stays trapped in the floor.

Installing underfloor electric radiant heat

There are two basic electric radiant heat systems: low-voltage mats and high-voltage cables. Cables are usually embedded in concrete and require some electrical skills to install. Mats, however, are easy to install and wire. Some have wires that double as thermostats: As the floor temperature rises, the ability of the wire to produce heat drops.

Mats made for above-the-floor installation need a layer of mortar for protection. Underfloor installations have to be insulated but otherwise need no protection.

Before starting an installation, check with an electrician to be sure your existing electrical system can handle the new circuit, if it needs one. In general you will need between 8 and 12 watts per square foot of heated floor. Make sure the floor you're installing under is suitable for radiant heat, and make sure the system is designed to account for climate and building insulation.

The system shown here is one of many available, and installation procedures vary from manufacturer to manufacturer. The system shown here is low voltage and uses a wire that acts as its own thermostat. Other systems require either a wall thermostat or one mounted directly in the floor. Always follow the manufacturer's recommendations.

Installing underfloor mats

1 **STAPLE THE MATS IN PLACE**

Unroll the mat material and cut it to length with scissors. Strip the insulation off an end of the two wires that run the length of the mat. Turn the mat so those ends are facing the wires that will bring power to it. Have a helper hold the mats against the bottom of the subfloor while you staple them in place. Don't install the 2 feet or so of mat to which you'll be attaching wire.

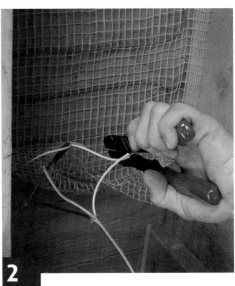

2 **CONNECT THE WIRES**

Crimp a black wire on one mat wire and a white wire on the other. You'll need a tinned copper sleeve for the job and a tool called a crimper. Slip the crimping sleeve over the wire at the end of the mat and put a 14-gauge stranded, tinned copper wire inside. Squeeze the crimping tool to crush the sleeve tightly over the wires. Cover the connection with electrician's tape.

Installing above the subfloor

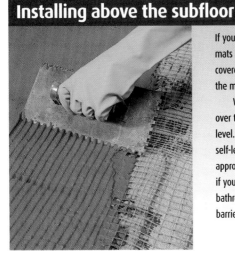

If you can't get to the underside of a floor, install electric mats above the floor. Keep in mind that they will have to be covered by a protective layer of gypsum or concrete. Staple the mats on top of the subfloor and wire as directed.

While some manufacturers advise spreading thinset over their mats, it can be difficult to keep the floor flat and level. Have the work done by a company that pumps a self-leveling gypsum mixture over the mats. Let it dry the appropriate length of time, then cover it with flooring as if you were installing the flooring over a concrete base. In bathrooms and kitchens, you'll need to install a moisture barrier to protect the gypsum.

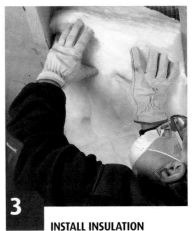

3 **INSTALL INSULATION**

Once all the mats are in place, install insulation between the joists, keeping it the recommended distance from the heating mats.

Installing an underfloor hydronic system

PEX tubing, the heart of a hydronic heating system, carries hot water along the length and width of a floor. PEX is short for cross-linked polyethylene, a plastic that has been manufactured specifically to remain flexible and withstand heated water.

Unlike electric mats, hydronic systems aren't prepackaged. Installation, however, is fairly simple. Work in the room below the floor you're going to heat. Start at a corner of the room and run tubing to the other side between the joists. Feed it into the bay between the neighboring joists through predrilled holes. When you've snaked tubing from one side of the room to the other, hold it in place with aluminum plates stapled to the subfloor. Some companies prefabricate the plates; others require you to bend your own. It's not all that difficult, but prefab is definitely quicker.

Have a professional design the layout: PEX comes in various diameters, and you want to make sure your system is properly sized. In addition, large areas or those with small spaces between the joists may require two sets of loops under the floor.

1 **DRILL THE HOLES FOR TUBING**
Drill a hole at one end of each bay so you can feed the tubing into the neighboring bay. Plan where each hole needs to be and drill them all before installation. Drill an oversize hole, as directed by the manufacturer, using a Forstner or similar bit. Spade bits aren't durable enough for a big job like this. Space will be tight and the drill bit will have a thick shank, so use a right-angle drill with a ½-inch chuck.

2 **THREAD THE TUBING**
Put a coil of PEX on the floor at one end of the first bay while a helper stands on the other end of the bay. Walk over to your helper while holding one end of the tubing. Put the tubing through the hole in the joist and pull it back to the other side of the room while your helper feeds it through the hole. When you reach the other side of the room, feed the tubing through the hole in the joist. Have your helper walk the tubing back to the other side of the room and feed it through the next joist hole. Continue until you've run tubing under the entire floor.

Above-the-floor installation

Like electric systems, you can install hydronic systems in a concrete, mortar, or gypsum bed. It's easier to install the tubing in specially made plywood with precut channels. Nail the plywood in place as you would a subfloor or underlayment. At the wall, install pieces with curved grooves that make a U-turn, and send the tubing back across the room in another groove.

You can install carpeting and wood flooring directly over the plywood. Vinyl requires underlayment, and ceramic and stone floors should be set in a mortar bed or on cement backerboard.

3 **FASTEN THE DISSIPATION PLATES**
Once the tubing is in place, go back to the beginning of the job. Hold the tubing against the underside of the subfloor and put an aluminum plate over it. Staple the plate to the subfloor. Space the plates along the tubing as directed by the manufacturer. If you have multiple loops, put a piece of tape on the ends of the tubing and label which end is connected to the heat source and which returns to the heat source. Have an installer connect the valves, manifolds, and pipes required to finish the job.

Preparing vinyl floors

Some resilient flooring (linoleum, vinyl, or vinyl-asbestos sheet and tile) can be used as a substrate for new flooring if it's well adhered to the subfloor or underlayment. In most cases, however, it will require some minor preparation as shown here.

The word on resilients

Resilient flooring can serve as a base provided it is of a single layer, is not of the cushion-vinyl variety, is not cracked, and is firmly adhered. Cushioned vinyl and multiple layers are too compressible to provide adequate support, while cracks may indicate an instability, which will cause failure in the flooring material as well.

To determine the nature of the existing flooring, remove a small sample from under a refrigerator or dishwasher and take it to a flooring store for identification. The existing flooring needs to be firmly adhered and installed over exterior-grade plywood at least ⅝ inch thick. If the subfloor is inadequate, screw a layer of ½-inch, CC-Plugged, Exterior-Grade plywood over the flooring.

You also need to determine whether the flooring contains asbestos. Don't start sanding until you are sure (see the "Safety Alert" at right). If subfloor and sheet flooring are OK, then remove any wax from its surface and roughen with 40-grit sandpaper. Remove the dust with a damp sponge.

SAFETY ALERT

ASBESTOS TILE
Resilient flooring installed before 1986 may contain asbestos. It's not a problem—until you try to remove it. Then the loose fibers can get into your lungs and cause serious health problems.
If you are planning to remove asbestos tile, talk to your state department of environmental affairs or department of health about its removal and disposal. You will have to either have the asbestos tile removed professionally or switch to a different type of flooring.

3

PREPARATION

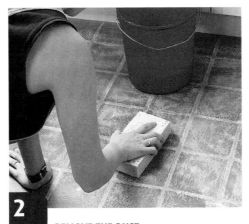

1 ROUGHEN THE SURFACE
Roughen the surface of soundly adhered, wax-free resilient flooring with 40-grit sandpaper. Be sure to wear a tight fitting dust respirator.

2 REMOVE THE DUST
Remove the sanding dust with a damp sponge. To test whether the adhesive will adhere, give the surface the "water-bead" test on page 82.

EMBOSSING LEVELER

Embossing leveler is a modified mortar product designed specifically to level out embossed patterns in vinyl flooring. With the surface leveled, well-adhered vinyl can be used as an underlayment for new vinyl without risking the old embossed pattern showing through.

Spread the leveler in a thin coat and remove the excess—all you want is to level the depressions in the surface. Work quickly—this stuff sets up fast. When it's dry, go back and lightly scrape off your trowel marks to smooth the surface.

Wood flooring

Wood is a traditional flooring material. Wood flooring today, however, is much different from the wide sawn planks of years past. Modern wood flooring is kiln dried and machined to standard dimensions. Tongue-and-groove edges ensure a tight installation with a level surface. In many cases, wood flooring is sold prefinished.

Wood flooring now comes in many forms: strips, planks, parquet, cork tile, and engineered products. Each brings to the home the warm look and comfortable feel underfoot that have always been associated with wood floors.

Installation has changed considerably, too, from the days when installers tacked it down loosely the first year, then nailed it down firmly once it had dried and shrunk. While most solid wood floors are still nailed in place, some types of wood floor can be glued down. And some flooring is not attached to the subfloor at all; it floats on top of a foam pad.

Each installation has its advantages: A floated floor goes down quickly and easily. A glued floor is also easy to install. (Glue is the only way you can hold down cork or parquet.) Sometimes only nails will do: You must nail down 3/4-inch solid-wood floors, for example.

Chapter 4 highlights

Whatever method you use, wood is one of the easiest floors to install. While other floors require mortar, stretching tools, or floor-size patterns, you can install wood flooring with tools you're familiar with: drills, saws, and hammers.

Wood must adjust to the "climate" of the room before installing it. Don't have it delivered on a wet day. Make sure all humidity-producing aspects of building and remodeling have dried before bringing the wood home. Acclimate the wood for five days prior to installation at a temperature of 65 to 70 degrees in the room where it will be installed. You can stack it log-cabin style or just spread it around the room.

Installing wood-strip flooring

PROJECT DETAILS

SKILLS: Basic carpentry
PROJECT: Installing an 8'×10' wood floor

TIME TO COMPLETE

EXPERIENCED: 4 hrs.
HANDY: 6 hrs.
NOVICE: 8 hrs.

STUFF YOU'LL NEED

TOOLS: Broom, tape measure, chalkline and chalk, jamb saw, drill with 1/16" bit, countersink bit, hammer, nail set, tablesaw, jigsaw, flooring nailer, pry bar, mallet

MATERIALS: 15-lb. tar paper or red rosin paper, flooring, flooring nails, transition strips

▲ Wood-strip flooring requires such a large number of nails that you should strongly consider investing in or renting a flooring nailer and compressor. The time saved and the quality of the finished job will be well worth the extra expense.

Wood flooring prep at a glance

- **Storage:** Keep temperature in room between 60 and 75 degrees during installation and for 5 days before and afterwards. Don't store directly on concrete: Provide 4-inch air space between flooring and concrete.
- **Location:** On or above grade. Do not install below grade.
- **Level/flat:** Within 1/8 inch over 6 feet.
- **Moisture:** Check subfloor with moisture meter. Subfloor moisture should not exceed 13 percent and should be within 4 percentage points of floorboard moisture.
- **Acceptable subfloors:** 3/4-inch CDX plywood preferred; 3/4-inch OSB acceptable. Minimum 5/8-inch CDX. Existing wood floor or tongue-and-groove solid wood subfloor also acceptable.
- **Trim:** Undercut door trim before installation. Remove baseboard, shoe molding, or both.

1 **LAY OUT THE FIRST ROW**
Prepare the subfloor as shown on page 80. Mark the walls to show the location of the floor joists. Cover the floor with 15-pound felt paper. For strength, run the strip flooring perpendicular to the joists. Start your layout at the longest uninterrupted wall that's perpendicular to the joists. At each end of the wall, measure out the width of a floorboard, plus 3/4 inch, and make a mark. Drive nails into the marks and stretch mason's line between them to lay out the first row.

Bring flooring samples home so you can examine your choices in context.

2 **PREDRILL FOR NAILS**

The first and last rows of flooring have to be nailed through the face of the boards. All the other boards are nailed through the tongue only. To prevent splitting face-nailed boards, drill 1/16-inch-diameter holes for the nails, 1 inch from the grooved edge. Space the holes so the nails hit a joist, or as directed by the manufacturer.

3 **FASTEN THE FIRST BOARD**

Align the first board with the layout line, with the tongue facing into the room. Put a 3/4-inch spacer against the adjoining wall, and slide the end of the board against it. Drive 6d or 8d flooring nails through the pilot holes, then drill additional pilot holes through the tongue. Countersink all the nails.

 TOOL SAVVY

NAIL GUNS

Nail guns make quick work of the countless nails you'll need in a wood floor. But quality is a benefit as well as speed. A pneumatic nailer will drive the nail at the same angle and to the same depth every time. Driving nails by hand, you're bound to leave a few nails a bit high in the tongue—making it difficult, if not impossible, to install the next board. Drive the nail a bit low, and you may as well not have a nail in the board at all.

You'll need two kinds of nailers—a face nailer and a side nailer—and given the cost, you may want to rent them. The face nailer is the tool you'll use on the first and last few rows of flooring, when there isn't enough room to use the side nailer. The side nailer, which drives the nail at an angle into the tongue, is the tool you'll use on the rest of the floor. Both use barbed flooring nails made especially for the job, so make sure you get them while you're at the store.

4 **CONTINUE THE FIRST ROW**

Put the next board in place along the layout line. Seat the end tongue and groove into each other, and push the two boards together for a tight seam. Nail down the board, moving down the row until you reach the side wall. Cut the last length to fit, leaving a 3/4-inch expansion gap, and nail it in place.

5 **RACK THE FLOORING**

Spread the boards from several bundles across the room. Mix bundles, and mix shades, colors, and lengths, using the natural variety in the wood to create a random pattern. Lay out the boards in the order you'll install them. Pros call this racking the boards. Flooring bundles tend to be uniform in color, and if you don't rack them, you'll create noticeable light and dark areas in the floor. Make sure you finish the process by arranging the joints so they are sufficiently offset across the floor.

6 **INSTALL THE NEXT ROWS**

Put the first board of the new row in place. Cut it, if necessary, so the end is offset from the end of the board in the previous row by a minimum of 6 inches. Put the end against a 1/2-inch spacer and seat the edge snugly against its neighbor. Drill pilot holes in the tongues, then nail and countersink them through the tongues (but not the faces) to hold the boards in place. Work your way down the rows, one row at a time.

7 **USE A FLOORING NAILER**

Switch to a flooring nailer as soon as you can. After installing the second or third row, you'll have enough room to get a flooring nailer between the wall and the board you're placing. Position the nailer so it will drive a nail through the tongue of the board, then hit it with a mallet to shoot the nail through the tongue. Adjust the air pressure as needed so the nail countersinks into the tongue.

8 **INSTALL THE REMAINING ROWS**

Work your way across the room, row by row, power-nailing the boards through the tongue. Leave a 3/4-inch expansion gap between the end board and the wall. Stagger the ends of the boards in adjoining rows by 6 inches and rack additional bundles as you go.

Changing directions

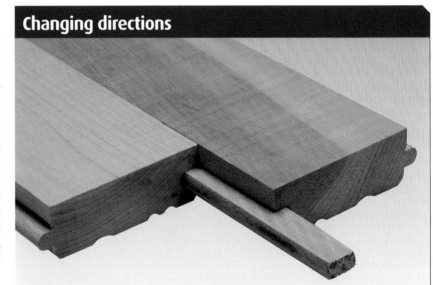

Flooring in a hallway should run the length of the hall regardless of joist direction. If the flooring will meet wood flooring in other rooms, install the hallway flooring first, then work your way into the adjoining rooms. In order to make this work, sometimes you'll need to join two boards groove edge to groove edge. If so, cut a strip of wood, called a spline, that is wide enough to fit into one of the grooves and about halfway into the neighboring groove. Glue it into one of the grooved boards and nail it to the floor. Slip the groove of the neighboring board over the new splined tongue.

4

WOOD FLOORING

9

STRAIGHTEN BOWED BOARDS

Even the best flooring comes with pieces that are not perfectly straight. Set these aside initially; if these end up as extras, you won't have to use them. If you must use a slightly bowed piece, drive a chisel into the subfloor and pry against the edge of the bowed strip to straighten it. If the piece is badly bowed, screw a piece of scrap to the floor about 1 inch from the strip. Tap a wood wedge into the gap, as shown, to straighten out the board.

10

FRAMING OBSTRUCTIONS

Often a floor will meet an obstruction such as a fireplace or counter. If so, miter boards to create a border that frames the obstruction. Position the boards so the tongue or groove mates with the rest of the floorboards. Cut off the tongue if it's on the edge that meets the obstruction. Apply the rest of the floor as you normally would, fitting the pieces into the frame as you go.

11

CUTTING CORNERS

Where the flooring meets a jog in the wall or a similar obstacle, cut corners to fit. Snug the piece of flooring against the obstacle and lay out the cut by marking where the edge of the obstacle meets the board. Allow for a 1/2-inch expansion gap at the end of the board and a 3/4-inch gap along the edges; make the cut with a jigsaw.

12

FACE-NAIL THE LAST ROWS

As you approach the wall on the far side of the room, it becomes difficult to use the flooring nailer. Once you don't have enough room to swing the mallet, begin drilling pilot holes for face-nailing, but nail only when you've laid down all the boards.

13

CUT THE LAST ROW TO FIT

You probably will have to cut the width of the boards in the last row to fit. Measure the space and subtract 3/4 inch for the expansion gap. Cut the boards to width on a tablesaw. Put the boards in place. Pry against a piece of scrap on the wall to seat the boards and close any gaps between them. Face-nail to hold the boards in place.

14

INSTALL THE TRIM

Install the baseboard and shoe molding to cover the expansion gap. Keep the lower edge of the baseboard even with the top of the floor, and nail the baseboard into the wall. Once the baseboard is in, set the quarter-round shoe molding on a piece of paper to keep it just a hair above the floor. Nail it to the baseboard, not to the floor or subfloor. Nail threshold or transition strips in place where the edge of the floor is exposed.

Installing a plank floor

Plank floors imitate the floors in colonial homes. Seventeenth-century builders didn't care how wide a board was, as long as it went from one side of the room to the other. Each row was typically a single board, often as wide as 20 inches, and the following row was the width of whatever board was next on the pile.

Modern random-width floors are a variation of the plank floor and usually are made from boards of three different widths. Each width is laid as a row, then the pattern repeats. In keeping with traditional floors, the boards are usually planks. To keep the planks from warping, they're often nailed in place, then screwed through predrilled holes. (You can drill your own, though doing so gets old by the 100th board.) Each screw is covered by a wooden plug that has to be sanded flush with the rest of the floor, so random-width floors are installed unfinished. If you're not interested in doing the finishing, any floor refinisher will be happy to take over.

1 MARK THE LOCATION OF JOISTS

Wide boards are more resistant to laying flat, and they also expand and contract more than narrow boards. Therefore, nail them through the subfloor and into the floor joists. On plywood subfloors, the nailing pattern should reveal the joist locations. On a tongue and groove subfloor, the nailheads won't be visible, so find the first joist with a stud finder. Snap chalklines to show the joist locations.

2 NAIL THE BOARDS

Even if the boards are tongue and grooved, face nailing is necessary on wide boards. Use a power nailer. Cut nails, with rectangular heads, hold well and look similar to those used on old floors. Use two nails across a 7-inch board and three nails on wider stock. Position all nails at least an inch in from the edge of the board to prevent splitting. Orient the nailheads so the long side is parallel to the length of the board.

Setting random-width planks

3 PLUG THE PLANKS

Plugging mimics the old practice of pegging a floor—drilling holes and anchoring the floor by inserting pegs into the beams below. The modern approach is to screw down the planks using counterbored holes and then plug the holes with wooden dowel plugs. Some planks come predrilled. If yours don't, use a counterbore bit to drill a stepped hole, so part of it is wide enough for the screw and part of it is wide enough for the plug.

4 TAP THE PLUGS

After the screws are in place, apply glue to the screw holes and tap in the plugs. Trim them flush with the floor. Sand and finish the floor.

To lay out the floor, measure out from the wall by the width of the widest board, plus ¾ inch for the expansion gap. Snap a chalkline and lay the widest boards along it. Blind nail the boards through the tongues. (Face-nail this row if there isn't enough room for the nailer.) Repeat the process across the floor, varying the widths of the planks and offsetting the joints.

Installing hardwood stairs

Stair installation varies widely from job to job. You may be covering existing stairs, or you may be covering stairs that consist only of a subfloor. The stairs may have one open side, two open sides, or no open sides. You may or may not have to install balustrade (the banisters, balusters, and newels).

Stair builders consider balustrade the height of the art. Stair-building manuals go on for pages about the balustrade, while devoting as little as one paragraph to installing the treads and risers. (Treads are the part of the stairs you walk on; risers are the vertical pieces at the back of each step.) If you're working on a stairway with fancy handrails, hire a pro. If you're working on stairs with a wall on each side, do it yourself.

When installing treads and risers on an unfinished stairway, the guts of the stairs are already built—and your aim is to make them pretty. If the treads on your stairs are rounded over and already overhang the risers, build them out as explained in "Installing engineered

stairways," page 106, before installing new risers and treads.

If you have stairs with existing banisters, the steps are probably hardwood, no matter how bad they look. If so, it makes more sense to refinish than to replace them.

Start by sanding them thoroughly with an orbital sander (a belt sander is too powerful), and use furniture stripper to remove any finish the sander misses. See page 121 for directions on applying finish.

GOOD IDEA

BEVEL THE RISERS

When you cut risers to size, cut an 8- to 12-degree bevel along the edge that meets the tread. Nail the tread in place so the short side of the bevel is against rough stairs and the long side faces out. The bevel keeps the edge above dirt, saw dust, and bumps that otherwise would cause a gap in the seam. You'll get a tighter-looking seam as a result.

1

CUT THE RISERS

Cut the risers one at a time. Measure each riser to determine its length and width. Cut the riser to width, then measure the length in a couple of spots. If the measurement differs, you'll have to cut an oversize tread, then trim it to match. Add $3/4$ inch to the largest tread length you measured. Cut the riser to this length. Put the riser in place, as shown, and set a compass so its legs are $3/8$ inch apart. Scribe along the wall with the compass, drawing a line on the riser. Cut along the line with a jigsaw. Once you've made the cut, scribe and cut on the other end of the riser too. Cut all the risers to size.

4

WOOD FLOORING

2

NAIL THE RISERS

Nail the risers into the pieces of framing beneath them, called stringers. You'll find a 2× stringer against the wall on each side of the stairs and one down the middle. Nail two 8d flooring nails into each stringer and drive them below the surface with a nail set.

3

TRIM THE TREADS

Begin with treads that have one rounded edge—they're available at home centers and lumberyards. Cut each tread to a width that will leave 1 inch overhanging the riser, then check the length, measuring in two places the way you did for the risers. For treads that need to be trimmed to fit, add $3/4$ inch to the longest measurement and cut the tread to this length. Put the tread in place and set a compass so the legs are $3/8$ inch apart. Trace along the wall with the compass, drawing a line on the tread. Cut along the line with a jigsaw. Once you've made the cut, scribe and cut the other end of the tread too.

4

INSTALL THE TREADS

Glue the tread to the steps with construction adhesive. Apply the adhesive to the step, rather than the tread, to minimize the squeeze-out onto the rounded edge. Install the tread, clean off any adhesive that squeezed out, then nail it in place with 8d flooring nails. Drive two nails into each stringer. Cut, scribe, and install the remaining treads.

Nailing an engineered floor

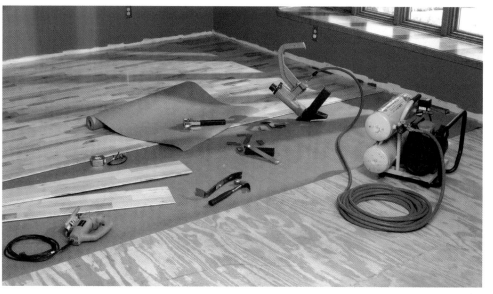

PROJECT DETAILS

SKILLS: Basic carpentry
PROJECT: Installing an 8'×10' floor

TIME TO COMPLETE

EXPERIENCED: 5 hrs.
HANDY: 7 hrs.
NOVICE: 10 hrs.

STUFF YOU'LL NEED

TOOLS: Jigsaw, trowel (for glue-down installation), flooring nailer, pneumatic nailer, or staple gun (for nail-down installation), pry bar, tape measure, chalkline and chalk, hammer, manufacturer's tapping block or scrap of flooring, hammer stapler, compass
MATERIALS: Flooring, nails or staples (for nail-down installation), engineered wood flooring adhesive and cleaner (for glue-down installation), foam underlayment, rosin paper or 15-lb. felt paper (for nail-down installation), blue painter's tape

You can glue down, nail down, or staple down engineered flooring. Some brands also can be floated, an installation in which the pieces are glued to each other but not to the subfloor. This creates a single large panel held in place by friction and its own weight. Without glue, nails, or staples to apply, this technique lets you install a wood floor over a wider variety of subfloors than would otherwise be possible. Acclimate the flooring at least 72 hours before installing it.

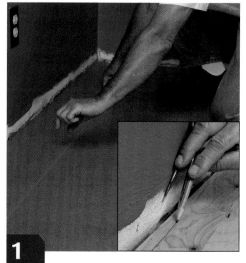

Engineered floor prep at a glance

- **Location:** Can be installed above, below, or on grade. Not for use in a full bath. In crawlspaces, must be at least 24 inches above ground with vapor barrier stapled across the bottom of the joists below the floor.
- **Subfloor:** Must be level and flat within $3/16$ inch over 10 feet or $1/8$ inch over 6 feet. May use a broad range of subflooring materials.
- **Plywood:** Use $5/8$ inch minimum, $3/4$ inch preferred. Joists 16 inches on center (OC). Exterior grade with long edges at right angle to joists. Ends staggered along different joists. Ends nailed with 6d threaded nails spaced 6 inches along outside edges, 10 inches along the interior. Allow $1/8$-inch expansion gap between panels.
- **OSB:** Use $3/4$ inch with joists 16 inches to $19\frac{1}{5}$ inches OC. Nailed and spaced to same specs as plywood.
- **Solid wood:** Use 1×4 to 1×6 pine, laid diagonally and nailed to joists 16 inches OC. Ends of boards cut parallel to joists and nailed.
- **Concrete:** Must be dry to manufacturer's specs year-round. For glue-down applications, sand off or remove any sealants applied to the floor.
- **Vinyl/ceramic tile:** Both are acceptable subfloors for floating application. Some vinyl types are not acceptable for glue-down. Loose-laid or perimeter-glue vinyl not acceptable for glue-down.

1

LAY OUT THE FIRST ROW

Staple down felt paper or rosin paper to moderate the effect of humidity beneath the floor. For a strong floor, install the planks perpendicular to the joists. If possible, start along one of the outside walls—they're usually the straightest. To lay out the first row, measure the width of a plank and add the size of the gap recommended by the manufacturer. Snap a chalkline this distance from the wall.

Lay a trial run of the first row, facing the groove along the starting wall. Put $1/2$-inch spacers between the wall and flooring. If at any point along the wall the space is less than $1/2$ inch, or is greater than the thickness of the baseboard you'll apply, you'll have to scribe the floor (see page 65).

4

WOOD FLOORING

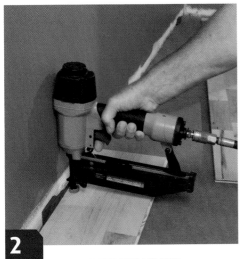

2 FACE-NAIL THE FIRST PLANK

Put the tongue of the first plank on the layout line and nail through the face of the board into the subfloor. Fasten each plank with at least two nails. Drive them 1 or 2 inches from the end of each plank and about every 8 inches in between.

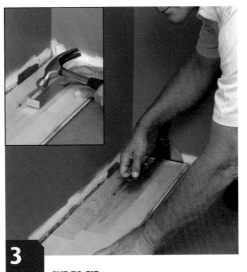

3 CUT TO FIT

Cut the last board of the first row to fit, leaving the recommended expansion gap. Push the board into place with a pry bar, as shown, protecting the wall with a putty knife or a scrap piece of wood. Some manufacturers make a special tool for this job, called a pull bar, which you tap with a hammer to seat the board (see inset).

⊙ TOOL TIP

HANG UP

All major manufacturers of engineered flooring recommend installing engineered planks with a pneumatic nailer, staple gun, or flooring nailer, so forget about using your hammer. Read the manufacturer's directions carefully, and use the recommended gun and adapters. Using the wrong tool risks scraping the finish or even damaging the flooring. You may also drive the nails too far or not far enough. The first leaves you with a poorly connected floor; the second causes damage to the board that fits over the nail.

4

WOOD FLOORING

4 CONTINUE LAYING THE FLOOR

Start the second row with the piece cut off the first row, unless the end would be within 4 inches of the end of the board in the first row. (The limit is 6 inches for some flooring; be sure to read the directions.) Slide the cutoff into place and push the boards together. Seat the board by tapping with a tapping block. Continue down the second row, putting the new planks tight against those already in place. Tap each plank to seat it against the previous row, then tap the end to join the planks together. Space the nails as before. As you approach the wall, cut the last plank to fit, leaving the required gap.

5 FACE-NAIL THE LAST ROW

Install the remaining rows, leaving the required gap at the walls and spacing the ends of neighboring planks as directed. When you reach the last row, measure, cut the planks to width, and face-nail them in place.

Gluing an engineered floor

1 **INSTALL A GUIDE BOARD**

Snap a chalkline parallel to the wall—outside walls are usually the straightest and best to use. Add together the width of several planks and the width of the recommended expansion gap between the flooring and wall. Snap a chalkline this distance from the wall. Nail a straight board between the line and the wall to use as a guide.

2 **APPLY THE ADHESIVE**

Spread a coat of engineered-wood flooring adhesive about two planks wide along the guideboard, using the notched trowel recommended by the manufacturer. The size and spacing of the notches controls the amount of adhesive you put down. Using the wrong trowel results in a coat of adhesive too thin to work, or one so thick that it creates a mess. Check your spread by pulling a board back up every now and then; about 80 percent of the glue should stick to the back of the flooring.

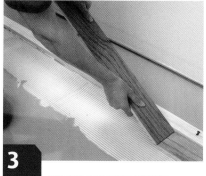

3 **INSTALL THE FIRST PLANK**

Put the groove of the first plank tight against the guideboard. Put the end of the next plank snugly against the end of the installed plank and push the two together. Slide the plank through the adhesive as little as possible—the adhesive tends to pull the plank back to its starting point. Work your way down the guideboard. Cut the last plank to length, leaving the proper expansion gap at the far wall.

Put the lid back on the adhesive as soon as you're done with it to prevent it from drying out.

4 **START THE SECOND ROW**

Begin the second row with the cutoff from the first row. This keeps the ends of the planks from lining up, creating both a stronger and better-looking floor. Maintain the expansion gap by butting the cutoff against a spacer at the wall. If using the cutoff results in a board that is awkwardly short, or if its end falls closer to the end of the neighboring plank than the manufacturer recommends, cut a new board.

5 **COMPLETE THE SECOND ROW**

Work your way down the second row, putting the ends of the boards together first, then sliding the edge of the plank into the planks of the first row. Clean off any glue that gets on top of the boards using the recommended cleaner. Cut the last piece of the row to fit, leaving the proper expansion gap between the plank and the wall. Push the board into place with a pry bar, as shown.

6
TAPE THE JOINTS FOR STRENGTH

Some manufacturers recommend taping adjoining rows together to keep them from spreading apart as you work. Use blue painter's tape, which removes easily without leaving marks, and apply the tape perpendicular to the seam.

Protect the wall from damage with scrap flooring.

🕐 TIMESAVER

GLUE, DON'T NAIL

Nailing a guideboard to a concrete floor with masonry nails is at least as hard as it sounds. Sometimes it's impossible. If you're having trouble driving the nails, snap a chalkline on the floor to mark where you want the first row of boards to go. (Snapping it on the edge away from the wall will make it easier to see.) Spread enough glue to lay the first row only, and put the boards in place along the line. Let the glue harden, and then use the first row as you would use the guideboard. Leave it in place when you return to that side of the room to finish installing the floor.

7
CONTINUE LAYING THE PLANKS

Spread more adhesive and work your way across the room, staying off the freshly laid planks. Always leave the manufacturer's recommended expansion gap between the ends of the planks and the wall. Trim the first plank in each row as needed to offset the ends of the planks by the amount the manufacturer recommends. If a board won't seat in its neighbor, coax it by putting a scrap against the piece and tapping on the scrap with a hammer.

9
REMOVE THE GUIDEBOARD

Once the adhesive has dried, remove the guideboard you nailed where you started the installation. Spread adhesive in the remaining space and lay flooring one row at a time. Measure and trim the last row as needed, leaving the same-size space you left along the other walls.

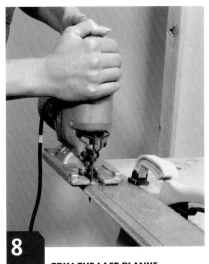

8
TRIM THE LAST PLANKS

When you reach the row against the wall, measure and cut the planks to width, allowing for the expansion gap. Spread the adhesive and put the planks in place.

10
PRY THE LAST ROW

Seat the last row against the preceding row with a pry bar. Protect the wall with a scrap of flooring. Pry all along the edge of the board.

Floating an engineered floor

4

WOOD FLOORING

WORK SMARTER

SPACING THE LAYOUT

If the last row of a floating floor is less than 2 inches wide and against the wall, it will create nothing but problems. Calculate the width of the row in advance. Divide the width of the room in inches by the width of a single plank, also in inches. If the remainder is less than two, the last row will be too narrow.

To solve the problem, make the first row narrower: The width should equal the width of the last row, plus the width of a full row, divided by two.

You can cut the board to width now if you want to, but it's best to measure the actual gap and cut the board then. Just remember the calculated width of the first row and use it in the next step.

1

SPREAD THE UNDERLAYMENT

If you're installing the flooring over concrete, lay 6-mil plastic sheeting over the concrete and overlap the seams by at least 8 inches. If the concrete is below grade, bring the plastic at least 4 inches up the wall. You will trim it off at the height of the baseboard once the flooring has been installed. Roll out the manufacturer's recommended foam underlayment, but do not overlap the seams.

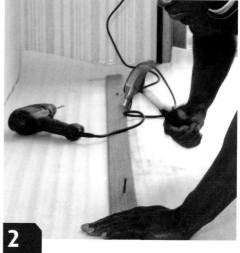

2

PUT DOWN THE STARTER BOARD

This is a straight board, temporarily nailed to the floor, used to align the flooring. To find the location, add the width of the first two rows to the size of the expansion gap the manufacturer says to leave at the edge of the floor. (Remember, the first row may not be full width if it's necessary to balance the first and last pieces of flooring.) Snap a chalkline this distance from the wall and nail the starter board along it.

Maintain the recommended expansion gap at all walls.

3

GLUE THE EDGES

Apply a bead of glue to the tongue on the end of the first plank following the manufacturer's specifications. Put the grooved edge against the starter board. Put the grooved end of the next plank against the glued tongue. Seat it by tapping with a hammer and a tapping block that's recommended by the manufacturer. (Using the wrong block can damage a plank.) Leave the recommended expansion gap.

4

LAY THE STARTER ROW

Lay the starter row, applying glue to the end tongues and cutting the last board to length. Seat the last board with a pull bar, as shown, leaving the recommended expansion gap.

5   INSTALL THE SECOND ROW

Start the next row with the cutoff from the first row, trimming it, if necessary, so that the end will be 24 inches from the end of the neighboring plank. Run a ⅛-inch bead of glue along the tongue of the previous row, put the cutoff against it, and seat with a tapping block.

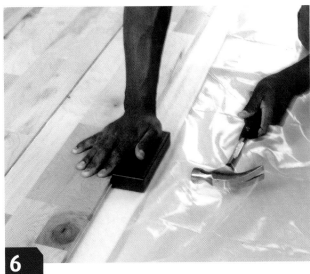

6   INSTALL THE REMAINING FLOOR

Glue and install the remaining boards. Apply glue to the tongues and nestle each board against its neighbor. Seat the edge with a tapping block, then seat the end. Cut the last board of each row to length and install it, leaving the required expansion gap.

7   TRIM THE FINAL ROW

Measure the width of the space for the last row and subtract the width of the expansion gap. Rip the boards to this width and temporarily put them in place. If the irregularities in the wall result in an expansion gap that is too small, scribe the boards as described on page 65. Apply glue and install the boards with the help of a pull bar.

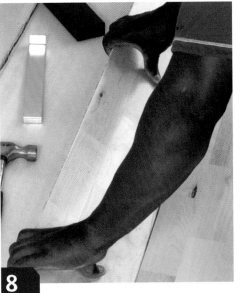

8   FINISH THE INSTALLATION

Remove the starter board and install the rows needed to fill in the resulting space. When you reach the row against the wall, rip it to width, as before, and scribe, if necessary. Install the boards and avoid walking on the floor for at least 8 hours until the glue dries. Install baseboard around the room to cover the expansion gap and protect the walls.

4

WOOD FLOORING

🌎 REAL WORLD

NAIL BASEBOARD TO THE WALL

A homeowner who drives the nails for the baseboard into the flooring soon discovers that a floor is nothing more than a big piece of wood. When the floor dries out during the winter heating season it contracts, pulling the baseboards away from the wall. The secret to applying baseboard is to let the floor float underneath. When you install it, put the baseboard on a piece of paper to keep it slightly above the floor. Then nail the baseboard to the wall, not the floor. You should be able to nail the lower portion of the baseboard into the bottom plate, a 2×4 that runs all the way across the bottom of the wall. Nail the upper portion to the studs inside the wall. Nail quarter-round molding or shoe molding directly to the baseboard.

Installing engineered stairways

1 BUILD UP THE RISERS

Stair treads usually have an overhang that extends beyond the riser by about 1 inch. The overhang interferes with installation of new, engineered flooring. Nail plywood to each riser so that the face of the riser is flush with the edge of the tread. If the top of the stairs meets an existing floor that you're not covering with engineered flooring, don't build out the top riser.

2 CUT THE BOTTOM RISER

Cut a piece of flooring to the width of the riser. Measure the length of the existing riser in two places. If the measurements are equal, cut the riser to size. If the measurements differ, cut a piece 1 inch longer than the longest measurement. With the riser in place, set a compass so the legs are $1/2$ inch apart. Trace along one wall with the compass, scribing a line on the riser. Cut along the line and repeat on the riser's other end.

3 CUT THE STAIR NOSING

Measure the front of the stair, and cut a nose to this length. (Because the nose is so narrow, you seldom have to scribe it.) Butt the bottom riser temporarily in place and put the nose in place over it. There is often a small lip in the bottom of the nose. Pull it tight against the riser to position the nose.

4 CUT THE FIRST TREAD

Measure from the riser at the back of the first tread to the back of the nosing. Subtract about twice the length of the flooring's tongue and cut this amount off the grooved edge of the flooring. Cut and fit it to length as you fit the riser in Step 2. When the pieces fit correctly, remove them from the steps, marking them so you don't confuse the riser and tread.

5 GLUE THE RISER AND NOSE

Spread the floor adhesive on the tread and on the riser below it. Use the same adhesive you used on the floor and spread it the same way. Put the riser in place with the cut edge up and put the nose over it. (The nose will hide any chips in the cut edge.) Nail the back of the nose into the tread.

6 INSTALL THE TREAD

Put the tread in place against the back of the stair. Slide it forward so that its tongue fits in the groove of the nose. Continue up the steps, always installing a riser, a nose above it, and then the tread.

Always work from the bottom of the stairs to the top. Not only is it easier, but any chips or dings that result from sawing the treads to size will be hidden by the riser.

Installing a medallion

PROJECT DETAILS

SKILLS: Basic carpentry
PROJECT: Installing a medallion

TIME TO COMPLETE

EXPERIENCED: Variable
HANDY: Variable
NOVICE: Variable

STUFF YOU'LL NEED

TOOLS: Tape measure, chalkline, drill and screwdriver bits, plunge router and flush trim bit, circular saw, mitersaw, utility knife, chisel, caulking gun, trowel, flooring nailer
MATERIALS: Medallion kit, adhesive, double-face tape, nails, white or yellow glue

Medallion prep at a glance

■ **Level/flat and moisture content:** Floor must meet the criteria set for a wood-strip floor. See page 94.
■ **Acclimation:** A week before installation, unpack the medallion and acclimate it at the job site.

 medallion comes packed in the template you'll need to install it. The router bit and a special corner chisel may come as part of the package too.

If you're laying a border, install it when you lay the floor. If you're putting in a medallion, you can do it either as the floor goes in or after it is installed. Carefully follow the manufacturer's instructions for either job.

2 FORM THE RECESS
Following the instructions with the medallion, install a guide bushing and bit in a router. Rout along the inside of the template with shallow cuts. Beware of nails—they will damage the router bit. Remove the flooring in the recess.

3 APPLY THE ADHESIVE
Apply construction adhesive to the recess with a caulking gun. Spread the adhesive evenly around the recess with a notched trowel, similar to the one used for cove molding.

4 INSTALL THE MEDALLION
Press the medallion into the adhesive. Walk across the medallion to seat it, then drive 1 $5/8$-inch drywall screws through the predrilled holes and into the subfloor. Apply white or yellow glue to the loose pieces of the medallion that cover the screws, and glue them into place.

1 MARK THE LOCATION
Remove the medallion from the template it comes packed in. Position the medallion on the floor, then trace around it with a pencil. Remove the medallion, and place the template over the marked outline. Fasten the template securely to the floor with brads or double-face tape.

4

WOOD FLOORING

 **BUYER'S GUIDE**

GET A KIT
Traditional border and medallion work is extremely difficult. Make sure you get a kit with a prefab medallion or border, a template, and the necessary router bits. If the floor is already finished, like this one, send a sample piece to the manufacturer and have them mill a medallion to the exact thickness and apply a finish. If the floor is unfinished, buy a stock medallion and sand it to the correct thickness when you sand the rest of the floor.

Installing an inlaid border

1 LAY OUT TWO EDGES OF THE INSIDE FIELD

Snap chalklines between the midpoints of the walls to find the exact center of the room. Check for square using a 3-4-5 triangle (see page 60), and adjust as necessary. Measure from the center point and lay out the lines that define the area inside the borders, called the field. Screw a straightedge to the center that runs in the same direction the floorboards will run. Screw a second straightedge to one of the adjacent lines that marks the end of the field. Make sure the straightedges are square with each other, and adjust as necessary.

2 INSTALL THE FIELD

Work from the center to create a balanced field. Start by putting the grooved edge of the first row against the center straightedge, and lay each row to cross the line marking the end of the field. When you reach the outside edge, remove the straightedge and begin laying the second half of the floor, again working from the center. If the manufacturer requires installing the center boards groove to groove, connect them with a spline.

3 TRIM THE LONG ENDS

Snap a chalkline across the floorboards, to mark the outer edge of the field. Align a straight board longer than the field so a circular saw will cut at the chalkline. Fasten the guide board to the subfloor with screws. Guide the saw along the board to trim the long pieces to the length of the field.

4 INSTALL THE CORNER STRIPS

Corner tiles that match your pattern are sold separately or as part of a border strip. If the corner tile is part of the strip, put it in place, aligning the inside corner of the tile with the corner of the field. If the corner tile is separate, put a border piece in place first, with the edge against the field and the end aligned with the corner. Put in loose splines if any parts of the floor meet groove to groove. Test-fit the corner tiles, and fix any problems. Apply construction adhesive to the underside of the tiles or border and tile, spread it, and press the pieces into place.

5 FILL IN THE BORDERS

Cut border pieces to fit in the empty areas, and secure them with construction adhesive. Fill in the area between the border and the wall with regular floorboards. Wrap the boards around the border one row at a time, mitering the corners with a power mitersaw. Leave a $3/4$-inch expansion gap along each wall.

Border prep at a glance

- **Level/flat and moisture content:** Floor must meet the criteria set for a wood-strip floor.
- **Acclimation:** A week before installation, unpack the border pieces and acclimate them at the job site.

Lay out the entire border in advance to make sure it fits together as planned.

WOOD FLOORING

4

Stenciling a floor

PROJECT DETAILS

SKILLS: Designing and cutting a stencil
PROJECT: Stenciling a border on an installed floor

TIME TO COMPLETE

EXPERIENCED: 3–4 hours, depending on size of the room
HANDY: 4–6 hrs.
NOVICE: 6–7 hrs.

STUFF YOU'LL NEED

TOOLS: Sander, utility knife, paintbrushes, pencil, straightedge, shop vacuum, measuring tape, ruler, single-edge razor blade, lamb's-wool varnish applicator
MATERIALS: Stencils, stencil paint, 180-grit sandpaper, painter's tape, paper plate palette, clear polyurethane

Stencils offer a foolproof method for applying uniform decorative patterns. Spice up a floor with decorative border stencils—to define space and highlight architectural features, such as doorways, a fireplace, or built-in furniture. The traditional way to achieve this effect is with costly inlaid borders, which is not practical for an installed floor. Border stencils work on any wood floor, from classic oak with a natural or stained finish to yellow painted pine floor.

Combining stenciling with faux-finishing techniques simulates wood inlays, adding another level of decorative accent to your floors. Stenciling a pattern on the floor is a classic decorating technique, and it's easy.

Floor stencils work well with almost any decorating style, but the technique really shines as part of a Southwestern, colonial, country, or Victorian scheme. Though kits are made especially for floors, wall border kits can be used on the floor as well. And, of course, you can make your own.

1 MAKE A SAMPLE STENCIL

Make a sample stencil to get a preview of both the pattern and the colors. If you have an extra piece of matching flooring, use that. Otherwise use a piece of plywood or cardboard. Tape the stencil to the sample material, and paint the sequence of colors.

2 SAND THE FLOOR

Slightly roughen the surface with 180-grit sandpaper so the paint will adhere better. Sand with an orbital sander or a hand sanding block. Thoroughly remove the dust.

3 MARK THE LAYOUT LINE

The stencil pattern usually looks better if it is spaced away from the wall. Measure out from the wall and mark several spots on the floor. Stretch a strip of painter's tape along the marks to make a stencil guide. The tape will be easier to remove than a pencil line or chalkline.

4

4 PLAN THE STENCIL LAYOUT

Start at the most visible corner of the room and work outward. Inevitably one or more of the corners will end up with an incomplete pattern, but they'll be less conspicuous. Map out exactly how the pattern will fall in the corners by making several photocopies of the stencil, cutting them out, and laying them along the wall. Find the best starting and ending point for your particular room.

5 POSITION THE STENCIL

When you decide on the best starting point, position the stencil on the layout line and tape it to the floor. Use masking tape or painter's tape to cover the parts of the stencil that don't receive the first color.

6 PAINT THE FIRST COLOR

Pour paint onto a paper plate. Lightly dip the stenciling brush into the paint and apply it to the floor. Use either stippling or swirling to apply stencil paint. Stippling maintains the stencil outline more crisply, and swirling looks more fluid and may allow some paint to bleed under the edges of the stencil. Experiment with the paint and the brush to decide which looks best; maintain that approach throughout your project.

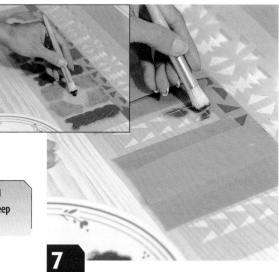

🎨 DESIGN TIP

PICK AN EASY PATTERN
A one-color pattern will keep decisions to a minimum.

7 PAINT THE ADDITIONAL COLORS

Remove the tape covering the stencil parts that receive the second color, and tape over the portion that received the first color. Use blue painter's masking tape, available in many widths with adhesive along only one edge, for this step. It covers a wide area and is easy to remove. Apply the second stencil paint. Repeat procedure until all colors have been applied.

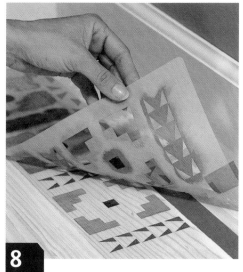

8 REMOVE THE STENCIL

After all the stencil colors have been applied, remove the tape and carefully lift the stencil from the floor. If some paint has bled under the stencil, allow the paint to dry thoroughly, and scrape off the excess paint with a single-edge razor blade. Do not blot the paint while it is still damp.

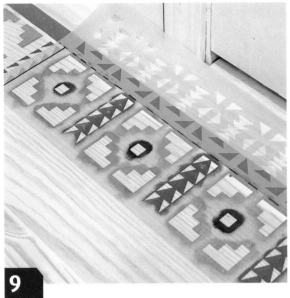

9 **REPOSITION THE STENCIL**

Align the registration marks that ensure regular spacing of the pattern (the solid line on the left side of the stencil), as well as the marks that align with the layout line (the broken line running lengthwise through the stencil).

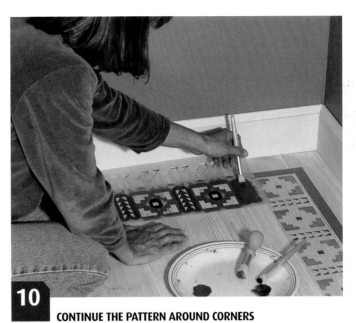

10 **CONTINUE THE PATTERN AROUND CORNERS**

Restart the stencil pattern when turning corners. Depending on the pattern, you may have to turn the stencil face down in order to match the pattern. If so, be sure to completely clean the painted side.

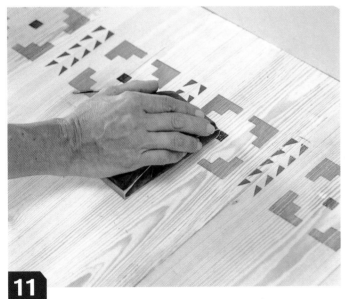

11 **SAND LIGHTLY**

Let the paint dry thoroughly for a day or two; then sand it lightly. If you want to impart a slightly aged look to the stenciling, sand a little heavier in some areas to simulate wear.

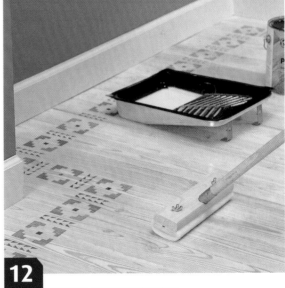

12 **APPLY A CLEAR FINISH COAT**

To lock in the crisp colors in the stencil and to prevent the paint from wearing off, apply a coat of clear polyurethane. If you apply the polyurethane to only the stenciled area rather than the entire floor, match the sheen that's on the rest of the floor.

Installing parquet tile

▲ **Parquet comes in preassembled tiles that simplify the installation of complicated-looking patterns.**

Parquet is wooden tile made up of narrow strips glued together to form a pattern. The most common pattern is a series of squares made of strips that change direction from square to square. Specialty houses sell elaborate patterns, which cost more but are no more difficult to install than the squares.

You can install parquet tile in either of two ways: Starting in the center of the room and laying the tile in a pyramid pattern or starting near a wall and laying the tile in a row. Both methods compensate for size variations that occur because each parquet tile is made of dozens of pieces of wood. Nestling each tile into a corner created by two other tiles helps compensate for this, as does carefully laying out lines.

The pyramid method is shown on page 115. The row method, shown starting on the opposite page, is recommended by some manufacturers because it's easier to achieve a square layout and involves less cutting along the walls.

Parquet floor prep at a glance

- **Storage:** Acclimate the tiles by storing them in the room where they will be installed. The room should be between 60 and 75 degrees and 35 to 55 percent humidity for two weeks prior to installation. If the surface is a concrete slab, create a 4-inch air space between the boxes of tile and the floor.
- **Location:** On or above grade only. Not for use with full baths. Crawlspace must be at least 24 inches above ground. Ground must be covered with 6–8 mil black polyethylene sheeting. Overlap seams 6 inches and seal with tape. A crawlspace must be ventilated with vent area equal to 1.5 percent of square footage.

- **Level/flat:** Within $\frac{1}{8}$ inch over 6 feet.
- **Moisture:** Floor must be dry or warping will occur. Check manufacturer's specifications.
- **Acceptable subfloors:** $\frac{3}{4}$-inch CDX plywood preferred. Also acceptable: $\frac{3}{4}$-inch OSB, solid wood floor, concrete, sheet vinyl, vinyl tile, cork flooring, $\frac{3}{4}$-inch wafer board or chipboard, ceramic, terrazzo, and slate marble. Some preparation required. Follow manufacturer's specifications.
- **Trim:** Undercut door trim before installation. Remove baseboard, shoe molding, or both.

WOOD FLOORING

4

Installing parquet in a perpendicular pattern

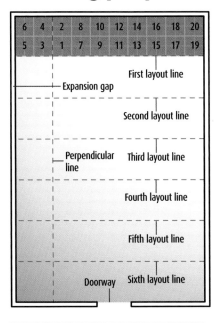

6	4	2	8	10	12	14	16	18	20
5	3	1	7	9	11	13	15	17	19

First layout line

Expansion gap

Second layout line

Perpendicular line — Third layout line

Fourth layout line

Fifth layout line

Doorway — Sixth layout line

1   **SNAP LAYOUT LINES**

Add the width of two tiles to the required expansion gap and snap a chalkline this distance from the wall opposite the door. Snap a second line the same distance from one of the side walls.

2   **SQUARE THE LINES**

Make sure the layout lines are square. Make a mark on one line 3 feet from where the lines cross. Make a mark on the second line 4 feet from where the lines cross. If the distance between the points is 5 feet, the lines are square with each other. If not, pivot one of the lines until the measurement is 5 feet.

3   **SPREAD THE ADHESIVE**

Spread the manufacturer's recommended adhesive between the first line you snapped and the wall. Use a notched trowel with the recommended size notches—the size and spacing of the notches controls how much adhesive is applied. Work in a well-ventilated area, opening windows and running fans as necessary.

4   **LAY THE FIRST TILE**

Mix tiles from several different cartons before you install any tiles. This distributes any color variations throughout the entire floor, making them less obvious. Place the first tile at the intersection of the two lines, carefully aligning it with them.

5   **LAY THE REMAINING TILES**

Install the second tile between the first tile and the wall. Carefully align the edge with the layout line. Push the tiles together with moderate pressure—hammers or other tools may force the tile out of position or out of square.

4

WOOD FLOORING

6 **CONTINUE TO THE WALL**

Continue until you reach the end wall. Follow the pattern shown in the illustration on page 113. Carefully align the tiles along the layout lines. If no layout line shows, nestle tiles in the corners created by their neighbors.

7 **MARK THE CUT LINE**

When you reach the wall, trim the tile, if necessary, to leave the required expansion gap between the tile and wall. Lay out the cut by setting a tile on one of the full tiles nearest the wall. Put a spacer the size of the expansion gap against the wall, then put a full tile against it. Trace along the edge to lay out the cut.

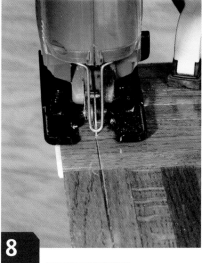

8 **CUT THE PARQUET**

In some brands of parquet, you'll find metal reinforcing bands embedded in each tile, so make the cut with a jigsaw to avoid injury. To avoid chipping the wood, guide a knife along a straightedge to cut along the line you drew in Step 7. Cut carefully, just on the waste side of the line.

9 **LAY OUT THE NEXT SECTION**

Snap a chalkline 24 inches away from and parallel to the first line you snapped. Lay parquet in this area, following the same pattern you used to lay tiles in the first area. Continue to lay out and install new sections of floor until you reach the wall opposite the starting wall.

10 **ROLL THE FLOOR**

Roll the floor, if necessary, depending on the adhesive you use. Follow the manufacturer's directions. With or without rolling, the adhesive takes time to set up, and the tiles will move if stressed too soon. Wait at least 24 hours before moving furniture into the room.

11 **INSTALL TRIM AND TRANSITIONS**

Install baseboard to cover the expansion gap between the parquet and the wall. Put the appropriate transitions between the new floor and existing flooring.

Installing parquet on a diagonal

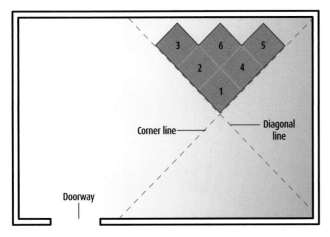

1 SNAP A DIAGONAL BETWEEN WALLS

Start by measuring an equal distance along two corner walls. A longer distance is better, so measure to the midpoint of the shorter wall, then measure the same distance along the longer wall. Snap a line between the two points. This will be one of the lines you follow when laying the pyramid.

2 SNAP A LINE FROM THE CORNER

To lay out the second line, find the midpoint of the first line. Snap a line from the corner, through the midpoint, to the opposite wall. Make sure the lines are square. Make a mark on one line 3 feet from where the lines cross. Make a mark on the second line 4 feet from where the lines cross. If the distance between the points is 5 feet, the lines are square with each other. If not, pivot the second line, leaving one end in the corner and sliding the other end along the wall until the measurement is 5 feet.

3 LAY THE TILES IN A STEPPED PATTERN

Spread adhesive in one of the quadrants created by the layout lines, following the manufacturer's directions. Lay the first tile at the intersection of the layout lines, aligning the edges carefully with the lines. Once the tile is in place, lay two more tiles along each of the layout lines. Lay the sixth tile between them to create a stepped pattern, as shown. Continue laying a tile along each line, then fill in the stepped pattern until you have filled the quadrant, except for the tiles along the wall.

4 FINISH THE QUADRANTS

Repeat, one quadrant at a time. Spread adhesive and apply tiles in the stairstep pattern. Small variations in tile size can cause the pattern to shift, and once it has, the only way to correct it is to start over. To avoid this, carefully align the tiles with the layout lines, and seat the tiles against their neighbors.

5 CUT EDGE TILES

Cut the edge tiles to fit. Put a full tile on top of one of the tiles in the row nearest the wall. Put ½-inch spacers against the wall, and put a full tile against them as shown. Trace the edge of the second tile to mark the cut. Use a jigsaw—the metal reinforcement strips embedded in the tile are dangerous when cut with a circular saw.

Combining materials

One of the attributes of flooring materials that is often overlooked is their design versatility in combination with other materials. Wood, especially lighter species finished with a clear varnish, brings the right degree of neutrality to other materials—not so much that it loses its own character, but just enough to provide the proper complement to stone or tile, for example.

Mixing materials—"juxtaposing" them would be more accurate—not only gives you an opportunity to create unusual, even stunning visual effects, it also provides you with a design tool that clearly separates one area of the room from another. For example, set off the conversation area in the family room from the balance of the ceramic tile with a large section of custom carpeting.

Or you can mix materials simply because certain combinations just look good together. Dropping a ceramic tile section in the center of a wood-strip floor adds interest to the room. It's also a good way to reduce the wear and tear on a wood floor in an entryway. It's an easy addition to your design, but you should make sure that the final tile height is about $\frac{1}{16}$ inch higher than the wood floor to make cleaning easier.

▲ Combining materials is a good way to bring the best out of both. Here the large expanse of the carpet provides a subtle contrast to the tile and clearly marks the areas of the room intended for different uses.

Installing tile with hardwood

1

INSTALL WOOD FLOORING

Lay out the floor for strip or plank material, outlining the area that is to be tiled. Install the flooring with a mitered border around the area to be tiled. You may have to make the grout joints a little wider or more narrow than usual so the tiled section is square and centered in the recess.

Cut backerboard to fit the opening ($\frac{1}{4}$ inch in many cases, to bring it slightly above the wood surface) and install it with the techniques shown on pages 156–159.

2

INSTALL CERAMIC TILE

Mark the backerboard with layout lines and spread thinset mortar at a thickness that will raise the tile slightly above the wood (you may have to experiment to get this right). Install the tile with spacers and grout it when the mortar has cured.

PARQUET AND ENGINEERED WOOD

Because engineered flooring is usually thicker than most parquet, the challenge with these materials is to make their surfaces level. You can add $1/8$-inch plywood (over a strong subfloor, of course) to make up the difference or increase the thickness of the parquet adhesive with a square-notched trowel. If that doesn't work, spread a coat of adhesive, lay in 30-pound felt paper and add another coat of adhesive.

STONE TILE AND HARDWOOD

For best results choose a tile that's $1/4$ inch thick. That way you can use $3/8$-inch backerboard or back-butter the tiles (spread thinset on back of the tiles) to bring them slightly above the hardwood floor.

VINYL TILE AND ENGINEERED WOOD

This combination is likely to be the easiest to install. It won't work well with peel-and-stick tiles, which are too thin. Use good quality tile (it's $1/8$ inch thick), and install it over $1/4$-inch plywood underlayment. That will make the thickness of the tile equal to the $3/8$-inch thickness of the engineered floor.

Refinishing a floor

PROJECT DETAILS

SKILLS: Using drum or vibrating sanders and edging sanders, basic carpentry skills, applying stains and finishes
PROJECT: Sanding and refinishing a floor

TIME TO COMPLETE

EXPERIENCED: 2 days
HANDY: 2 days
NOVICE: 3 days
VARIABLES: Depending on the size of the room, allow 4 to 8 hours for prep, sanding, and cleanup. Follow the manufacturer's instructions for application of stains and finishes, as well as drying times. Second and third coats will extend the project timetable.

STUFF YOU'LL NEED

TOOLS: Plastic sheeting, pry bar, hammer, nail set, putty knife, drum sander and sandpaper, vibrating sander and sandpaper, edge sander or random-orbit sander and sandpaper, dust mask, shop vacuum, paint tray, lamb's-wool applicators (for varnish), clean rags, tack cloth, paintbrush or foam brush, ventilating respirator
MATERIALS: 8d finishing nails, latex wood putty, wood stain, 220-grit sandpaper or #000 steel wool, varnish, blue painter's masking tape

WORK SMARTER

TOO THIN TO SAND?
Pull up a floor vent or take off the threshold or the baseboard to reveal the edge of a floorboard. You can sand until you're just above the tongue and groove.

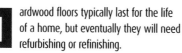

Hardwood floors typically last for the life of a home, but eventually they will need refurbishing or refinishing.

Refinishing
If the floors are simply dirty from years of use but aren't worn through to bare wood, you can probably clean them with household detergent and elbow grease, or you can rent a floor-buffing machine with an abrasive pad. Remove all the dirt and wax from the floor but not the finish itself, then apply a new finish coat.

Refurbishing
If your floors are in bad shape, you can often sand them back to their original state. Solid wood-strip floors can be sanded and refinished several times. Engineered wood floors, however, are made from laminated wood products and can be sanded only once and only with great care. Examine an edge of the floor—under a threshold, for example—to determine the floor's thickness. If the floor is laminated wood, leave the job to professionals.

If the floor is reasonably flat and free of dips and gouges, all you need to do is remove the finish with a vibrating sander. Vibrating sanders work on the same principle as handheld finishing sanders: The machine's

flat pad with sandpaper vibrates and oscillates to remove the old finish. Vibrating floor models are bigger and heavier, of course, but easy to control.

If the floor is uneven or has scratches or deep gouges, you need to use a drum sander. (Don't use drum sanders on maple, birch, or cherry. They leave burn marks.) If you're not comfortable running the machine, call a professional to do the sanding, then do the finishing and staining yourself.

Floor sanders at a glance

Drum sander   Vibrating sander   Edge sander

Drum and vibrating floor sanders and edgers are rental items. Drum and edge sanders are powerful tools, and it takes some practice to operate them properly. Many rental companies offer a training demonstration, so take advantage of the opportunity. After class you're on your own. To minimize potential damage to your floor, start by using fine sandpaper on a small area to become familiar with the machine. Later switch to coarse paper and start the real sanding. Sandpaper comes with the rented sanders but you'll pay for each piece. Get more than you think you'll need—you can return unused paper for a refund when you return the sander.

1

REMOVE THE SHOE MOLDING

A floor sander may bang against base molding, so remove it. Usually all you have to do is remove the shoe molding—the quarter round that runs along the floor. Pry it off as shown, protecting the baseboard with a piece of scrap wood. If there is no shoe molding, either remove the base molding or take care not to damage it with the sanders.

2

FIX SQUEAKS AND SHORE UP THE FLOOR

Check for squeaks and nail loose floorboards. The best approach is to nail into a floor joist, not just the subfloor, with 8d finishing nails. Find protruding nails by sliding the blade of a putty knife across the floor. Set the nails and fill the holes with latex wood putty.

3

CONTAIN THE DUST

To prevent dust from spreading throughout the house, close off doorways and ductwork with plastic sheeting. Stick strips of masking tape around the edges of closet doors. If possible, pull the dust out a window with a box fan. Wear a dust mask when sanding.

4

ROUGH-SAND THE FLOOR

Rough-sand with a drum or vibrating sander. If the floor itself is in bad shape, start with a drum sander. If refinishing is all that's necessary, use a vibrating sander (Step 6) instead. Get advice from the tool rental company. When drum sanding, start with the coarsest sandpaper grit—typically 36- or 40-grit—then switch to 60-grit. Finish with 80- or 100-grit. Move the sander so it travels along the length of the boards with the grain of the wood. Work the drum sander forward and back over 3-foot to 4-foot lengths of floor, overlapping the strokes by at least one-third of the belt.

4

WOOD FLOORING

5

SWEEP AND VACUUM

Sweep and vacuum between sandings. The sanding dust eventually gets in the way of the sanding process and must be removed. Always sweep and vacuum before moving on to the next grit of sandpaper. Doing so not only cleans the floor, it picks up any debris left by the sandpaper that would scratch the results of the finer-grit paper.

6

FINE-SAND THE FLOOR

Fine-sand with a vibrating sander (optional). These sanders level minor unevenness left by drum sanders. If you use both tools, use the drum sander for the two coarse grits (36 and 60), then use the vibrating sander for the medium and fine grits (80 and 100). If you use only the vibrating sander, start with 60-grit, then sand with 80-grit and, finally, with 100-grit.

To keep a lamb's-wool applicator from drying out overnight, store it in a tightly sealed plastic bag. When it's time for the next coat, unwrap the applicator and you're ready to go.

GOOD IDEA

TRIAL RUN

A drum sander is difficult to maneuver until you get the hang of it. Ask the rental company for a demonstration and some operating tips, and practice on an old sheet of plywood before you start on your floor. Start with fine sandpaper, then switch to coarser grades when you're more comfortable.

TOOL TIP

A DIFFERENT DRUMMER

A sander drum is usually made of rubber that's wedged between two discs held in place by a nut. To lock a roll of sandpaper in place, tighten the nut, squeezing together the sides of the drum. This increases the diameter just enough to prevent the sandpaper from slipping off. Loosen the nut to remove the sandpaper.

7

SAND THE EDGES AND CORNERS

Sand corners and edges with an edge sander. The edge sander usually comes as part of the rental. Use 80-grit paper to reach areas that the large sanders fail to reach: in corners, under radiators, in small closets, etc. Edge sanders can be difficult to control; practice on a hidden area, such as the inside of a closet, until you get the hang of it.

8 FINISH-SAND THE EDGES

A random-orbit sander is easier to control than an edge sander. Use it to finish tight places such as corners. Random-orbit sanders are less aggressive and less likely to gouge. They do an excellent job, at a slower pace.

9 APPLY STAIN

Apply a wood stain (optional). When the sanding is done, vacuum up all the dust and follow up with a tack cloth. Apply wood stain with a foam applicator pad. Work one manageable area at a time—4 square feet, for example. Always stain in the direction of the wood grain.

10 WIPE OFF EXCESS STAIN

Most manufacturers recommend removing excess stain as you go—usually a few minutes after you apply it. Use clean cotton cloths or paper towels. Some finishers prefer wiping the floor with a cotton cloth wrapped around a dry applicator pad.

11 APPLY FINISH

Allow the stain to dry as recommended before applying the first coat of varnish. Polyurethane, either oil-base or water-base, is a reliable finish for floors. Apply the finish with a lamb's-wool applicator. Sand the floor lightly with 220-grit paper or #000 steel wool. Vacuum up the dust. Apply three coats of oil-based finish or four coats of water-base finish, sanding in between.

4

WOOD FLOORING

Maintaining wood floors

echnological advances in the production of floor finishes have created products that the pros of 50 years ago wouldn't have thought possible. In addition to the ease of application, modern wood finishes can stand up to a whole lot more abuse than older finishes. But modern finishes share at least one thing with the older products—floors still need to be cleaned regularly.

How you clean your floor will depend somewhat on whether it has a surface finish only or is waxed. These differences are sometimes hard to spot. To tell if your floor is waxed, drop a little water in an out-of-the-way corner. If white spots appear after about 10 minutes, the floor is waxed. Remove the white spots by buffing with #0000 steel wool and a little wax.

Cleaning surface finishes

Dust or vacuum the floor regularly and clean up spills immediately with a damp cloth. Use a general-purpose floor cleaner to clean the floor—or a product recommended by the finish manufacturer. Don't wax urethane-finished floors. The wax doesn't stick to this finish and actually makes it slippery. If a urethane coat is dull, what

it may need is a sanding and a recoat. Some urethanes can be recoated without sanding.

Cleaning waxed floors

Dust or vacuum regularly. Remove spills immediately with a damp cloth, and buff with a soft, dry cloth to return the shine. Buff only the dull areas of the floor. Clean the floor once a year with a solvent-based cleaner (water-based cleaners will fog the finish). Then wax and buff the floor.

Some basic floor repairs

Although wood is among the toughest flooring materials, it can suffer damages—splits, cracks, or moisture damage in one area can usually be repaired without tearing up the floor. Some damage may be confined to the surface

or finish; refer to the chart below for suggestions about repairing surface damage. Replacing damaged sections of wood flooring is fairly straightforward, as illustrated on these pages.

REAL WORLD

REPAIRING WOOD FLOORS

Problem	Remedy
Chewing gum, crayon, candle wax	Pop off with ice in a bag, scrape with plastic scraper. Seep cleaning fluid under chewing gum.
Cigarette burns	Burnish with fine steel wool or scrape charred area. Wax, or sand, stain, and refinish.
Dents	Cover with dampened cloth and press with an electric iron.
Scratches	Wax the area or hide the scratch with a thin coat of dusting spray rubbed into scratch.
Seasonal cracks	Increase humidity in dry season—install humidifier, boil water, open dishwasher after rinse.
Surface stains	Remove with sandpaper or steel wool, feathering edges; or clean with one of these solutions:
Heel marks	Wood cleaner or wax.
Oil and grease	Try wood cleaner first. Then, on waxed floor, use TSP or soap with high lye content. On surface finish, use TSP.
Pet stains	Wood cleaner, followed by mild bleach or household vinegar for up to an hour. A remaining spot is not likely to sand out. Cover damage with rug or remove, replace, and refinish.
Ink	Use same procedure as for pet stains.
Mold, mildew	Floor cleaner. If wood fibers are stained, remove and refinish.
Water spots	Buff lightly with #0000 steel wool, then wax. If necessary, sand with fine paper, stain, and recoat.

Replacing damaged strip or plank flooring

1 **OUTLINE THE DAMAGE**
Use a framing square to outline the damaged area.

2 **DRILL OUT THE DAMAGE**
Use a $5/8$-inch spade bit to drill out the inside edges of the damaged section.

3 **PLUNGE-CUT THE DAMAGED SECTION**
Set your circular saw so it just cuts through the flooring and not the subfloor. Set the saw on the flooring at an angle and start it. Lower the saw blade into the flooring and cut toward the holes you drilled.

4 **CLEAN THE CUTOUT WITH A CHISEL**
Square the drilled edges of the cutout with a sharp chisel, bevel facing the edge.

5 **CUT A HARDWOOD PATCH**
Cut a replacement board, removing one side of the groove to help make it fit. Test-fit the patch.

6 **ANCHOR THE PATCH**
Spread a thin coat of construction adhesive on the back of the patch and tap the patch into place.

Repairing damaged parquet tile

Parquet is the fine furniture of wood floors. If you treat it as such, it will give you years of service. If you mistreat it, it soon can look deteriorated and shabby. One of the best things you can do for this floor is to clean it with a product either made by or recommended by the manufacturer. Never clean a parquet floor (or any wood floor, for that matter) with water or water-based products.

The same general standards for maintenance of wood floors apply to parquet. Wipe up spills immediately with a damp cloth and dry the area with a dry cloth. Old T-shirts are excellent for this purpose. Do not use cleaners that contain abrasives, caustic chemicals, bleach, or ammonia. For routine cleaning, it is best to use a solvent-based cleaner or a one-step cleaner/polish combination.

Most prefinished parquet tile comes with a durable acrylic or polyurethane finish. Some finishes are no-wax, others benefit from waxing. Check the manufacturer's directions before you purchase cleaning products. Acrylic waxes are not generally recommended for wood floors, and some polyurethane finishes must never be waxed.

Almost all wood finishes change color over time. You can slow this process somewhat by keeping the drapes closed. Areas covered with rugs won't be subject to color changes and the color difference will be revealed if you decide to move the rugs later.

Preventative maintenance for parquet

Regular vacuuming is the best thing you can do for a wood floor. Aside from water, nothing ruins a wood floor more quickly than the abrasiveness of tracked-in dirt and dust. Vacuuming removes these offending particles and keeps them from residing in the joints (which brooming or dust-mopping won't do).

To help keep the grit from getting on the floor in the first place, set slip-resistant mats (with nonstaining backs) at your doorways, use casters or felt pads under furniture legs, and avoid walking with any kind of spiked shoes (athletic or heels).

Floor mats in front of stoves, refrigerators, and sinks help prevent stains. Use them in the bathroom too.

Always use the cleaner that the manufacturer recommends. Generally these are solvent-based solutions, but several new environmentally friendly cleaners are showing up on the market.

1

SCORE THE DAMAGED TILE
Put a fine-toothed blade on your circular saw and set it so it just cuts through the parquet and not the subfloor. Make a series of plunge cuts in the damaged tile about 2 inches apart.

Refinishing parquet

Parquet tile, especially a quality product with a thick veneer, is an excellent candidate for refinishing. Refinishing methods, however, differ substantially. First, use a pad sander. A drum sander is too aggressive and may strip the veneer from the tile. Secondly, begin sanding on the diagonal. Work the sander from one side of the room to the other. Then shift directions and sand along the other diagonal of the room. Make a final pass parallel to and along the longest wall of the room. Repeat this three-pass process with successively finer grits of sandpaper.

Stain and varnish the floor with the product of your choice, either a penetrating or surface finish. Penetrants sink into the wood pores; they won't wear out unless the wood does. Surface finishes don't soak into the pores of the wood; they stay on top and generally are less durable.

2
CHISEL OUT THE DAMAGED TILE
Starting at one of the plunge cuts you made, chisel out the damaged sections. Clean the recess completely and scrape out any leftover adhesive.

3
CUT AND FIT A REPLACEMENT TILE
Cut a replacement tile to fit the recess (you may have to cut the tongues and the bottom off the grooved sides). Apply the same adhesive in the recess you used to lay the floor and set the tile in carefully.

4
WEIGHT UNTIL THE GLUE DRIES
Press down on all parts of the tile to make sure it seats properly. Clean off any excess adhesive that seeps out. Make sure the tile is dry. Lay some waxed paper over the tile (in case more adhesive seeps through) and weight the tile with books or other heavy objects till the glue drys.

Laminate flooring

ou can buy laminate flooring that resembles any of a number of more-expensive flooring materials, from exotic woods to stone. Laminates are also light, strong, durable, and easy to install. And because laminate planks are two or three times wider than the natural materials they resemble, you can cover a lot of floor in a short time.

Most laminate flooring materials are designed to snap together without glue or nails. (Some brands can be glued, but even those usually have snap-together edges.) Laminate floors float—that is, they are not attached to the subfloor.

Instead, laminates lay on foam underlayment, which makes the flooring easier to install. The subfloor must still be smooth and level, but the foam underlayment makes the flooring more forgiving of small subfloor imperfections. (The foam also helps deaden the sound underneath and gives the surface a bit of cushion underfoot.)

The most common underlayment is green or blue plastic foam that rolls out over the subfloor. Rubber-backed underlayment is more expensive, but makes the floor more resilient and thus more comfortable. Some laminate planks now come with underlayment already attached to the back.

Chapter 5 highlights

If you're installing laminate flooring over a concrete slab in a basement or in any other place where moisture might be a problem, you'll need some kind of waterproofing membrane under the foam. One solution is to lay 6-mil polyethylene sheeting over the floor before you put down the underlayment. This will keep moisture out of the underlayment and flooring, but requires a two-step application.

Or you can install 2-in-1 foam underlayment, which is more expensive but has its own moisture barrier so it installs in one step. If you use this underlayment, be sure the film side faces the slab.

Installing snapped laminates

PROJECT DETAILS

SKILLS: Basic carpentry
PROJECT: Installing a snap-together laminate floor

TIME TO COMPLETE

EXPERIENCED: 3 hrs.
HANDY: 4 hrs.
NOVICE: 5 hrs.

STUFF YOU'LL NEED

TOOLS: Metric tape measure, level, jigsaw, trim saw, circular saw or tablesaw, rafter angle square, hammer, bucket, installation strap clamps, spacer, tapping block, pull bar
MATERIALS: Foam underlayment, flooring, manufacturer's recommended glue for glued applications, sealant or mildew-resistant silicone caulk, floor-leveling compound (if needed)

SAFETY ALERT

WATCH YOUR STEP
Some laminate flooring manufacturers include thorough directions for installing stairways made with laminate flooring. Check with your building inspector before installing them. In many areas, laminate stairs fail to meet code.

Laminate floors mimic a variety of materials, including wood, stone, and tile. They can be glued or snapped together. This snap-together plank floor looks like its glue-together cousin, but takes a fraction of the time to install.

Laminate flooring has many advantages: It's quick to install, durable, and easy to clean. It is ideal for installation over old resilient flooring that may contain asbestos because it can be installed without disturbing the original floor.

For many years the primary method of installing laminate flooring was to clamp and glue the pieces together. Recently glueless snap-together systems that are far more user-friendly have been introduced. The glue-together planks are still popular in commercial applications where heavy foot traffic affects wear and longevity, but for the majority of do-it-yourselfers, snap-together technology is the best way to go. Both types are floating floors—they

aren't nailed or glued to the subfloor. They sit on a foam underlayment and are held in place by their own weight.

Because of its construction, laminate can be installed either perpendicular to or parallel to the flooring joists. For the best-looking floor, position the planks so they're parallel to the main light source. If light enters the room through a window on the north wall, for example, run the planks from north to south. If the window is on the east wall, run the planks from east to west. In narrow spaces, run the planks parallel to the long wall—in a hallway, for instance, run the planks the length of the hall.

Laminate flooring prep at a glance

- **Location:** Use above or below grade. Glued planks are generally approved for use in full baths; snap-together planks are not. Seal edges of floor with caulk or sealant if used in bath. Seal edges of floor if likely to get wet in kitchen. Never install over any floor that has a drain or sump pump.
- **Crawlspaces:** Cover ground or underside of joists with 6-mil plastic.
- **Subfloor:** Fill any depressions greater than $3/16$ inch. Floor must be level within 1 inch over 6 feet.
- **Concrete:** Test by taping plastic patch to surface for 72 hours. If dry, cover with 6-mil vapor barrier. If wet, contact manufacturer for advice.
- **Other subfloors:** All subfloors are acceptable, except carpet. Wood and parquet flooring installed over concrete must be removed before installation.
- **Prep:** Remove baseboard and replace after installing floor. Undercut door trim so floor will fit underneath it. Acclimate boards by putting the boxes in the room at least 48 hours before installation.

1
INSTALL MOISTURE BARRIER
Install a moisture barrier over concrete by lining the floor with polyethylene sheeting. Most laminate requires a sheet 6 mil thick, but use whatever your floor manufacturer recommends. Overlap the seams by 8 inches or as recommended. Do not install a moisture barrier over a wood subfloor—this will result in mold, mildew, and a warped floor.

2
ACCLIMATE THE PLANKS FOR 48 HOURS
Two days before you begin work, take the packages of laminate into the room you're flooring. Set the thermostat at a normal temperature for the time of year. Put the unopened boxes flat on the floor, or stack them three or four high, log-cabin style. After 48 hours, they will have adjusted to the temperature and humidity of the room.

3
UNDERCUT THE JAMBS
Instead of trying to cut flooring to fit around door moldings, installers cut away part of the jamb and slip the floor underneath. To do this, put a piece of flooring upside down on foam underlayment next to the jamb. Put a trim saw on the plank and cut at least $1/2$ inch into the jamb. Pop out the waste with a screwdriver or chisel.

4
CALCULATE END-PLANK WIDTHS
Divide the width of the room by the width of the plank. This ensures that the last plank, which generally must be cut to width, will be at least 2 inches wide. Unless you enjoy dividing fractions by fractions, make the measurements with a metric tape measure. (You don't have to understand metrics to do this.) If the remainder is less than 50 mm, the last plank will be less than 2 inches wide. You'll need to trim the first plank to make the last plank wider. Use the formula in the next step to plan the cut.

5
TRIM THE FIRST ROW
Even if you don't need to adjust the width of the final plank, cut the tongues off the planks you'll use for the first row. If you need to adjust the width or would simply like planks to be the same width at either end of the room, add the width of a plank to the width you calculated in the previous step. Again, use the metric system. Divide by 2 to get the plank width, then lay out the cut using the metric tape measure.

6

START THE SECOND ROW

Cut the first plank in the second row so the ends of the planks are offset from row to row. Cut the plank to length as directed by the manufacturer. If making the cut with a circular saw, guide the saw with a layout square, as shown here. Set the plank aside.

7

ROLL OUT THE UNDERLAYMENT

Some planks have underlayment that is already attached. Other planks require you to roll out the underlayment separately. Roll a single strip of underlayment alongside the wall where you'll start laying flooring.

8

INSTALL THE FIRST PLANK

It's easiest to assemble the first two rows when they're a couple of feet away from the starting wall, and then slide them into place. Start with a full-length plank (tongue removed in Step 5) with the groove facing into the room. Snap the tongue of the piece you cut to length in Step 6 into the groove in the edge of the first plank.

9

SNAPPING THE PLANKS

Snap the third plank into the end of the first plank. Put down a fourth plank, snapping the end into the end of the second plank, and leaving a slight gap between the long edges of the two planks. Kneel on the first plank to hold it in place while you work. Lift the edge of the third plank about 1 inch off the floor. Pull the plank towards you, while pushing down on the first plank right next to the seam. The planks should snap together. Repeat on the next two planks.

⊙ CLOSER LOOK

THE RIGHT FIT

Different brands of flooring fit together differently, so follow the directions that come with the flooring you buy. For the brand shown here, put the tongue into the groove, with the groove plank flat on the floor, and angle up the edge of the other plank. Press the plank flat to snap the pieces together. The pieces snap together on both the ends.

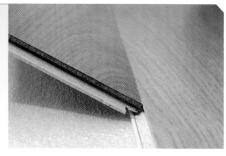

10

CONTINUE INSTALLING THE FLOOR

Continue laying the first two rows across the length of the room. When you get to the last plank, put a spacer against the wall, and cut a plank to fit in the opening. Put the plank in place, then snap it into the end groove, as shown, using a hammer and pull bar (made by the manufacturer). Slide the assembled rows against the starting wall.

11

SCRIBE THE WALL CONTOUR

Because this is the first time that the rows are rigid, it's also the first time you can see how the first row fits against the wall. If the gap between the wall and the planks is wider than the expansion gap, scribe the wall contour on the planks in the first row. Do this by setting a compass to the dimension of the largest gap, plus about 1/2 inch. Guide the compass along the wall to mark the planks.

12

CUT THE PLANKS

To cut along the line, disassemble the rows, following the manufacturer's directions. Number the bottom of the boards in the first row so that you can reassemble them in the same order. Cut along the scribed line using a jigsaw with a laminate blade, which is designed to minimize chipping. Reassemble the rows when you're done cutting.

13

START THE THIRD ROW

Once the first two rows are in place, begin the third row. Cut a plank to length so the end falls at least 8 inches from the end of its neighbor in the second row. Put a spacer against the wall, put the plank against the spacer, and snap the plank into the edge of the second row. Work your way across the room, laying a single row. Snap the ends of the planks together first, then join the sides.

WORK SMARTER

MAKING THE CUT

Laminate flooring chips easily. Making a cut with a minimum of chipping depends on the tool.

■ **Jigsaw:** Cut with the jigsaw on the good side of the board and use a laminate blade. Laminate blades are designed to minimize chipping.

■ **Circular saw:** Cut with the good side down and saw riding on the surface that will be against the floor. A circular saw causes chipping on the surface facing up.

■ **Tablesaw:** Cut with the good side up. Tablesaws cause chipping on the surface against the table.

14

SNUG THE GAPS

If you see a gap anywhere along the edges, close it by tapping the edge with a hammer and block. When you reach the end of a row, cut plank to fit, and put it in place against a spacer as before. Work your way across the room, installing one row at a time. Unroll additional underlayment as you need it. Butt underlayment seams, but never overlap them. Tape the seams if recommended by the manufacturer.

15

TRIM THE FINAL ROW

Trim the final row to fit. Start by assembling a row directly on top of the row just laid. Take a piece of scrap, and if the bottom lip of the flooring is wider than the top lip, break off the bottom lip. Hold the scrap against the wall, put a marker against the opposite edge, and pull the scrap and marker along the wall to mark the planks. Trim the planks with a jigsaw. Caulk the edge with silicone caulk.

5

LAMINATE FLOORING

Installing glued laminates

The planks of glued laminate are glued to each other but not to the subfloor. This is a floating floor, and its advantages include durability and ease of installation.

Because the boards are glued together, the seams are stronger than those that just snap together. As a result, glue-together flooring is the favorite in commercial installations. If your rec room is destined for high-caliber table tennis matches and square dances, glued planks may be the answer. Many manufacturers of laminate flooring also require that the edges of their products be glued in bath and kitchen installations. The glue helps waterproof the joints.

The surface laminate, the core, and the liner on the bottom of glue-together planks are the same as those in snap-together planks. In many brands, the joint is simpler, but in others it is the same as for snapped laminates.

Installation of glued laminates is somewhat different from snapped floors. Placement of the first few rows is crucial, so you'll cut and fit them before you start gluing. Once they're in place, take them apart and start gluing. The water-base glue is easy to apply and easy to clean up. Most manufacturers sell their own glue and will void the warranty if you don't use it. (They put tracers in it so they can tell.)

Because you'll use glue, you'll also need clamps. At the minimum, you'll need to secure the first three rows together with clamps recommended by the manufacturer. Some manufacturers recommend that you clamp the rest of the rows too—ask about this before buying the floor.

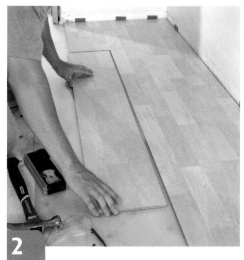

1

PLACE THE UNDERLAYMENT
Roll out the underlayment. If you're applying the floor over concrete, roll out 6-mil vapor barrier first, overlapping the edges as directed by the manufacturer. Then roll out a strip of underlayment from wall to wall.

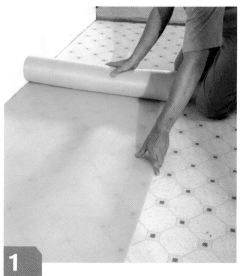

2

TEST-FIT THE FIRST THREE ROWS
Before gluing, test-fit the first three rows. Put the first plank in place with ¼-inch spacers between the plank and the wall. Put the groove of the next plank over the tongue of the first. Begin the second row with a plank cut to two-thirds its full length and the third row with a plank one-third its full length. When all three rows are in place, number each plank with labels to show its location and take the floor apart.

Laminate flooring prep at a glance

- **Locations:** Above or below grade. Glued planks are generally approved for use in full baths. Snap-together planks are not. Seal edge of floor with caulk or sealant if used in bath. Seal edges in areas of floor likely to get wet in kitchen. Never install over any floor with drain or sump pump.
- **Crawlspaces:** Cover ground or underside of joists with 6-mil plastic.
- **Subfloor:** Fill any depressions greater than 3/16 inch. Floor must be level within 1 inch over 6 feet.
- **Concrete:** Test by taping plastic patch to

surface for 72 hours. If dry, cover with 6-mil vapor barrier. If wet, contact manufacturer for advice.
- **Other subfloors:** All are acceptable, except carpet. Wood and parquet flooring installed over concrete must be removed before installation.
- **Prep:** Remove baseboard and replace after installing floor. Undercut door trim so floor will fit underneath it. Acclimate the boards by putting boxes in the room at least 48 hours before installation.

3

GLUE THE FIRST PLANK

Put glue in the end groove of the first plank and position it against spacers on the wall. Put the second board of the row in place, seating it with a hammer and tapping block. Continue down the row, gluing the grooves and assembling. When you reach the end board, seat it with the help of a pull bar.

4

FINISH THE FIRST ROW

When you reach the end, cut a plank to fit. If the plank meets a wall, cut the piece to fit between the last full plank and a spacer placed against the wall. If the plank meets another floor, cut the piece to fit the transition molding, as directed by the manufacturer. Put the plank in place and seat it by tapping on a pull bar. The minimum length for the last plank is about 8 inches, depending on the manufacturer. If your plank is shorter, cut a few inches off the previous plank to make the last plank longer.

5

START THE SECOND ROW

Put glue in the edges and end grooves of the first plank of the second row. Put it in place with a spacer between it and the wall, and put the groove over the tongue of the preceding row. Work your way down the row, gluing and assembling as you go.

6

INSTALL THE THIRD ROW

Install the third row the same way you installed the second row. Once all three rows are installed, clamp them together with belt clamps made by the flooring manufacturer. You can purchase or often rent the clamps from your home center or flooring supply store. Put the hook of one end over one edge of the floor, and the other hook over the other edge. Pull the loose end of the belt until it's snug (but don't pop the joints), then tighten with a wrench.

7

CONTINUE TO THE LAST ROW

Fit and install the last row. If the last row is narrower than the width of a plank, scribe to lay out the necessary cuts. First put a row of full-width planks directly on top of the last full row you laid. Put a full-width scrap against a spacer and trace along the wall to mark the planks. Cut along the line with a jigsaw. Apply glue and put the planks in place, seating them with the help of a pull bar.

💡 GOOD IDEA

MIRRORING THE CONTOUR OF THE WALL
If the wall dips or juts out at any point, you may have to trim or scribe the entire first row of planks to maintain the required ¼-inch expansion gap. Set a compass so the points are about 1 inch apart. Pull the point of the compass along the wall, marking the flooring with the pencil leg. Cut along the line with a jigsaw.

Some manufacturers call for different-size spacers and different length starting boards. Follow their directions carefully.

Caring for and cleaning laminate flooring

Regular vacuuming with a floor attachment will keep your laminate floor looking as beautiful as the day it was installed. Grit and debris left on the surface can damage the floor.

Preventive maintenance

To keep your floor shiny and clean, do a little preventive maintenance. Start by putting a mat or rug at each entrance to the room to collect dirt. Put a rug over the floor in high-traffic areas too, such as the area in front of the kitchen sink. Any rug laid on a laminate floor should have a rubber backing to keep it from slipping. If the rubber discolors the laminate, wipe the area with ammonia to clean it.

Vacuum the floor immediately after installation to remove any construction debris that might scratch it. Put felt pads on the feet of chairs, tables, and other furniture to avoid scratching the floor. Replace plastic or metal casters with rubber casters.

Clean it right

Vacuum or dry-mop instead of sweeping. If you dry-mop, shake the mop out thoroughly to avoid rubbing dirt across the floor the next time you mop. If you vacuum, use an attachment designed for wood floors. Running a vacuum with a beater block across the floor damages the floor.

When the floor needs to be washed, mop it using the no-wax cleaner recommended by the manufacturer. Regular detergents and soap products will build up on the floor, making it look dull.

Clean up stains caused by chocolate, grease, juice, or wine with the no-wax cleaner. To remove tar, crayon, lipstick, shoe polish, or nail polish, use mineral spirits, nail polish remover, or denatured alcohol. Do not rub with steel wool.

Laminate floors don't require wax and won't benefit from having it applied. In fact, wax leaves a film on the floor that deadens the shine.

REAL WORLD

THE ICEMAN COMETH

The kitchen was looking pretty good as one do-it-yourselfer started putting everything back together. The painting was done, the cabinets were in, and now, at last, so was the floor. There were protective felt pads on the table and chair legs. The last appliances to place were the refrigerator and stove. A neighbor helped heave the refrigerator onto a blanket and slid it across the floor—no problem until they got to the wall where they had to either slide the fridge off the blanket or leave the blanket under the fridge. It was in the last few blanketless inches that they scratched that new floor. At least the scratch was small—once you've run a refrigerator through the finish on laminate, you can't do much to repair it.

There's a way to avoid that problem: Rent an air sled. It's a rubber mat that slips under the fridge just like the blanket. But when you attach an air sled to the blower that comes with it, air shoots out of the bottom of the mat and lifts the refrigerator a fraction of an inch off the floor. Once the fridge is hovering, you can push it with one hand. When it's in place, you turn off the blower and slide the deflated mat out from under the fridge.

Repairing minor damage

1 SQUARE THE DAMAGED AREA

Square off the damage. You can patch damaged areas ¼ inch in diameter or smaller with finishing putty sold by the manufacturer. Make sure you get the putty that matches your floor. Cut along the edges of the damage with a utility knife to create a spot that has four straight edges. Vacuum up the debris.

2 APPLY FINISHING PUTTY

Put tape around the hole, as shown, to make cleanup easier. Squeeze some putty onto the damaged area and level it off with a plastic putty knife.

3 REMOVE THE PROTECTIVE TAPE

Remove the tape. The putty shrinks as it dries and should now be flush with the floor. Wipe up any putty on the floor with a damp cloth.

Repairing major damage

Repairing major damage in a laminate plank requires replacing the plank. All major manufacturers of laminate recommend leaving the job to a pro. Here's what's involved.

First lay out lines that are about an inch from each edge and both ends of the damaged plank. Then draw lines connecting the corners of the rectangle with the corners of the plank. Each of these lines represents a cut that will be made; a few pieces of tape will show exactly where to stop the cut.

Once the lines are drawn, cut out the rectangle formed by the first four lines, then remove the section with a suction cup. Make careful cuts along the diagonal lines to break the rest of the plank free.

To replace the plank, cut off the tongue and the underside of the groove from a matching plank. Glue it in place. Lay sandbags on it to hold it down until the glue dries.

Vinyl flooring

he only difference between vinyl tile and sheet vinyl is the size. Both are made of the same materials and in the same way, and both require the same subfloor.

When it comes to installation, however, vinyl tile is the less intimidating of the two. You install it one small piece at a time, and it often comes with a peel-and-stick backing. It's easy to trim, and if you make a mistake, you've wasted only a single tile. Besides, you can also use it to create a wide variety in your floor design. You can mix and match tiles to create patterns, or you can buy tiles with patterns that are almost identical to those found on sheet vinyl.

So should homeowners stay away from sheet vinyl? Not necessarily. With a little patience, and taking one thing at a time, cutting a room-size sheet is not that difficult. At least one

Chapter 6 highlights

manufacturer sells an inexpensive installation kit that guarantees either a perfect cutting job or new sheet vinyl to replace the error. And several companies make a sheet vinyl product that is even easier to install. It sits on the floor like a rug, with no adhesive. Instead, strips of double-sided tape hold it fast at doorways and under appliances.

It goes without saying that because vinyl is thin and pliable, it will conform to every defect in the surface under it. So besides requiring a surface that's clean, it needs the smoothness of underlayment-grade plywood. The subfloor must be dry too. Unlike wood floors or carpet, which can let a certain amount of moisture pass harmlessly through them and evaporate, vinyl will trap moisture and cause mold and rot. If you live in a humid climate, add a waterproof underlayment to your list of materials.

Because the adhesive that holds vinyl tile in place is water soluble, mopping with too much water will, over time, dissolve the adhesive, and the tile corners will start to lift. A little forethought at mopping time will keep your floor down for a long time.

Installing sheet vinyl

PROJECT DETAILS

SKILLS: Making a pattern, spreading adhesive, cutting vinyl
PROJECT: Installing sheet vinyl

TIME TO COMPLETE

EXPERIENCED: 20 min.
HANDY: 1 hr.
NOVICE: 2 hrs.

STUFF YOU'LL NEED

TOOLS: Utility knife, tape measure, framing square or combination square, marker/pencil, compass, scissors, straightedge, hook-blade (linoleum) knife, notched trowel, floor roller, broad knife, rubber gloves
MATERIALS: Roll of butcher or kraft paper, masking tape, installation kit (optional), cloth rag, vinyl flooring adhesive, double-sided tape, duct tape, seam sealer, adhesive cleaner

A proper subfloor is more important to a vinyl floor installation than to any other. Because it is a resilient flooring, wear causes bumps and ridges to show through the way a penny shows through paper when rubbed with a pencil. Read "Installing underlayment," page 86, and any directions that come with your flooring carefully, and do exactly what the manufacturer requires. As a general rule, avoid lauan underlayment. Some species contain stains that bleed through to the surface of the vinyl, and there is no way to distinguish one species from another. No warranty covers lauan stains or any other problem created by a defective subfloor.

Vinyl floors are commonly installed in bathrooms and kitchens, which have more obstructions than living rooms or dens. Remove all the obstructions you can, including toilets and sinks. Turn off the water first and disconnect the lines from any fixture you're removing (see page 71). Drain the water from toilet bowls and their tanks with a small bucket and sponge. Remove the bolts that hold the toilet to the floor, and lift the toilet out of the way with a helper. Remove sinks from vanities and unscrew vanities from the wall to remove them. Pedestal sinks may need to be unscrewed from both the floor and the wall.

Installation begins with making a pattern the shape of your floor, minus about 1 inch in each direction. Make the pattern carefully and trace around it in pencil before cutting it. Be sure to use a pencil or a ballpoint pen; other markers may leave stains that will travel through the vinyl.

◀ **The trick to installing sheet vinyl is to make a pattern that exactly matches the shape of the room. Baseboard will cover any irregularities along the edge of this floor. In a room with existing baseboard, install quarter round to cover any gaps.**

Vinyl flooring prep at a glance

- **Storage:** Acclimate materials by storing them in the room for 48 hours before installation at a minimum of 65 degrees. Keep the room at a minimum of 65 degrees during installation and for 48 hours afterward.
- **Location:** On, above, or below grade.
- **Level/flat:** Not only must the floor be level, it must be flat. If you are installing new vinyl over old embossed vinyl, fill the pattern with an embossing leveler recommended by the manufacturer.
- **Moisture:** Test for both moisture and pH to make sure the floor meets manufacturer's standards. Problems with either will prevent the floor from bonding well.

ACCEPTABLE SUBFLOORS

- **Wood:** Double layer of plywood with a combined thickness of at least 1 inch; or $^3/_4$-inch wood covered by $^1/_4$-inch underlayment.
- **Existing vinyl:** Above grade you can apply sheet vinyl over existing sheet vinyl as long as it is no more than one layer thick. Vinyl must be cleaned with the manufacturer's recommended wax-free product. Fill existing embossed vinyl with an embossing leveler.
- **Concrete:** May be applied directly to concrete above, below, or on grade. Floor must be clean, dry, and structurally sound. Test for moisture and pH.

- **Ceramic tile:** Vinyl may be applied to ceramic tile. Abrade the surface of the tile, fill grout lines, and level the surface by pouring a latex-modified portland cement-based underlayment over the tile.

  Do not apply over chipboard, wafer board, oriented strand board, particleboard, or lauan. Floor must be absolutely smooth, as any irregularities will show through the vinyl.
- **Trim:** Undercut door trim before installation. Remove shoe molding.

Making a template

1 CUT A TEMPLATE

To make a paper template, start with a roll of butcher or kraft paper. Run it along the longest wall, about 1 inch away from it. Cut small triangles in the paper with a utility knife. Remove the triangles and tape the paper to the subfloor through the holes. Treat large counters or cabinets that you couldn't remove as if they were walls: Run the paper parallel to them, leaving a 1-inch gap between the paper and the obstruction. Lay paper on the entire floor, taping it in place.

2 MEASURE FOR CUTOUTS

When you come to pipes or obstructions, such as toilet drains, tape paper to the floor all around the obstruction and to any neighboring paper you've already laid. Measure the distance from the wall to the center of the pipe, using a framing square or combination square.

3 MAKE THE CUTOUTS

Lay out the cut out on a separate piece of paper. Measure from the edge of the paper and make a mark where the center of the pipe will be. With a compass, center a circle the diameter of the obstruction on the mark and cut a hole with scissors or a utility knife. Cut a slit from the edge of the paper to the hole. Trim the edge that will be nearest the wall so that when the paper is in place, there will be a 1-inch gap between it and the wall. Put the paper around the obstruction and tape it to the neighboring strips of paper.

4 LAY OUT DOOR CUTS

You can undercut door trim the same way you undercut it for other flooring so that you can slip vinyl underneath it. (See "Installing flooring around doors," page 67.) Unlike other floors, however, vinyl is thin and easy to cut. Instead of cutting the trim to accommodate the vinyl, cut the vinyl to fit the trim. Lay a piece of paper against the trim and push against it to create a fold that follows the outline of the trim. Cut along the crease with scissors. Tape the paper in place so that the cut edge is snug against the door trim.

5 MARK THE CONTOUR

Put a straightedge against the wall and trace along it to draw a line on the template paper. (This creates a line that follows the contour of the wall exactly. Subsequent steps will help you cut vinyl to the true size of the floor.) Work your way around the room, drawing a line on the paper as you go. If you see gaps between the straightedge and the wall, substitute a short block of wood for the straightedge. Once you've finished, remove tape from the triangles but not from the seams. Roll up or loosely fold the template and set it aside until you've unrolled the sheet vinyl in another room.

Installation kits

At least one sheet vinyl manufacturer sells a complete installation kit that includes everything necessary to construct an accurate flooring template. Such a kit normally includes a roll of heavy paper, masking tape, a trimming knife, and a complete set of instructions. Also among the tools is a small tracing wheel you run along the wall to draw a line marking the path of the wall; a spacer called a transfer guide helps you lay out a second line that creates the proper gap between the pattern and the wall.

The installation kit is easy to use, and the manufacturer will replace it and any damaged vinyl if you make a mistake. Although you can create a template for any brand of sheet vinyl with the kit, the guarantee covers only the manufacturer's brand.

Cutting a one-piece vinyl sheet

1 UNROLL THE VINYL SHEET

Take the vinyl to a room larger than the one in which you'll install it. A garage or basement works well as long as the floor is smooth and absolutely clean. Unroll the vinyl, design side up, and let it sit for a few minutes until it is flat on the floor. Reroll the vinyl with the design side inside and leave it briefly if the manufacturer calls for it.

2 SET THE TEMPLATE

Put the template on the vinyl. If the design has noticeable straight lines, such as grout lines, align the edge of the pattern with the lines. Tape the template to the vinyl through the triangular cutouts you made earlier.

3 TRANSFER THE TEMPLATE

Place a straightedge along the edge of the template. Use it to accurately trace the cut on the vinyl. Make the marks in pencil or with a ballpoint pen. Felt-tip markers create stains that will be impossible to remove. If the pattern includes cutouts for door trim or obstructions, carefully trace freehand along the cutout. Remove the template once you've drawn the lines.

4 CUT THE VINYL

Make the cuts with a hook-blade (linoleum) knife, which is hooked and cuts as you pull it. Hold the knife straight to avoid creating a beveled edge. You can guide the cut along a straightedge if it makes you more comfortable, but because trim will cover the edges, a freehand cut works equally well. Be careful not to cut into the flooring surface underneath.

5 CUT OUT THE CUTOUTS

Cut out the openings you laid out for pipes and drains. Trace around the layout lines of small holes with the knife. Cut out larger holes with scissors. Cut a slit between the cutout and the edge of the vinyl so you'll be able to fit it around the obstruction.

6 ROLL UP THE VINYL

Wash off any remaining layout lines with a damp cloth. Apply duct tape diagonally near inside corners to prevent rips. Roll up the vinyl around the tube it came on, rolling it so the design faces out and the narrowest section of floor will be the first to unroll. Apply the vinyl within 2 hours or it will lose its ability to stretch and hide any small gaps.

6

VINYL FLOORING

Laying a one-piece vinyl sheet

1 UNROLL THE VINYL

Take the vinyl to the room it will be installed in and position it in such a way that, when you unroll it, it will be in its final position. Tuck the vinyl under the door trim or align it with the trim, depending on how you laid out the template. Make any necessary corrections.

2 CHECK THE EDGES

Walk around the room, taking note of the expansion gap. If the gap is too small, or if the vinyl won't seat because it is catching on the wall, trim the edge. Put a straightedge over the vinyl to lay out the cut—a drywall broad knife works well. Guide the knife along the edge to make the cut.

3 APPLY THE ADHESIVE

Fold the vinyl back on itself, exposing half of the floor. Apply vinyl flooring adhesive with a notched trowel, following the manufacturer's directions. It's important that you use the recommended notch size and that you let the adhesive cure according to the manufacturer's specs. Notch size controls how much adhesive remains on the floor. The adhesive is cured and ready to hold sheet vinyl when you can touch it without getting any on your hands. Applying the vinyl any earlier could cause the bond to fail.

4 ADHERE THE FIRST HALF

Fold the first half of the sheet into the adhesive. Then fold back the other half and apply adhesive to the exposed floor. Let it cure and fold the vinyl into it. Roll the floor immediately to push the vinyl into the adhesive and prevent it from bubbling. Start in the middle of the floor and work out to the edges.

WORK SMARTER

SO CLEAN YOU COULD EAT OFF IT. . .

Cleanliness brings success when laying vinyl. Stones trapped under the vinyl eventually work their way to the top, ruining the job. Dust and dirt weaken the vinyl adhesive, causing trouble down the road. To make sure the floor is clean, sweep it, vacuum it, then wipe it with a damp—not wet—rag. Let the floor dry thoroughly before applying the vinyl.

Installing a perimeter-laid floor

Some types of sheet vinyl, those that are perimeter laid, require vinyl adhesive only around the edges of the room. Perimeter-laid sheet vinyl is vinyl-backed, as opposed to felt-backed vinyl, which is glued to the entire floor. Perimeter-laid sheet vinyl allows the floor to expand and contract, and it compensates for normal movement in wood and concrete. It seems like it would be easier and cleaner to work with, especially if you tend to get adhesive on your hands while you work. In reality, though, perimeter-laid floors are trickier to install because they must lie completely flat without the help of adhesive.

Cutting a two-piece sheet

Vinyl comes in sheets that are either 6 or 12 feet wide. If your room is wider than 12 feet, you'll need to lay out and cut a seam. Avoid running it down the middle of your room where everybody will see it. Choose an inconspicuous spot in an area of the room that gets the least amount of traffic. Plan a seam that is as short as possible and at least 6 inches away from a parallel joist or seam in an old floor that you're covering.

When you make a two-piece floor, you'll make a two-piece template and apply it over two pieces of vinyl that overlap at the future site of the seam. You'll install the floor with the pieces still overlapped at the seam, then you'll make what's called a double cut through the seam. Holding the knife straight up and down and guided by a straightedge, you'll cut through both pieces of vinyl at the same time. The resulting pieces will match perfectly.

1 LAY OUT THE SEAM

Lay out a template as you would for a one-piece installation. Overlap the paper by about 2 inches wherever it crosses the seam, and tape the pieces together. Make several "witness marks" across the seam so, when you move the template, you can reassemble it along the seam. Once you have completed the template, remove the tape that holds it to the floor and the tape across the seam. Roll up each half and temporarily set the template aside.

2 SET UP THE SEAM

Spread the vinyl out, design side up, on a smooth, clean surface. Cut the vinyl to create two strips long enough and wide enough to place the seam where you want it. Leave the strips on the floor in the same position as when they came off the roll. If the vinyl has a pattern match, as shown above, overlap the pieces by 2 inches. Match the pattern, as shown. If the vinyl has no pattern match, turn one of the pieces end for end. Overlap by 2 inches. In either case, tape the pieces together in several places.

3 SET UP THE TEMPLATE

Unroll the template, align the witness marks, and tape the template back together. Position the seam over the double layer of vinyl, then tape the template to the vinyl through the triangular cutouts. Then cut the perimeter of the vinyl as you would for a single piece. Wait to cut the seam.

4 ALIGN THE SEAMED EDGES

Take the vinyl into the room where you'll install it, one half at a time. Overlap the pieces at the seam. Slide the pieces as needed to create a pattern match. Tape across the seam to hold the pieces together.

5 CUT THE SEAM

Cut the seam along the overlapping pieces of vinyl. Choose a path that camouflages the seam, such as along an apparent mortar line in a brick pattern. Cut the seam with a new blade in a utility knife, guiding the cut with a straightedge. Hold the knife straight up and down as you cut to avoid creating a beveled edge. When you've finished the cut, roll back the vinyl and remove the scraps.

Laying a two-piece sheet

1 MARK THE SEAM LOCATION

Roll back one piece of vinyl to reveal the floor underneath the seam. Trace along the edge of the other piece to draw a line on the floor. Draw the line in pencil—inks might bleed through the vinyl and stain the surface. Draw two more lines, each one 12 inches on either side of the line that marks the seam.

2 LINE UP THE SEAM EDGES

Fold back the vinyl over the lines. Align the seams so the pattern matches the way you want it to, and tape the seam firmly in place.

3 SET THE ADHESIVE

Fold back the vinyl at right angles to the lines you drew so you can see all three lines. Apply vinyl adhesive along the exposed section of floor, except for the area between the lines, using the trowel specified by the manufacturer—the notch size controls how much adhesive is applied. Fold back the vinyl into the adhesive, then press the vinyl with a floor roller.

> **Always seal the seams. Make sure you get a sealer that matches the sheen of your floor.**

4 ADHERE THE SECOND HALF

Fold back the other half of the vinyl to expose the section of floor that has no adhesive. Apply adhesive as before, leaving the space between the lines bare. Fold the vinyl into the adhesive and roll it with a floor roller. Remove the tape from the seam.

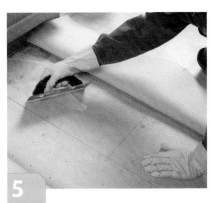

5 ADHERE THE SEAM

Roll back the vinyl on one side of the seam until you come to the adhesive that's already been applied. Trowel on adhesive in the exposed area and let it dry for the amount of time the manufacturer recommends. Fold back the vinyl into the adhesive and roll it. Clean up any adhesive that squeezes out with the cleaner specified by the manufacturer.

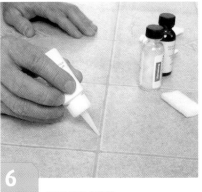

6 SEAL THE SEAM

You must seal the seams to keep out water and dirt. Make sure you get a sealer that matches the sheen of your floor—the choices are usually matte and glossy, but check with your flooring dealer. Clean the seam with seam cleaner—it's usually packaged with the sealer. Put the sealer in its applicator bottle and mix it with water as directed. Apply a 1/8-inch bead of sealer along the seam. Let excess sealer dry, then let it wear off naturally. Wiping it off while wet will leave a line. Keep traffic off the floor for a few hours.

6

VINYL FLOORING

Installing modified loose-lay vinyl

Modified loose-lay sheet vinyl is another way of saying "no adhesive required." Modified loose lay has other advantages. Once you cut and unroll the floor, it's installed. You can install it over surfaces like painted concrete, to which adhesives won't stick. You can roll it and then unroll it—something you might do to let it and the subfloor dry if the washer overflows.

Modified loose-lay vinyl has a heavy fiberglass backing that causes the sheet to lay flat on the floor without the help of glue.

It's far from a specialty item—you can purchase or order it from most suppliers—but it is special. Don't attempt a modified loose-lay installation with vinyl designed for something else. Not surprisingly, modified loose lay is derived from regular loose lay, which requires absolutely nothing in order to stay flat. In the system described here, you put a piece of double-sided tape under the vinyl at doorways. It's a slight change that keeps the floor from curling up in high-traffic areas.

WORK SMARTER

KEEP IT CLEAN

The absence of adhesive doesn't forgive the presence of dirt. Like gelatin, vinyl is resilient. It springs back when you push it and conforms to whatever surface you put it on. If the surface is a needle, for instance, the vinyl will flow over it. The surface above the needle will be slightly elevated. As you walk over the spot, you'll wear through the elevated area and create a ghostlike image of the needle. If the surface is a tiny piece of gravel, however, walking over it will wear a hole right down to the stone. Sweep the surface before you go to work and vacuum it carefully to remove any grit or grime that will show through the vinyl.

1 CUT A TEMPLATE

Lay out and cut a template as you would for regular vinyl. Your particular modified loose lay may require a slightly different expansion gap, so read the manufacturer's directions carefully. Spread out the vinyl on a clean floor that is larger than the template, tape the template to it, and cut the vinyl to shape. If the installation requires a seam, cut it and lay it out as you would on other vinyl. (See pages 142–143.)

2 LAY ADHESIVE TAPE

Apply double-sided tape at doors and under appliances. The surface must be clean and dry. Apply tape specifically designed for loose lay, as other types may cause stains that bleed through to the surface of the vinyl. In doorways, cut the tape and stick it to the floor. In areas that support appliances, use tape to make an X slightly larger than the appliance. Do not overlap the tape at the center of the X—use four pieces. Wait to remove the protective paper from the top of the tape.

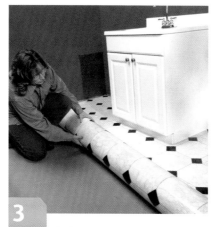

3 UNROLL THE VINYL

Roll up the vinyl and take it to the room where you'll install it. Unroll it and smooth it with a clean push broom. Modified loose lays usually require an expansion gap. Check the manufacturer's specifications, and trim the edge of the sheet to create the gap, if necessary. If the floor has a seam, roll back the pieces and apply double-sided tape to the floor along the entire length of the seam. Remove the protective paper from the tape and press the seam in place.

4 ADHERE THE EDGES

Roll back the vinyl so you can get to the taped areas one at a time. Remove the protective paper, roll the vinyl back over it, and move on to the next taped area.

6

VINYL FLOORING

Transitions

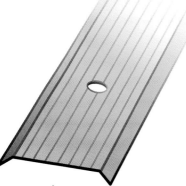

SADDLE THRESHOLD
Because vinyl is so thin, you can usually install trim made for other flooring right over it to handle any transitions. You can also install specialty moldings. A saddle threshold screws down to protect exposed edges of vinyl. Some saddle thresholds will go over concrete.

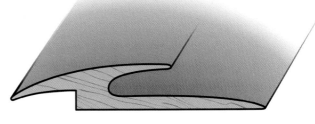

CARPET- OR WOOD-TO-VINYL MOLDING
If your vinyl floor meets a glue-down carpet, a vinyl molding like this one handles the transition. Install the molding during carpet or wood installation, then lay the tile up to it.

Vinyl cove molding

Vinyl molding is an easy-to-apply baseboard that goes up quickly in a room with no trim. It's resilient and hard to scuff, so it makes a durable molding in areas that get substantial abuse. Vinyl molding comes in strips 4 inches high and about $^1/_{16}$ inch thick. Two styles are available: one that is flat and comes in rolls, and one that has a small curve (called a cove) at the bottom. The cove molding is the better of the two because the cove sweeps out slightly from the wall to cover the expansion gap at the edge of the floor.

Installation tools are few: a utility knife, a framing square, and a caulking gun with a special tip designed for cove molding.

1 CUT TO LENGTH
Start in a corner of the room. Spread the recommended adhesive on the back of the molding using the caulking gun with a special cove-molding tip. Push the molding against the wall and press along the entire surface to attach it to the wall. If you need more than one length, butt two pieces together. If you need to cut a piece of molding, make repeated cuts across the back using a utility knife guided by a straightedge.

2 CUT THE INSIDE CORNERS
Run molding into the corner on one of the walls. Carve away the cove on the other piece of molding so it nests against the first piece, then glue it in place. The technique described for outside corners in Step 3 also works on inside corners, though it may be difficult to get the molding all the way into the corner.

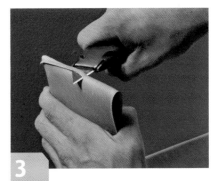

3 CUT THE OUTSIDE CORNERS
Put the molding in place and trace along the wall to mark where the piece will turn the corner. Bend the piece face-to-face at the mark and trim away about half the thickness of the molding along the line. Test-fit to make sure the recess is over the corner and that the piece will bend into place. Warm with a hair dryer to make it flexible. Apply adhesive and install.

Laying vinyl tile

Vinyl tile is made of the same materials as sheet vinyl, and you can pick a pattern that gives your room much the same look as sheet vinyl. However, with vinyl tile, you can choose different color tiles to create borders or checkerboard patterns. You don't need a template of the room to lay tile, and you need not worry about cutting seams.

When buying tiles, you'll have to choose between self-stick tiles and tiles that you set in adhesive applied to the floor. Most ordinary tiles are self-stick, while specialty tiles are set in adhesive.

Self-stick tiles should be set on a clean subfloor that has been primed with a floor primer designed for vinyl tile. Let the primer dry thoroughly before applying tiles.

Plan the layout so tile joints fall at least 6 inches from joints in the subfloor or underlayment.

▲ Vinyl tile is either self-stick or set in a mastic that you spread on the floor. Layout begins in the center of the room so that tiles trimmed to meet the walls will mirror those on opposite sides of the room.

Vinyl tile prep at a glance

- **Storage:** Remove tile from carton and store materials in the room for 48 hours before installation, keeping the room at a minimum of 65 degrees during that time, as well as during installation and for 48 hours afterward.
- **Location:** On, above, or below grade.
- **Level/flat:** Level is not an issue with most vinyl floors, but the floor must be flat. If installing over embossed vinyl, fill the pattern with an embossing leveler recommended by the manufacturer.
- **Moisture:** Test for both moisture and pH to make sure the floor meets the manufacturer's standards. Problems with either will prevent the floor from bonding well.

ACCEPTABLE SUBFLOORS

- **Wood:** Double layer of plywood with a combined thickness of at least 1 inch; or 3/4-inch wood covered by 1/4-inch underlayment. Leave 1/32-inch gaps between sheets of underlayment and keep the ends of the underlayment at least 6 inches from the ends of the subfloor panels. Fill all gaps, as well as the indentations left by nails, and sand smooth.
- **Existing vinyl:** Above grade, you can apply self-stick tile over existing sheet vinyl as long as it is no more than one layer thick. Vinyl must be cleaned with the manufacturer's recommended wax-free product. Fill existing embossed vinyl with an embossing leveler.
- **Concrete:** May be applied directly to concrete above, below, or on grade. Floor must be clean, dry, and structurally sound. Test for moisture and pH.
- **Ceramic tile:** May be applied over ceramic tile. Abrade the surface of the tile, fill grout lines, and level the surface by pouring a latex-modified portland cement-based underlayment over the tile.

  Do not apply over chipboard, wafer board, oriented strand board, particleboard, or lauan. Floor must be absolutely smooth, as any irregularities will show through the vinyl.
- **Trim:** Undercut door trim before installation. Remove shoe molding.

Laying tiles in adhesive

CLOSER LOOK

SHUFFLING AND ARROWS

THE SHUFFLE

Tiles come in dye lots. Colors sometimes vary from lot to lot, and frequently within the lot. To keep this from affecting the look of your floor, intermingle the boxes of tiles before laying them. Put the boxes near your starting point and mix their contents randomly. This way you'll spread color variations evenly throughout the floor.

THE ARROWS

Some tiles have a grain. It is virtually invisible to the naked eye, but the shade of the tile changes depending on the angle at which light hits the grain. If your tile has a grain, the arrows on the bottom of the tile tell you which way the grain runs. For a floor that has a uniform shade, lay the tiles so the arrows all point in the same direction. For a checkerboard look, turn every other tile 90 degrees. Check by making a test run before you get the glue out so that you're sure you'll like the look.

1

APPLY THE ADHESIVE

Lay out the floor in quadrants as shown on page 60. Apply adhesive in one of the quadrants using the notched trowel recommended by the manufacturer. Wait about 15 minutes, and when the adhesive feels tacky but doesn't stick to your hand, set the first tile at the intersection of the chalklines (see inset). Lay all tiles with the arrows pointing in the same direction, or turn every other tile 90 degrees, depending on the design you want to create.

2

LAY THE TILES

Put the second tile to one side of the first tile, carefully positioning it along the chalkline and tightly against the first tile. Set it exactly where you want it to go—sliding will cause adhesive to roll over the top of the tile. Install the third tile the same way along the other chalkline. Work diagonally from line to line to set tiles in the remaining adhesive, as shown above.

3

MARK THE EDGE TILES

You will probably need to cut the tiles against the wall to fit. To allow for expansion of the subfloor, cut the tiles to leave a 1/4-inch gap at the walls. Lay out the cut by putting a 1/4-inch spacer upright against the wall. Place the tile you'll cut directly over the last full tile. Place a scribing tile against the spacer and over the tile you'll cut. Mark the tile as shown and cut it with a flooring or utility knife. Lay out corner tiles the same way, putting the spacer tile against each wall in turn.

4

MARK CORNER CUTOUTS

Lay out cuts for tiles that have to fit around an outside corner with two tiles—the one you'll cut and a spacer tile. Start as if you were cutting a border tile: Put the tile you'll cut on top of the last full tile in the row. Put a scribing tile on top of that and slide it against a 1/4-inch spacer at the wall. Draw a line on the tile you'll cut by tracing along the edge of the scribing tile. Lay out the other half with a straightedge. Put 1/4-inch spacers against the corner wall, and put a straightedge along the spacers. Draw a line along the straightedge to lay out the cut on the tile (see inset).

Make the cut by guiding a utility knife along the straightedge. Start the cut at what will be the corner of the cutout and work toward the edge.

5

ROLL THE FLOOR

Clean off the adhesive as soon as you have installed the tiles. Latex-based adhesive usually cleans up with soap and water, but read and follow the directions on the can. Don't soak the floor—it will ruin the glue bond. Set the tiles firmly in the adhesive by rolling the floor in both directions with a floor roller. Install baseboard, quarter-round molding, or both to cover the gap at the edge of the floor.

6

Applying self-stick vinyl tile

Much of the vinyl tile sold today has a peel-and-stick backing. It's a good product that makes the job of installation a little easier, which is why homeowners love it. Installing it is much like installing other vinyl tiles, except you have no adhesive. (For information on layout, see "Laying tiles in adhesive," page 147.) What the manufacturer's directions often fail to tell you, however, is that you need to prime the floor with a latex floor primer first. Unlike adhesive that you trowel, the adhesive on self-stick tiles never truly dries. This seldom presents a problem, as long as the floor is properly primed. The primer creates a surface to which the adhesive clings, an especially important factor when the subfloor is porous plywood or concrete.

Like other vinyl tiles, self-stick tiles vary slightly in color from batch to batch. To camouflage any shifts in color, alternate between two boxes when applying the tile. Have an empty box handy to hold the paper backing as you peel it off the tiles.

1 PREP THE FLOOR

You can apply self-stick vinyl over concrete or a 1/4-inch plywood underlayment (other than lauan). If you're applying over concrete, make sure it's smooth and clean. If you're installing over any other subfloor, cover it with a 1/4-inch underlayment that's smooth and clean. Space the panels 1/32 inch apart and stagger the seams. Fill the gaps with a filler recommended by the tile manufacturer. For more on preparing subfloors, see "Installing underlayment," page 86.

2 PRIME THE FLOOR

Buy the primer that the manufacturer recommends and apply it as directed. If the manufacturer doesn't recommend a primer, ask your retailer to recommend one. It's generally not a paint product, but a thinner mixture that seals the pores of the subfloor and creates a surface that the tile will stick to easily. A typical application requires two coats—a coat diluted with water, followed by a full-strength coat. Pour the primer into a roller pan and apply it with a long-handled paint roller.

3 MARK LAYOUT LINES

Snap chalklines across the room to find the center. Check for square with a 3-4-5 triangle and move the end of one of the lines, if necessary, to bring the lines into square. Lay a trial run of tiles to gauge the size of the tiles that will meet the wall. If they will be less than half a tile wide, move the lines as needed, until the tiles at the edges are the same width on both sides of the room.

4 SET THE FIRST TILE

Before you apply the first tile, flip it over and look for arrows indicating grain direction. Arrange the tiles so that all the arrows point the same way, alternate, or face in random directions (depending on the look you want). Peel off the back and put the corner of the tile at the intersection of the layout lines, and the edges of the tile along the lines. When the tile is in the right spot, press it against the subfloor and press down the edges by rolling with a wallpaper roller.

5 USE A STEPPED PATTERN

Work diagonally from one layout line to the other, applying the tiles in a stepped pattern. This helps to keep the floor square: Each tile is nestled between two others. Apply as shown, filling one quadrant of the floor before going on to the next. Press down each tile once it's in place and roll the edges as before. Roll the entire floor with a floor roller when you're done.

6

VINYL FLOORING

Laying a cork floor

1

PRIME THE FLOOR AND SET THE LAYOUT LINES
Prepare and prime the floor as directed by the manufacturer, using the primer or thinned adhesive as specified. Begin the layout of the floor by finding the midpoint of each wall. Snap chalklines between them, dividing the room into four equal sections.

M ost manufacturers recommend that you offset the joints when laying a cork floor so the joints in one row don't align with the joints in neighboring rows. This helps hide the minor irregularities in size that occur in cork simply because it's a natural product.

Other than that, manufacturers' directions vary widely. Some require an expansion gap between the wall and the floor; others don't. Some recommend an adhesive that rolls on; others recommend one you apply with a trowel. While the general procedures here outline the basic approach, always check the manufacturer's recommendations for specifics.

Cork floor prep at a glance

- **Storage:** Acclimate the tiles by removing them from their cartons and putting them in the room where they'll be installed 48 to 72 hours before installation. Room temperature must be between 60 and 85 degrees. (Some brands set the upper limit at 70 degrees.)
- **Concrete:** Cork can be applied to concrete floors on or above grade. Test for moisture with plastic sheeting for 72 hours (see page 82) to make sure the floor meets manufacturer's standards. Fill all cracks with cement patching compound. The floor must be level within $\frac{1}{8}$ inch over 10 feet and should be flat.
- **Wood:** Cork can be applied directly over any smooth wood floor (except oak) or over a wood or plywood subfloor. If the surface is irregular, cover the floor with $\frac{1}{4}$-inch underlayment. Nail every 4 inches around the edges with $1\frac{1}{4}$-inch ringshank nails and on a 6-inch grid over the face of the panel. Leave a $\frac{1}{8}$-inch gap between panels to allow for expansion, fill the gaps with a latex filler, and sand smooth. Above crawlspaces, floors must be at least 18 inches above ground. Cover the floor with 6-mil polyethylene.
- **Primer:** Seal the old floor with a primer or thin coat of adhesive as directed.

2

SQUARE THE LAYOUT

Make sure the lines are square with each other. Mark one layout line 3 feet from where it crosses the other line. Mark the other layout line 4 feet from the intersection. If the distance between the marks is 5 feet, the lines are perpendicular. If not, adjust one of the lines until they are. Prime over the lines if the directions call for it. The primer is clear, so you'll still be able to use your chalklines for reference.

3

APPLY THE ADHESIVE

Apply adhesive in one quadrant with a trowel or roller, as recommended by the manufacturer. Let it dry thoroughly. Never apply cork to wet adhesive.

4

LAY THE FIRST ROW

Take tiles from three or four boxes and mix them together so any color variations will be distributed randomly. Lay the first tile in the corner formed by the intersection of the chalklines. Work your way down the chalkline, butting the tiles together. At the wall, cut the tile to fit using a utility knife and straightedge. Leave an expansion gap if the manufacturer calls for one.

5

LAY THE SECOND ROW

Return to the middle of the room to begin the second row. Lay the first tile of this row so the middle straddles the chalkline. Work your way down the row. At the wall, cut the last tile to fit, leaving an expansion gap if one is required.

6

FINISH THE QUADRANT

Continue in this manner until you've laid tile in the entire quadrant. Repeat in the remaining quadrants, one at a time.

7

ROLL THE FLOOR

Roll the floor with a 100-pound roller several times in several directions at half-hour intervals. Let the floor sit overnight, then roll it a final time. If the manufacturer calls for a protective coat in addition to the finish that's already on the tile, apply as directed.

Maintaining vinyl and cork

Vinyl is easier to care for than most people think. As a result, it tends to be overmaintained, which does it no favors. When you wash it, for example, simply use a nonrinsing cleaner that leaves no film. Most products sold as vinyl cleaners fit the bill.

- DON'T flood the floor with water. Water will work its way into the seams and edges of the floor, causing the glue to fail and the edges to curl.
- DON'T use abrasive cleaners—spray or powder. Abrasive cleaners scratch the floor, and there is no way to undo the damage.
- DON'T use dishwashing soap. While it may leave your crystal sparkling bright, it will leave a film on your floor.
- DON'T use oil-based floor cleaners. The film they leave will be worse than the one left by the dishwashing soap.

GOOD IDEA

PREVENTIVE MAINTENANCE

To keep your vinyl floor looking beautiful, follow these simple tips.

- Put felt pads on chair legs, table legs, and other furniture to avoid scratching the floor.
- Don't put rubber-backed rugs on the floor—the rubber stains the floor.
- Put a heavy-duty doormat at the door and encourage everyone to wipe their feet. This is especially important if you have an asphalt driveway. The chemicals in asphalt cause vinyl flooring to yellow.
- Run the air-conditioner if the temperature rises above 100°. Heat causes the tiles to expand and the adhesive to melt. Extended exposure will ruin the floor. To protect the floor in a summer home, set the air-conditioner on its lowest setting and let it run while you're away.

No wax means no wax

Unlike wood, vinyl is unable to absorb wax. To give vinyl its shiny look, it's made with a top layer that looks like wax. If you try to put wax over it, the wax will build up, collect dust, and look terrible. If you want to put a nice shine on the floor, apply a finish made by the floor manufacturer. It's usually available in two sheens—matte and high gloss. Buy some while you're buying the tile so you're sure to get the right one for your floor. Apply with a mop as directed.

Removing stains from vinyl

Stain	Remove with
Asphalt, shoe polish	Citrus-based cleaner or mineral spirits
Candle wax	Scrape carefully with plastic spatula
Crayon	Mineral spirits or manufacturer's cleaner
Grape juice, wine, mustard	Full-strength bleach or manufacturer's cleaner
Heel marks	Nonabrasive household cleaner; if stain remains, use rubbing alcohol
Lipstick	Rubbing alcohol or mineral spirits
Nail polish	Nail polish remover
Paint or varnish	Wipe with water or mineral spirits while still wet.
	If dry, scrape carefully with a thin plastic spatula.
	If stain still shows, rub with rubbing alcohol.
Pen ink	Citrus-based cleaner, rubbing alcohol, or mineral spirits
Permanent marker	Mineral spirits, nail polish remover, or rubbing alcohol
Rust	Oxalic acid and water (1 part acid to 10 parts water); extremely caustic; follow all directions

After removing any stain, wipe the area with a damp cloth to remove residue.

Replacing a vinyl tile

6

VINYL FLOORING

1 WARM THE TILE

The key to removing a damaged vinyl tile is heat. Set a hair dryer on high heat and concentrate the heat for a minute or so on one edge of the tile. Insert the blade of your putty knife and work it back and forth, pushing forward to break the adhesive bond.

2 SCRAPE OUT THE PIECES

Warmed-up tile will tear and leave small pieces stuck in the adhesive. Warm and scrape each piece until you have removed all of them.

3 APPLY THE ADHESIVE

Notch the end of a plastic scraper and use it to comb adhesive in the recess of the damaged tile. Make sure the adhesive covers the entire area of the recess.

4 INSTALL THE NEW TILE

Eyeball the pattern of the tile so you can match its grain with the rest of the floor. Otherwise, it will stick out noticeably. Set the tile at an angle with one edge tight against the other and lower the tile into place.

5 ROLL THE REPAIR

Make sure the new tile adheres tightly to the adhesive by rolling it with a rolling pin. Warm the surface slightly before you roll it. The heat will soften the adhesive and help bond the tile.

Preventing dents and scratches

Resilient flooring is softer than other flooring materials and will dent, scuff, and scratch more easily. With resilients you can't remove the damages. The best care for a resilient floor is preventative maintenance. Here are some ways to prevent dents:

- Protect the floor when moving appliances. Lay plywood panels on the floor and "walk" the appliance across the panels.
- Use floor protectors to keep furniture legs from denting the floors; the heavier the furniture, the wider the protector should be.
- Avoid furniture with rolling casters. If you must have casters, use double rollers.
- Keep dust and dirt outside the house—use mats or rugs at entrances but avoid rubber-backed rugs. They can discolor resilient flooring.
- Keep the floor clean with regular sweeping or vacuuming but don't use vacuums with beater bars.

The iron-off alternative

You can do little to repair a damaged tile, and most of it isn't worth doing. But you can replace a vinyl tile with a few low-tech tools. The first is an iron—you may want to buy one at a thrift store solely for this purpose. Set the iron on medium to high and put a rag over the tile you're replacing. Iron the rag for 10 or 15 seconds to warm the tile and the adhesive that holds it in place. Keep the iron away from the neighboring good tiles to avoid ruining the glue beneath them. Once the tile is warm, slip a wide putty knife under it and try to pry it up. If it won't budge, iron a bit more and try again. If you damage a neighboring tile, remove it after you remove the first tile. Scrape away any adhesive with a putty knife. Clean the area thoroughly and spread glue in the opening with the recommended trowel. Let the adhesive cure for about 15 minutes or as recommended on the can. Just before you put the new tile in place, put the rag over it and warm it with the iron to make it more pliable. Then set—don't slide—the tile in place.

Cleaning cork tiles

1
VACUUM THE FLOOR

Vacuum the floor with a canister vacuum, not an upright vacuum or canister attachment with beater bars—doing so can tear up the surface of the tile.

2
MOP THE FLOOR

Damp-mop the floor. Don't overwet the surface—you'll warp the tile and weaken the adhesive bond. Because cork is a wood product, don't use commercial cleaners on it. Purchase a cleaner made by the manufacturer.

Refinishing cork tiles

Even though modern cork flooring products come with a wear-resistant varnish, it must periodically be renewed. Clean the floor as described at left and let it dry. Then use a sponge or lamb's wool applicator to reapply the varnish. Never use a generic product—always use a solution made especially for cork.

Ceramic and stone flooring

 eramic and stone tile are the heaviest flooring materials and require a substantial floor structure to support their weight. Although you can install these materials over existing tile laid on a slab, old tile installed on a wood-frame subfloor should be removed before putting the new floor down.

To maximize its strength and durability, this material needs to get adjusted to its environment, just like other flooring materials. Bring it into the room at least a day before installation. Arrange the cartons so you can reach them easily, but in a place they don't interfere with your working space.

Procedures for laying ceramic and stone products are similar, but stone comes with some idiosyncrasies. Stone has to be cut on a wet saw. If you try to snap-cut or nip it, it will fracture along its natural grain lines. Stone layouts can prove a little more fussy also. Because most stone tile looks best with 18-inch grout joints, layouts can be a little more complicated.

This chapter covers the basics of big tiles, small tiles, borders, and even stone. Of all the floors in this book, these are the ones likely to last the longest. They're also the kinds of materials most homeowners know little about. Mortar, grout, and backerboard are materials you seldom work with around the house. Don't be

Chapter 7 highlights

intimidated. If you have learned to cut wood or drywall—or even if you haven't—you can learn to cut backerboard too.

Unlike woodworking, where you race the clock to assemble cabinets before the glue dries, very little happens quickly in laying ceramic or stone tile. If you make a mistake with the mud, simply scrape it up or add more. If you make a mistake with a tile, just pick it up and fix the problem. You learned the basics of carpentry when you drove your first nail, so don't be afraid to learn the basics of masonry. It's only dirt, baked clay, stones, and mud.

Installing backerboard

PROJECT DETAILS

SKILLS: Basic carpentry
PROJECT: Preparing an 8'×10' area for tile installation

TIME TO COMPLETE

EXPERIENCED: 2 hrs.
HANDY: 2.5 hrs.
NOVICE: 3 hrs.
VARIABLES: Time includes mixing and spreading mortar, positioning sheet, cutting, screwing, and fitting around obstructions.

STUFF YOU'LL NEED

TOOLS: Tape measure, straightedge, trowel with ¼-inch square notches, margin trowel, drill with screwdriver bit, drywall scoring tool, utility knife, carbide-tipped hole saw, mortar mixing paddle and ½-inch drill, dust respirator, safety glasses, knee pads
MATERIALS: Latex-modified thinset mortar, backerboard, backerboard screws, fiberglass backerboard tape

TOOL TIP

CUTTING BACKERBOARD
- The sand in mortar quickly dulls a utility knife, so use a carbide scoring tool designed for the job.
- Score the board on both sides instead of just one. If the board has a mesh surface, cut all the way through it when you score.

The quality of your finished ceramic tile project depends on the quality of the surface beneath it. For best results use backerboard to create a smooth and level underlayment.

To avoid cracking, tile needs a stable bed to rest on. Backerboard, a rigid panel that creates that solid substrate for tile, is made of cement, fiber concrete, gypsum, plywood, or plastic depending on the manufacturer. Use the manufacturer's recommended thickness and application.

Backerboard is part of a system of products that acts as a bed for the tiles. The bed begins with a lather of wet mortar applied to the floor. The backerboard is set in the mortar while it's still wet, then screwed to the subfloor. Any gaps between sheets of backerboard and the floor are taped and mortared. Once this has dried, a layer of mortar is set on top of the backerboard and the tiles are set in it.

When you buy fiberglass tape for the joints, make sure you get backerboard tape. Drywall tape can't stand up to the lime in the mortar. Backerboard screws are also a must. Drywall screws will rust.

Tiling translated

- **Admix:** A liquid added to mortar to make it stronger.
- **Backerboard:** A ½- or ¼-inch-thick rigid panel sometimes reinforced with fiberglass mesh; the mason's version of drywall.
- **Latex-modified mortar:** A mortar mix to which latex has been added. The latex improves adhesion, increases strength, and gives the mortar greater flexibility.

- **Polymer-modified mortar:** Similar to latex-modified, except that long-chain molecules (called polymers) substitute for latex.
- **Thinset:** Mortar that's designed for use over backerboard. The mortar itself isn't thin, but the layer you apply over the backerboard is. Thinset is available in several grades, with and without additives. Always follow the manufacturer's recommendations.

Cutting backerboard

1 **LAY OUT THE CUT**
Measure and lay out each end of the cut with a felt-tip pen or with a carbide scoring tool. Draw a line on each side of the panel. Use a straightedge to guide the carbide scoring tool along the layout line. Score several times with moderate pressure on one or both sides of the panel, depending on the manufacturer's instructions.

2 **SNAP THE PANEL**
After scoring, press down with your hand and knee near the score line. Lift the edge to snap the panel. Cut through the backside if you haven't yet scored it.

Drilling holes in backerboard

1 **LAY OUT THE HOLE**
Measure and lay out the center of the hole. Or if you and a helper can manage the board fairly well, you can mark the hole with lipstick. Rub some lipstick on the stub of the pipe (or other obstruction), then carefully align the backerboard above it. Lower the backerboard gently onto the stub to make a mark where you'll need to drill. For best results, use one method and double-check it with the other.

2 **DRILL THE BACKERBOARD**
Drill the hole with a carbide-tipped hole saw. Drill slowly and press lightly to avoid cracking the panel. Cut only about halfway through then turn the piece over to finish cutting the hole. The drill bit in the center of the hole saw is longer than the cutting arm itself, so when you flip the board you'll see the hole to use as a guide to finish the cut. Wear safety glasses and a respirator to avoid inhaling crystalline silica, which is harmful to lungs.

3 **CUT LARGE HOLES**
If you need to cut a large hole, start by laying it out on the panel. Put a $1/2$-inch-diameter carbide bit in your drill, and drill a series of holes as close together as possible just inside the layout line. (Instead of drilling, you can drive a screwdriver through the surface along the layout line.) When you've made all the holes, knock out the waste piece with a hammer. Wear a respirator and safety glasses.

Laying backerboard

1 LAY OUT THE PANELS

Plan the layout so the backerboards span the joints in the subfloor and reinforce them. Start every other row with a half panel so the corners of panels never meet. Snap chalklines to show where each panel will go.

2 PREPARE THE MORTAR

Use latex-modified thinset mortar. Mortar has a working time of about 2 hours once it's mixed, so mix about half the bag following the manufacturer's directions. Start by putting the water (or the recommended liquid admix) in a large bucket and have a helper slowly pour in the mortar.

3 MIX THE MORTAR

As your helper pours in the mortar, mix it with a paddle specifically designed for mortar—don't use a paint paddle. The paddle has a lot of work to do, so the shank is $\frac{1}{2}$ inch in diameter, and you'll need a drill with a $\frac{1}{2}$-inch chuck to power it. Mix slowly to a smooth paste consistency. The mortar is properly mixed when you can form a ridge in it with a trowel. If the ridge slumps, add more mortar to the mix. If it crumbles, add water. Once it's mixed, let it slake, or rest, for about 10 minutes, then mix again.

4 MORTAR THE SUBFLOOR

Pick the best spot to start your installation and cut a panel to fit within the layout lines, if necessary. Apply mortar within the layout lines for the panel, using a $\frac{1}{4}$-inch square-notched trowel. (The notches control how much mortar you apply.) Follow the backerboard manufacturer's specs when choosing a trowel. Press the mortar into the plywood with the face of the trowel, holding it at a slight angle, then start building the bed. When you've applied a bed about $\frac{3}{32}$ to $\frac{3}{16}$ inch thick (depending on the manufacturer), hold the notched edge 45 degrees to the subfloor and rake out the mortar.

5 BED THE BACKERBOARD

Put the backerboard in the mortar bed as soon as you've laid the bed. Put spacers at the walls to leave a gap between the walls and backerboard. (The size of the gap varies depending on the manufacturer.) Walk gently on the panel to set it in the mortar. If you don't put the panels into a wet mortar bed, gaps between the floor and the panels will form in some places, and the tiles will crack when you walk over the voids.

7

CERAMIC AND STONE FLOORING

6 FASTEN THE PANEL

Fasten the panels to the floor with 1¼-inch backerboard screws. Place the screws across the face of the panel as recommended by the manufacturer, and drive the heads flush with the surface. Keep screws at the perimeter of the panel ½ inch away from the edge, spacing them as recommended by the manufacturer.

7 INSTALL THE SECOND PANEL

Apply mortar within the lines for the second panel just as you applied it for the first. Put the panel in place, using spacers at the wall to leave the proper gap. Leave a ⅛-inch gap between panels using 16d nails as spacers—you'll fill the gap with mortar later to tie the panels together. Screw the panel in place.

8 LAY THE REMAINING PANELS

Work your way around the room spreading mortar, laying panels and screwing them in as you go. Continue to leave ⅛-inch gaps between panels and a ¼-inch gap at the wall. Remove the spacers once the panels are installed.

9 MORTAR THE JOINTS

When you've laid all the panels, fill the spaces between them with mortar. Smooth it on with a margin trowel, forming a 3-inch-wide band that's centered on the joint.

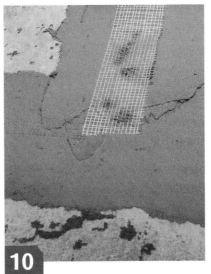

10 TAPE THE JOINTS

Put tape across all the seams and embed it firmly in the thinset.

11 MORTAR THE TAPE

Apply the mortar, then smooth it out with a trowel. You won't be able to get it flat without exposing the tape, so simply smooth the mortar with the trowel. Feather the edges. When the mortar has dried, lay out the floor, using the techniques shown on pages 60–63.

Setting ceramic tile

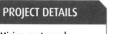

PROJECT DETAILS

SKILLS: Mixing mortar and cutting tiles
PROJECT: Installing ceramic tile

TIME TO COMPLETE

EXPERIENCED: 5 hrs.
HANDY: 6 hrs.
NOVICE: 8 hrs.
VARIABLES: Time does not include installation of backerboard.

STUFF YOU'LL NEED

TOOLS: Tape measure, chalkline, plastic mixing bucket, mortar mixing paddle and ½-inch drill, notched trowel, margin trowel, rubber gloves, safety glasses, beater block and rubber mallet, tile cutter or wet saw, abrasive stone file, rubber grout float, sponge, knee pads
MATERIALS: Ceramic tile, latex-modified thinset mortar, grout (unsanded grout for stone), tile spacers, silicone caulk

Ceramic tile is the most durable flooring you can install. It stands up well to water, making it popular in kitchens, baths, and entry halls. It's also low maintenance, making it popular with all those who clean floors.

Installation, however, is labor-intensive. Even if you don't have to install backerboard (not necessary on a slab floor or patio), there's mixing mortar, setting tile, applying grout, and sealing the tile.

Tile installers are a skilled lot, but patience is a good substitute for skill. Read the directions here carefully, then read all the directions that come with the grouts and mortars you buy. Mix them carefully, and once you're ready to go, follow your layout lines with precision.

WORK SMARTER

AVOID COLOR PROBLEMS WITH GROUT
Don't assume you can just mix a colored grout and it will be consistent over the entire floor. Read the recommendations and directions on the grout bag carefully to ensure that you know the proper method of application. Avoid mottled colors and grout lines that change by:
- Mixing the powder before you add water to distribute the pigment uniformly. If you're using more than one box, mix the boxes.
- Using the same ratio of water to grout in each batch. Changing the mixture can change the color.
- Making sure the grout dries for about two hours after you buff the haze off the tile with a rag. (And remember to buff immediately.) Wipe the floor with a clean rag, lightly dampened in clean water. Immediately cover the floor with kraft paper, making sure neighboring pieces overlap. Leave the paper in place for three days. If this is impractical, spray the floor with a fine water mist several times a day for three days.

Tile flooring prep at a glance

- **Location:** On, above, or below grade.
- **Level/flat:** Within ¼ inch over 10 feet.
- **Acceptable subfloors:** Minimum of $^{19}/_{32}$-inch exterior-grade plywood on joists spaced 16 inches on center. Cover plywood with mortar and set cement-based backerboard in the mortar while still wet. Screw to subfloor with approved screws. Spread mortar over backerboard and set tiles in mortar.
- **In bathrooms and other wet locations:** Install a waterproof barrier above the backerboard.
- **Trim:** Undercut door trim before installation. Remove baseboard, shoe molding, or both.

CLOSER LOOK

GROUT LINES
You get to decide how much space to leave between tiles. Here are a few guidelines:
- **Quarry tile:** Tiles are customarily spaced ¼ inch apart.
- **Large, uniform machine-made tile:** Space the tiles ⅛ to ¼ inch apart.
- **Large handcrafted tiles, such as saltillo:** Space the tiles ½ to ¾ inch apart so their irregular edges are less noticeable and less problematic when laying the tile.
- **Marble and granite:** Butt tiles and fill chamfered edges with unsanded grout.
- **Ceramic and porcelain:** Space tiles ⅛ to ¼ inch apart.

BUYER'S GUIDE

MASTIC ISN'T MAGIC
Avoid mastic adhesive when installing ceramic floor tile. The best installation is a plywood subfloor covered by a cement-based backerboard that bonds with the mortar and tile to create a single, strong unit.

Always buy grout with a latex or polymer-modified additive. It forms a stronger bond and is less likely to crack.

7

CERAMIC AND STONE FLOORING

Laying ceramic tile

1 MIX THE MORTAR

Use the latex-modified thinset mortar specified for your tile. If you're installing porcelain tile, buy mortar made specifically for porcelain. It mixes and goes on like other mortar but sticks better to porcelain's nonporous surface. Pour about three-quarters of the recommended amount of water into a plastic mixing bucket, and have a helper slowly add the mortar. While the helper is pouring, mix with a mortar paddle (a paint paddle will break) driven by a 1/2-inch drill. Add water as you mix until the mortar has a smooth, pastelike consistency. Wear safety glasses, a dust mask, and rubber gloves to protect your skin from the mortar, which is caustic.

Test the mortar. Put some mortar on a scrap piece of plywood or on the floor, and use your trowel to form a peak. If the peak holds its shape, the mortar contains the right amount of water. If the peak slumps, add mortar to the mix; if it crumbles, add water. Continue adding, mixing, and testing until you achieve the right consistency.

2 SPREAD THE MORTAR

Start in the center of the room and spread mortar right up to the edge of one of your layout lines. Apply the mortar first with the straight edge of the trowel, then comb it with the notched edge. Use a trowel with the notch shape and size recommended by the manufacturer—the notches control the amount of mortar on the floor. Comb the mortar into straight lines.

Water, water everywhere: Installing waterproof barriers

Although water has little effect on ceramic tile, ceramic tile doesn't necessarily stop water from leaking to the subfloor. This is OK for a floor that gets only the occasional mopping, but it can be a real problem in other places, especially around bathtubs, where water can warp the subfloor or even leak through to the ceiling below. In places that are likely to see a substantial amount of water, put a good moisture barrier beneath the floor. Choose from two ways to do it: with a waterproof sheet or with a trowel-on moisture barrier.

On walls you can use tar paper or plastic sheeting, which must be installed behind the backerboard in order to work correctly. On floors the backerboard must be mortared directly to the subfloor; consequently, tar paper and plastic are out of the question. Instead use a special membrane that is applied to the top of the backerboard. The membrane is made of a waterproof material sandwiched between layers of polyester. It doubles as an isolation membrane, helping to prevent cracks in concrete floors from working their way into the tile. To apply, install the backerboard as you normally would, then trowel on latex thinset with the recommended trowel. Unroll the membrane into the mortar. If you need more than one width of membrane, overlap the strips and glue them together with glue used for PVC. (Use the manufacturer's brand.) Roll the membrane into the mortar with a floor roller. Let the mortar dry, and apply mortar and tiles on top.

Trowel-on membranes are exactly what you'd expect them to be: flexible, watertight compounds that you trowel over the subfloor. Some are premixed; others you mix yourself. Some require two coats; others require only one. The final coat is about 1/16 inch thick. Tile can be installed as you normally would once the membrane has dried, which usually takes 4 to 6 hours. Follow the manufacturer's directions.

3 SET THE TILE AND CHECK THE SPREAD

Put two tiles next to each other in the mortar, with a spacer in between. Press both firmly into the mortar. Double-check the consistency of the mortar by pulling a tile up and looking at the bottom. The back of the tile should be covered with mortar. If you see only parallel mortar lines, the adhesive is too dry. If mortar squeezes up between the tiles, the bed is too thick and you need to drop the angle of the trowel as you comb. If the ridges in the adhesive have left more or less solid lines on the tile, the bed is too thin and you need to raise the angle of your trowel. If the mortar on the floor fails to stay in ridges, it is too wet.

4 SET THE FIRST TILE

Comb out the area of mortar that you tested, adding more mortar if necessary. Lay the first tile at the intersection of the guidelines. Twist the tile back and forth slightly to make sure it is embedded in the adhesive. If the tiles are 12×12 inches or greater, comb the mortar into straight lines with the trowel. Then put the tile in place and move it back and forth between $1/8$ and $1/4$ inch, perpendicular to the direction in which you combed. This helps fill any voids created by an uneven back.

5 SET THE SECOND TILE

Set spacers next to the first tile and place the second tile alongside the first, twisting it slightly. Continue laying tiles until you have filled the layout section (see page 115). Twist each tile as you set it.

6 CLEAN THE TILES

Dried mortar on top of the tiles will be difficult to remove. Wipe off the face of the tiles with a damp sponge as you go. Use a sponge that's just wet enough to wipe up stray mortar but not so wet that it leaves the rest of the mortar runny.

WORK SMARTER

WORKING WITH SALTILLO

Because they are handmade and fired at low temperatures, saltillo tiles need extra attention. Grout can stain saltillo, so begin by sealing the face of the tiles by brushing on a commercially made tile sealer.

Saltillo is especially porous, so once the sealer has dried, soak the tile in a bucket of water to which you've added two drops of dishwashing soap. This keeps the tile from absorbing all the water from the mortar and causing it to fail. The face of the tile may turn a whitish color as a result of soaking, but this disappears once the tile is fully dry.

Saltillo tiles have irregular backs with nooks and crannies that may be difficult to fill with mortar. Back-butter the tile (apply a coat of mortar onto the back) to make a smooth surface and eliminate voids between it and the backerboard. Set the tile in the mortar just as you would any other tile.

CLOSER LOOK

EXPANSION JOINTS

Subfloors expand and contract with changes in weather, and the movement can force tile into the wall. Avoid damage by leaving a 1/4-inch caulked gap between the tile and the wall. If you're installing a floor that's more than 36 feet in either direction, you'll need an expansion joint in the middle as well. To make the joint, leave one of the grout lines empty. Fill the void with a foam backer rod and caulk over it with caulk that matches the grout. For quarry and cement-bodied tile, make the joint the same width as a grout joint but no narrower than 1/4 inch. For other tiles, 1/4 inch is preferred, but you can make the joint as narrow as 1/8 inch.

7

CERAMIC AND STONE FLOORING

7
BED THE TILES

As soon as you've installed three or four tiles, lay a short length of 2×4 or a beater block on top of the tile. Tap lightly with a rubber mallet to level the tiles and embed them firmly in the mortar.

8
LAY THE NEXT SECTION

After you finish the first layout section, move on to a neighboring section in the same quadrant. Spread mortar in the grid and lay the tiles. When each section is finished, move to the next. Keep laying tiles until you reach a point where the space between the tiles and walls is less than a full tile width, but don't tile yourself into a corner. If you run into pipes, corners, or other obstructions, see pages 64–67.

9
MARK THE EDGE TILES FOR CUTS

Spacer tile

Scribing tile

Tile to be cut

Cutting line

To mark a cut quickly and without measuring, put the tile you're going to cut on top of the last full tile near the wall. Put a spacer tile against the wall and lay another full tile on top of the one to be cut. Slide that tile, the scribing tile, up to the spacer tile. Mark along the edge of the scribing tile on the tile to be cut, and cut the tile. To avoid confusion, lay out, cut, and install one tile at time.

10
SET UP THE SNAP CUTTER

Cutting tile on a snap cutter is a two-step process. You score it, then you snap it. To score the tile, put it in the cutter and align the cutting wheel with the layout line. Lift the handle to bring the scoring wheel down onto the line. Push or pull the cutting wheel along the top of the tile with a single firm stroke.

11
SNAP-CUT THE TILE

Put on a pair of safety glasses. Press down on the handle to move the cutting wheel out of the way. Press down farther to snap the tile.

12
SET THE EDGE TILES

If you haven't already, spread mortar between the last full tile and the wall. Put the tile in place and set it just as you set the others. Work your way along the wall, one tile at a time.

Cutting tile on a wet saw

A wet saw is a power tool that uses a water-cooled diamond blade to make quick work of cutting tile. Although you can cut tile with a snap cutter, a wet saw is better to use when a job requires a lot of cutting. Wet saws usually have a sliding table that feeds the tile into an overhead blade. A pump sprays a stream of water over the blade while it's running. The water and tile dust make quite a mess, so you should set up the saw outside or in a garage, if possible.

Professional-grade wet saws cost several hundred dollars, so rent one instead of buying. For a few dollars more than the rental price of a professional's saw, however, you can buy a homeowner's wet saw like the one shown here.

1

ALIGN THE TILE IN THE SAW
Set the fence so that when the layout line is at the blade, the widest part of the tile is between the blade and the fence. This keeps your hands as far away as possible from the blade during the cut. Put on a pair of safety glasses, back the tile away from the blade, and turn on the saw.

2

CUT THE TILE
Holding the tile with both hands, feed it along the fence and into the blade. Push slowly, letting the saw do the work and keeping your hands away from the blade. Push the piece between the blade and fence until it completely clears the blade.

Cutting notches

1

MAKE TWO STRAIGHT CUTS
Lay out and mark the sides and the end of the notch. Make a cut along one side of the notch. Reset the fence to make the other cut. Stop each cut when the blade reaches the line marking the end of the notch.

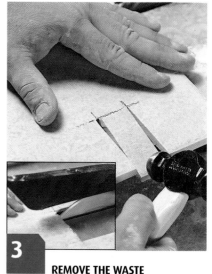

2

CUT AWAY THE WASTE
If the notch is wider than 1 inch, reset the fence to make a series of parallel cuts spaced about 1/4 inch apart. Stop each cut when it reaches the line that marks the end of the notch.

3

REMOVE THE WASTE
Break off the individual pieces between the sides of the notch. To trim the remaining jagged edge, put the tile back on the saw with the blade just touching the end of the notch. With the blade running, slide the tile sideways, keeping pressure on the tip of the blade to smooth the jagged edge (see inset).

Cutting curves

When you're laying tile around pipes, you will end up having to cut some curves.

If the pipe falls on the edge of the tile, you can cut the curve with a pair of tile nippers. If the pipe falls in the middle of the tile, you'll have to drill a hole with a carbide-tipped hole saw. Rod saws, which look like coping saws that have extra-thick blades, are great for cutting wall tile. Unfortunately, they're not up to the job of cutting floor tile, which is thicker.

🔵 TOOL TIP

WOOD SAWS WON'T CUT IT
The hole saw used to install a door lock isn't tough enough to cut through ceramic tile. You'll need a saw with carbide grit on the cutting edge. Such a saw fits in a standard ³⁄₈-inch drill and costs just a little more than a standard hole saw of the same diameter.

Cutting curves with nippers

1
START THE CUT
Start at one end of the curve. Bite into the tile using about one-quarter of the jaw. Widen the cut by nibbling away at the tile.

2
FINISH FROM THE OTHER END
Move to the other end of the curve and make a cut. Work from both ends toward the middle until you've removed a strip of waste along the edge of the tile. Repeat the process until you've cut out all the waste.

Cutting holes with a hole saw

Smoothing edges

Use an abrasive stone file or rotary grinder to smooth the edges of tiles cut with nippers or a snap cutter. Tiles cut on the wet saw are smoother and don't need to be filed.

1
MARK THE CENTER
Drill bits wander across hard, slick surfaces like the glazes on ceramic tiles. Prevent wandering by tapping a center punch ever so gently with a hammer to break through the glaze. This gives the bit enough purchase to start the hole.

2
DRILL THE HOLE
Drill the hole with a carbide-grit hole saw. Clamp the tile to a piece of scrap plywood. Put the center bit on the divot you made in the glaze. Drill slowly, exerting light pressure to avoid breaking the tile.

Grouting ceramic tile

1 MIX THE GROUT

Mix the grout at slow speed in a plastic mixing bucket with a mortar paddle and a ½-inch drill. Some grouts have latex in the powder mix; others require a latex admix. If you fail to include a required admix, the grout will eventually need to be replaced. After you've mixed the grout, let it rest, or slake, for 10 to 15 minutes, then remix.

2 SPREAD THE GROUT

Apply masking tape to protect the baseboard, trim, and neighboring floors. Spread the grout with a rubber grout float. Hold the float at a shallow angle and work on three or four tiles at a time. Press the grout into the joints to fill them. For joints wider than ³⁄₈ inch, use a grout bag.

📖 WORK SMARTER

SEAL OUT DIRT

Porous tile, unglazed tile, and stone require a little extra attention to prevent grout from staining them. Before you grout, apply a sealer that will prevent the grout from soaking into the surface of the tiles. Let the mortar cure for 72 hours (or as directed) after you've installed the tile. Then apply the sealer with a new mop, brush, or sponge. Let the sealer soak into the tile for 10 to 15 minutes, then wipe off the excess. Apply a second coat. Test 2 hours later by dribbling drops of water onto the tile. If the water soaks in, apply more sealer. If the water beads up, apply the grout.

Use nonsanded grout if the space between tiles is less than ¹⁄₈ inch. Otherwise use sanded grout.

3 REMOVE EXCESS GROUT

Hold the float at a steep angle. Sweep it across the tiles diagonally to avoid dipping into the joints. Remove grout along the edge of the floor with a margin trowel.

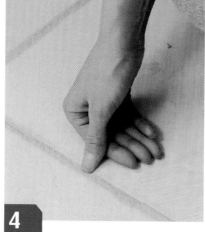

4 LET THE GROUT SET UP

Once you've removed as much grout as possible with the float, let the grout cure. Test it by pressing it with your thumbnail. When this leaves no impression, the grout is solid enough for the next step.

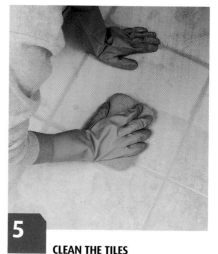

5 CLEAN THE TILES

Grout leaves residue on tiles. Use a damp sponge to wipe it up. Dip the sponge in clean water frequently and wring it out thoroughly before wiping up more of the residue.

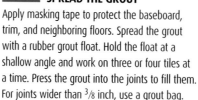

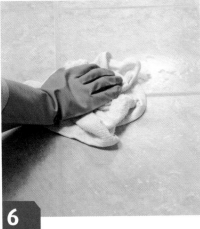

6 REMOVE THE HAZE

Once the water from sponging has dried, most likely a slight haze will remain on the tiles. Buff it off with a clean, dry rag.

7 SLOW-CURE THE GROUT

Instead of drying, grout undergoes a chemical reaction called curing. A slow cure results in stronger grout. Twenty-four hours after you've applied the grout, spray it with water once or twice a day for three days to slow the cure.

8 APPLY TILE AND GROUT CLEANER

Sponge the cleaner on, then scrub the surface with a stiff brush. Rinse thoroughly and let the floor dry before applying sealer.

9 SEAL THE GROUT

Apply sealer after the grout has cured a minimum of three days. Some grouts need to cure much longer before being sealed, so follow the manufacturer's directions. Using a sponge, apply sealer to 6 to 8 square feet at a time. Wipe up the excess before it dries and move on to the neighboring tiles. Apply a bead of caulk in the gap between the tile and the wall.

📖 WORK SMARTER

SLING A GROUT BAG

A grout float works poorly on joints wider than $3/8$ inch or on tile with irregular edges. Apply grout with a grout bag instead. The bag is like a pastry bag and has interchangeable tips. Pick one that's the same width as the joint. Fill the grout bag from the top by troweling in grout with a margin trowel. When the bag is about two-thirds full, roll up the top to close it, squeezing the rolled material firmly with one hand. Put the nozzle between the tiles and squeeze with your other hand. Smooth out the joint with the rounded end of a trowel or a similar object.

⊙ TOOL TIP

SEALER APPLICATOR

Instead of applying grout with a sponge or brush, use a sealer applicator that is more precise and cuts down on cleanup. It has a small wheel that runs along the grout line, controlling both the amount of grout applied and where it is applied.

For important information on minimizing discoloration when applying grout see "Avoid color problems with grout," page 160.

Installing mosaic tile

The tiny, individual tiles you often see on the floors in older homes are indeed little tiny tiles. And not long ago each of these tiles was, in fact, set individually. Not so since the invention of mesh-backed mosaics. Now these mosaic tiles are mounted on a 12×12-inch mesh sheet that is laid as if it were a single tile.

This makes the job considerably easier, but you still need to watch out for a few things. Make sure the entire sheet, not just portions of it, is set in the adhesive. Make sure the sheets are properly aligned with their neighbors. If one sheet is a little bit crooked, every sheet after it will be equally crooked. It's also easy to install a sheet that's slightly higher or lower than its neighbor, so watch for this too.

It's virtually impossible to lay this kind of tile without some mortar squeezing up to the surface between tiles. Because you won't be able to successfully clean out the mortar, use a mortar that matches the grout. This way, the color will be uniform.

1 PREPARE AND MORTAR LAYOUT GRIDS

Prepare the floor as you would for any tile job. Snap layout lines that divide the floor into quadrants and sections. Square the lines and make sure you have edges of equal widths.

2 SET THE FIRST SHEET

Spread mortar in one of the sections and set the first sheet of tile into one of the corners. Press it into place with a beating block, a small rectangle that you tap with a hammer to set the tiles in the mortar.

3 CHECK THE MORTAR SPREAD

Lift the sheet up to see how much mortar is on the back. If parts of the back are bare, switch to a trowel with a larger notch. Recomb the mortar and reset the first sheet. Some mortar will squeeze up between the tiles; it's unavoidable. If it gets on the surface of the tiles, wipe it off with a damp sponge.

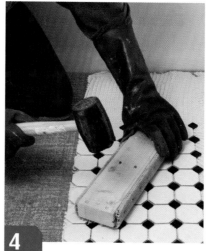

4 SET AND BED THE NEXT SHEET

Install the next sheet the same way. Then press on both sheets with the beater block to make sure they are flat and at the same level. Make sure the sheets are spaced properly and that gaps are equal in width.

5 FINISH THE FIRST SECTION

Continue across the mortar. Make sure each piece is flat, level with its neighbors, and properly aligned. When you've finished the first section of floor, lay mortar for the next. Work your way across the floor until you've covered it with tile. Grout and seal normally.

Installing a border

A border is easy to install and adds emphasis to the floor. You can create your own border using tiles that contrast with or complement the rest of the floor, or you can buy commercially available patterned border tiles. The border need not travel along the wall. Place it several feet away to purposely emphasize one part of the room, or use it as a transition between differing tiles.

The key to borders is laying them out correctly. Never assume that the room is square and that you can simply run the border along the wall. If the room isn't square—and few are—the tiles that meet the wall will have to be cut to different sizes. This isn't obvious if they're plain tiles, but it's terribly noticeable in the case of border tiles. If the lines you draw during layout tell you you're going to have trouble, move the border away from the wall by a tile or two to hide the problem.

1 **FIND THE CENTER OF THE ROOM**
Snap a chalkline from the midpoint of one wall to the midpoint of the opposite wall. Repeat on the neighboring walls. The lines cross in the center of the room. Lay tiles and spacers, but not mortar, along the lines. If the tiles that meet the wall will be less than half a tile wide, shift the appropriate line by half the width of a tile. For more on layout, see "Laying out a floor for tile," pages 60–63.

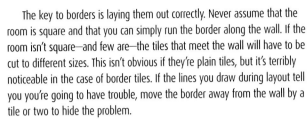

2 **LAY OUT THE BORDER**
With the tiles and spacers aligned along layout lines, choose a spot for the border that ends on a full grout line. Measure and snap a chalkline this distance from the layout line on this and the opposite side of the room. Repeat on the neighboring sides of the room.

3 **TEST-FIT THE BORDER**
Lay tiles and spacers for the border all the way around the room. Adjust as necessary. If the border is against the wall in a room that's badly out of square, the width of the border tiles will change noticeably along at least one of the walls. If the difference is objectionable, move the border at least one tile away from the wall but parallel to layout lines. Any tiles you have to trim will be in a less noticeable part of the floor.

4 **LAY TILE UP TO THE BORDER**
Snap a grid on the floor, marking small rectangular sections that you'll lay one at a time. Trowel on mortar in a center rectangle and lay tiles in it. Working in one quadrant of the room, lay tiles across the floor until you've laid the entire quadrant inside the border. Move on to the next quadrant and repeat until you've laid all the tiles inside the border.

5 **LAY THE BORDER**
Trowel on mortar and lay small sections of the border. If there will be tiles between the border and the wall, install them as you go. Let the floor dry, and grout and seal it as you normally would. For more information, see "Grouting ceramic tile," pages 166–167.

Setting a pattern

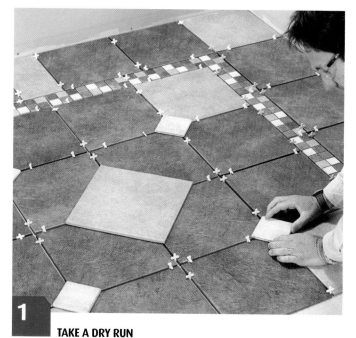

1 TAKE A DRY RUN

Prepare the floor and install backerboard (see pages 156–159). Then use graph paper to draw the pattern to scale, accounting for all the tiles. Use this drawing to guide you as you install the pattern. Snap layout lines that represent both the interior and exterior areas of the border and the tiles within the field. Using your drawing as a guide, dry-lay all the tiles, making sure that the layout will not produce tapered rows.

2 CUT A GUIDE BOARD

Cut a piece of 1/2-inch plywood to the dimensions of the interior of the border. Spread and comb thinset on the area just inside the border and across to the nearest wall. Set the plywood guide on its layout lines and arrange the border pieces in order on top of it. Set the border pieces in the thinset.

3 TEST THE INSETS

Dry-lay the centerpiece on its layout lines and dry-lay the surrounding tiles. Where there are inset cuts to make, cut cardboard templates, test-fit them, and if they're right, use them to cut the tile itself.

4 CUT THE INSETS

For every diamond inset, hold the pattern tile centered on the corners of the cut tile and trace a cut line around the edges. Cut all these tiles at the same time.

5 INSTALL THE REST OF THE TILE

Pull up the plywood guide board and trowel thinset in the central area. Set the pattern in place, using your drawing as a guide. Let the mortar cure, grout and clean the tiles, and seal them if necessary.

Setting a tile base

1 LEVEL THE BASE TILES

Even on out-of-level floors you'll have to install the tiles with their top edges on the same plane. Here's how. Lay the bullnose tile against the wall with spacers between them. Adjust the tile heights with plastic wedges (available at your tile supplier) until all tiles are level. Mark the wall at both ends of the line of tiles.

2 MARK THE LAYOUT LINE

Take up the tiles and snap a level chalkline between the marks you made. Mark all the walls with chalklines in a similar fashion. Mix enough thinset to cover the area in which you'll be working. Back-butter each tile.

3 SET THE TILE

Set each tile in place, inserting spacers between them. Keep the top of the tiles level with the line using the plastic wedges. Gently remove excess mortar from the joints with a utility knife and clean the surface. Set and clean corner tiles and let the mortar cure overnight before grouting.

Setting tile corners

4 CAULK THE EDGES

Grout the trim tiles and sponge-clean the surface at least twice and wipe off the haze with a clean rag. Caulk the joint at the floor and along the top edge of the trim. Smooth the caulk with a wet finger or sponge.

1 START AT AN OUTSIDE CORNER

Dry-set the tiles in place and mark a line to designate where the top of the tile hits the wall. Remove the tiles, spread thinset to the line, and starting with a full tile at the outside corner, reset the tiles. When you get within two tiles of the inside corner decide whether the last tile will be less than a full tile. If it will be, cut the last two tiles larger than half but sufficient to fill the space.

2 CUT THE FOOT TO FIT

At the inside corner, you will need to make an angled cut off the edge of the cove in order for it to fit against the foot of the tile on the adjacent wall.

7

CERAMIC AND STONE FLOORING

Installing stone tile

Applying stone tile is much like applying ceramic tile. Prepare the floor as you normally would, installing backerboard over a wood subfloor or applying directly to a concrete floor.

When choosing stones, avoid black and green marble. They stain easily and require professional installation with epoxy-based mortars.

Other stone tiles are easier to install, but make sure you buy a mortar and an unsanded grout designed for stonework. Other mortars may show through the tile, and sanded grout may scratch the tile.

Because it is a natural product, stone tile is uneven. Using an ordinary tiling procedure, it is difficult to lay each tile at the same level. Compensating for this involves back-buttering the tile—applying mortar to the back of the tile in addition to what's already on the floor. The extra mortar provides a cushion that you can push a tile into, if necessary, to align it with its neighbors.

Stone tiles with a highly polished surface usually have a chamfer along the edge. Set them edge to edge, then fill the chamfer with grout. Set tumbled stone tiles like those shown here with a much wider space between tiles.

1

DUST OFF THE TILES

Stone tile often has a coat of dust on its back from the milling process. The dust keeps the stones from bonding as well as they should. Wipe off the backs with a damp cloth and let them dry.

2

SEAL THE TILES

Seal the tiles before you install them to protect them from stray mortar. Wipe on the sealer, wait 10 to 15 minutes, then wipe off the excess. Repeat. When the surface is dry, gather the tiles randomly to spread out any color variations, and put them in piles or in boxes.

3

SET THE TILES

Mix the mortar and spread it one section at a time as you would for ceramic tile. To keep the surface of the floor flat, back-butter the tiles (put a coat of mortar on their backs), and put the tiles in the mortar bed.

4

BED THE TILES
Each time you put a tile in the adhesive, bed it with a beater block and rubber mallet. Make sure each tile is level with its neighbor, tapping with the mallet to adjust as necessary.

5

GROUT THE TILES
Let the mortar dry for at least 24 hours, then mix a nonsanded grout designed for use with stone. Spray the tiles with water from a spray bottle before you spread the grout to prevent the tile from absorbing all of the water from the grout. Apply and seal as you normally would.

Romancing the stone
Some tile lines come with bullnose and trim tile. Others don't. If your selection doesn't come with them, you can make your own by rounding the edges with a rubbing stone.

Hone the edge of a cut tile with a rubbing stone to duplicate the chamfered edge that comes from the factory.

Cutting edge tiles

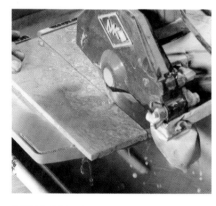

SAW EDGE TILES
Measure the dimensions of each edge tile—it's unlikely they will all be the same size. Cut the edge tiles with a wet saw and lay them in a mortar bed, back-buttering each tile as you go.

Cutting holes in tiles

1

SAW THE SIDES OF A HOLE
Mark the outline of the hole (for an electrical outlet box, for example) with a china marker (not a felt-tip, which may bleed). Using a dry-cutting saw equipped with a diamond blade, lower the saw into the middle of the line. Work the saw forward to one end of the line, then back to the other corner.

2

KNOCK OUT THE CENTER
Knock out the cut piece with tile nippers and trim the corners. Don't worry if the cut line is slightly errant; it will be hidden under the wall plate.

7

CERAMIC AND STONE FLOORING

Maintaining ceramic and stone

Although many ceramic tiles will stand up to normal use without staining, some of the softer tiles will need special attention. No matter what kind of tile you have on your floor, regular cleaning is mandatory.

When you need to remove a stain, start with the procedures described in the chart below. If one of these doesn't work, ask your tile dealer how to get the stain out. Some will recommend a commercial stain-removal agent made for your tile.

You can often get out stubborn stains with a mixture of cleaning agent and baking soda, plaster of Paris, or refined clay. Deodorant-free cat litter works well. Mix the ingredients into a wet paste and apply it to the stain. Tape a plastic bag over the paste and let it sit for a couple of days. Then brush off the paste.

Unglazed tile almost always requires a sealer, and even presealed tile may need periodic stripping and resealing. Penetrating sealers soak into the tile bisque and preserve the natural color of the tile. Topical sealers lie on the surface of the tile and may lighten or darken the tile colors or change its sheen. Topical sealers wear off and sometimes require yearly reapplication. When tiles look dull it is probably time to strip and reseal them.

Stripping tile

1

STRIP OFF THE OLD SEALER
Resealing your tiled floor requires removal of the old sealer first. Flow stripper on the surface with a mop. Scrub the area with a brush or with a floor-scrubbing machine. Do not let the stripper dry on the surface.

2

REMOVE THE RESIDUE
Some water-based strippers allow removal with a wet-dry vacuum. If not, remove the residue with a sponge or rags. Rinse thoroughly with clean water and wipe dry. Old residue mixed with new sealer will create a gummy, clouded surface.

Removing stains from tile

Stain	Cleaner and method
Ink, coffee, blood	Start with a 3 percent hydrogen peroxide solution; if that doesn't work try a nonbleach cleaner.
Oil-based products	Use a mild solvent, such as charcoal lighter fluid or mineral spirits, then household cleaner in a poultice. For dried paint, scrape with a plastic (not metal) scraper.
Grease, fats	Clean with a commercial spot lifter.
Rust	Use commercial rust removers, then try household cleaner.
Nail polish	Remove with nail polish remover.

Always rinse the stained area with clear water to remove residue.

⊘ SAFETY ALERT

FLOOR CARE PRODUCTS CAN BE TOXIC
Many strippers and sealers are solvent-based and highly caustic. Even water-based products contain harmful chemicals. All floor care products are potentially dangerous—observe the manufacturer's safety precautions.

Wear rubber gloves, old long-sleeve clothing, pants, and eye protection. Wear a respirator to avoid breathing toxic fumes and put a fan in the window to provide adequate ventilation. Perform tile maintenance tasks when children are out of the house.

Sealing tile

1 VACUUM THE FLOOR

If you've just stripped an existing floor, allow 48 hours for the surface to dry before sealing. On existing floors vacuum the surface thoroughly to keep dirt and dust from becoming embedded in the new sealer.

2 CLEAN THE TILE

Clean the tile with a commercial tile-cleaning product following the manufacturer's directions. Rinse with clear water.

3 APPLY THE SEALER

Apply sealer with a sponge applicator, paint pad, brush, or mop, as required by the manufacturer. Do not let sealer puddle or run on walls. Some sealers can't be overlapped. Some may require wiping with a clean rag. Allow time to dry between coats. Apply one or two additional coats.

WORK SMARTER

SHINE UP TILE WITH WAX

Some unglazed tiles benefit from wax application, especially if the wax contains pigments that enhance the tile color. But like sealers, waxes need periodic renewal.

To properly renew a waxed floor, strip the old wax and wash the surface thoroughly with a mild detergent. Rinse with clear water and let it dry completely.

Apply the wax in thin coats, letting each coat dry thoroughly, then buffing it before application of the next coat. Repeated thin coats leave a brighter shine than one thick coat; they also reduce wax buildup.

A dull shine may just need a cleaning and buffing. Clean the floor with a soap-free cleaner and buff with a cloth or rented machine. When using a buffer, start in the middle of the floor with the brush level. Tilt the handle up or down slightly to move it from side to side. Don't push the machine. Buff across the surface.

Repairing grout

Regrout an entire floor only when you have to: It's an enormous job. Stained, discolored, and even mildewed grout is better cleaned than replaced. Buy a special grout cleaner from the tile department of your local home center or hardware store. You must repair small sections of damaged grout, however, by removing and replacing the grout. If the floor has colored grout, expect the repaired area to be a slightly different color. Each dye lot has a slightly different shade, and the chances of matching one to the other are minimal at best.

If you're installing a tile floor, save some of the grout in an airtight plastic container, and note the ratio of water to grout you used when mixing it. If you have to make a repair, the grout will match the original color of the grout you installed. Some variation in color may remain, however, simply because your floor's grout has been exposed to sun, dirt, and soap.

To remove the grout in a large area, cut it with a rotary hand tool.

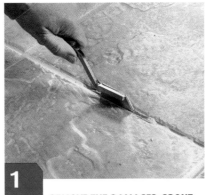

1

REMOVE THE DAMAGED GROUT
Cut out the grout from the damaged area with a carbide-tooth grout saw. The cut must be at least $1/16$ inch deep to hold the new grout—the deeper the better. Vacuum up the debris and clean with a grout cleaner recommended by the manufacturer of the grout you're using.

2

MIX NEW GROUT
Mix the grout with a latex additive. If you're using a powdered grout, some (but not all) call for a latex admix. If so, follow the directions exactly. Grout fails without a latex admix, which may be the reason you're having to repair the grout in the first place. Some grouts are available premixed in plastic buckets. If you use one, make sure that it contains a latex admix and that it is recommended for repair work.

3

GROUT THE TILES
Apply the grout as you normally would. Spread it with a rubber grout float. Hold the float at a shallow angle and work on three or four tiles at a time. Press the grout into the joints to fill them. Grout has a long pot life, so it probably will stay moist in the bucket as long as you keep stirring it. Do not water it down if it hardens.

4

CLEAN THE GROUT
Clean the grout and keep it damp. Wait 15 minutes, or until the grout is firm, then immediately sponge off excess grout. Let the grout dry completely and buff off the remaining haze. Some grouts need to be kept damp constantly while curing; others air cure. Follow the directions on the container.

Cleaning tile

A pass with a wet mop is usually enough to clean a ceramic tile floor, but stone, especially marble, stains easily. Clean stone tiles with stone tile cleaner, which you usually apply directly to the floor and wipe up with a sponge or sponge mop. If grout lines are difficult to clean, apply a grout cleaner using the applicator on the bottle. Avoid using abrasive cleaners on tile or stone.

Replacing a tile

1 **REMOVE THE GROUT**

Grout locks a tile in place, making it harder to remove and increasing your chances of damaging a neighboring tile. Remove the grout from around the tile with a grout saw or rotary tool, cutting as deeply as you possibly can.

2 **SCORE THE TILE**

Put a straightedge across one of the diagonals. Guide a scoring tool along the straightedge, scratching a line in the tile. Repeat until the line is at least $1/16$ inch deep. Repeat on the other diagonal.

3 **BREAK UP THE TILE**

Put on your safety glasses and strike the center of the tile with a center punch. The tile will begin to break up. Put a cold chisel on the diagonal near the center and strike it with a hammer. Repeat along the entire length of both diagonals until you're able to remove all of the tile pieces.

4 **REMOVE THE MORTAR**

Chisel away the mortar with a bricklayer's chisel. Remove as much mortar as you can. You can leave some mortar, as long as it is firmly attached and there is enough room for a new layer of thinset.

5 **APPLY THINSET**

For the strongest bond, use a mortar made specifically for repair work. Mix it according to the directions on the box, and spread and comb it on the floor with the trowel specified by the manufacturer. Back-butter the replacement tile, spreading just enough mortar to cover the back; too much will cause the tile to sit high on the floor.

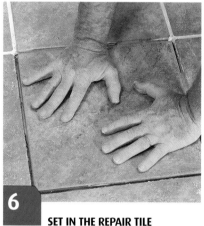

6 **SET IN THE REPAIR TILE**

Put the tile in place and twist it back and forth to spread the mortar. Tap the tile down with a flat board and mallet. Remove excess mortar that squeezes into the joints. Let the mortar cure, then grout and seal the joints.

Buy cold chisels with plastic safety handles to protect your hand from misplaced hammer blows.

Carpet

n a cold day, there's nothing like getting out of bed and stepping onto a warm carpet. Tile may be durable. Wood may be traditional. Vinyl may be colorful and low maintenance. But carpet is the flooring that invites you to walk barefoot or stretch out in front of the fire. Besides, carpet installation requires few if any layout lines.

Once the carpet is delivered, store it on a clean, dry surface. If the surface is damp, protect your carpet with a sheet of plastic under it. When you finally get to its installation, you can carry it into the room in which you're installing it and cut it oversize there, but it's easier to measure the room and cut it oversize off-site.

If your room has in-floor hydronic radiant heat, be careful not to puncture a heating pipe when you nail down tackless strip. Dampen the perimeter of the floor and turn the heat up. The water will dry first to show the pattern of the piping. Mark the pattern with a permanent marker. Fasten tackless strip so there's a gap between the strip and the wall equal to about two-thirds the carpet thickness. This allows you to tuck the carpet in along the edges of the room.

Chapter 8 highlights

Carpet installation has largely been left to the pros. But now that rental shops carry the tools, there's no reason most average homeowners can't install it themselves. Some carpet installs easily, exactly like self-stick tiles, while other carpet installs like sheet vinyl—no tacks needed.

Most methods, however, begin with an oversize piece of carpet that's trimmed after it's installed. If this is your first installation, stick with a plain carpet rather than one that's patterned, and don't buy berber—it requires extra skill to install.

Laying one-piece tacked carpet

▲ Laying carpet requires some specialty tools. The knee kicker in the foreground and the extension pole (called a power stretcher) are items you can rent along with cutters and trimmers. Knee kickers can be dangerous if used improperly; see the Safety Alert below.

You can attach carpet to the floor in one of three ways—tacks, tack strips, or glue. Tacks have largely been replaced by tack strips but you may still encounter them when removing or repairing carpets. Glue is discussed in "Installing glued and seamed carpet," pages 186–188.

Tack strips are thin, narrow pieces of wood that have two or three rows of closely spaced tacks that stick up out of the wood. (Despite the tacks, they're sometimes called tackless strips because you no longer have to tack the carpet.) Prior to installation, you nail the strips around the edge of the room, points up. You then stretch the carpet, hooking it over the strips to hold it in place.

You begin laying carpet in a corner of the room, anchoring the carpet to a few feet of tack strips against the longer wall. Staying in the same corner, you then anchor the carpet to a few feet of tack strips along the shorter wall. You anchor the rest of the corners as the job progresses, but the overall picture looks like this: The installer anchors carpet on the long wall of the starting corner, followed by the adjoining short wall. The remaining long wall is next, followed by the remaining short wall.

The exact order of work is shown on page 183. Short arrows indicate where you push the carpet with the knee kicker. Long arrows show the angle and starting point of the power stretcher. Once you've attached the carpet near either the kicker or stretcher, reposition the tool and work your way along the wall.

Carpet comes in 12-, 13½-, and 15-foot-wide rolls. If your room is wider than 15 feet, it will require a seam. No seam is invisible, and looped carpets show seams more than others, but a good job is less visible than a bad one. If your carpet requires a seam, practice with a few feet of scrap before deciding against professional installation. When you're planning the seam, run it in the direction of the light source. For information on seaming, see "Installing glued and seamed carpet" on pages 186–188.

1 CUT TACKLESS STRIPS

Cut the tackless strips to fit the perimeter of the room. Tackless strips are made for concrete or wood and vinyl and come with the proper nails in place. At doorways, wrap the strips around the door frame but do not extend them across the opening. Position and nail the strips with the points facing the wall. Keep a space equal to about two-thirds the thickness of the carpet between the walls and the strips, using a piece of carpet as a guide.

2 LAY THE PAD

Padding comes in 4½- or 6-foot-wide rolls. Unroll the padding so the seams, if any, will be at right angles to those in the carpet. Tape neighboring pieces together with 2- to 3-inch masking tape or as directed by the manufacturer. Staple along the pad every 10 to 12 inches in each direction. (A hammer stapler makes quick work of the job.) Work toward the tack strips, smoothing the pad and stapling as you go. Staple the pad against the edge of the tack strip. Run a carpet knife against the strip to trim the pad.

3 CUT THE CARPET

Measure the room. Snap chalklines across the back of the carpet to outline a piece that's 6 inches longer and wider than the room. Put a piece of scrap wood under the carpet with the layout lines facing up. Use a straightedge to guide a carpet knife along each line. Change blades frequently.

⚙️ **TOOL TIP**

GET SOME HELP FROM A "DEADMAN"

In a large room, or a room with obstacles such as a radiator or baseboard heater, a power stretcher may be unable to reach from wall to wall. If that's the case, use a "deadman." Nail two lengths of tack strip to the face of a 2×10 with the teeth facing the same way. Put the teeth of the strip into the carpet so they slope away from the head of the stretcher and have a helper stand on the 2×10. Put the foot of the stretcher against the deadman and push against it as if it were a wall.

4 CENTER THE ROUGH-CUT

Center the carpet in the room with the backing against the floor. Make relief cuts at the corners so the carpet lies flat. Cut from the top using a carpet knife.

5 ANCHOR THE LONG WALL

At the long wall near a corner of the room, put the toothed end of a knee kicker in the carpet about 1 to 3 inches from the wall. Push the padded end, then push down with a stair tool, as shown above, to anchor the carpet on the tack strips. Using the stair tool, tuck the carpet between the tack strip and wall. Push, hook, anchor, and tuck carpet along about 3 feet of the wall.

6 ANCHOR A SHORT WALL

Repeat on the short wall of the same corner. Push the carpet over the tack strips with the knee kicker, and anchor and tuck the carpet with the stair tool. Anchor and tuck the carpet along about 3 feet of the wall.

7 POWER-STRETCH THE FIRST CORNER

Put the foot of the power stretcher against a 2×4 or 2×6 laid against the short wall of the starting corner. The 2×4 protects the wall from damage and should be about 48 inches long and padded with a piece of scrap carpet. Run the stretcher at about a 15-degree angle toward the opposite corner. Set the head of the stretcher about 6 inches from the wall. Push on the handle to stretch the carpet about 1 to 1½ percent. (This translates to between 1¼ and 1¾ inches over a 10-foot span and is the amount of stretch you want each time you power-stretch.) Hook, anchor, and tuck the carpet along about 3 feet of both of the corner's walls.

8 ANCHOR THE LONG WALL

With the knee kicker, push the carpet against the long wall between the two installed corners. Anchor and tuck with the stair tool.

Push, but don't kick, the knee kicker with the section of your leg just above your knee.

9 POWER-STRETCH THE SECOND CORNER

Put the foot of the stretcher against the 2×4 and the long wall of the starting corner. Run the stretcher at about a 15-degree angle to the corner, as shown. Stretch, anchor, and tuck the carpet along about 3 feet of both walls that form the corner.

10 ANCHOR THE SHORT WALL

Use the knee kicker to push the carpet against the short wall, attaching it to the tack strips. Anchor and tuck, then work your way along the short wall, pushing and attaching the carpet as you go.

11 POWER-STRETCH THE OPPOSITE LONG WALL

Power-stretch from the long wall of the starting corner to the opposite long wall, running the stretcher at about a 15-degree angle. Hook, anchor, and tuck the carpet over the tack strips near the head of the stretcher. Moving the stretcher along the wall, stretch, hook, anchor, and tuck the carpet section by section.

12 POWER-STRETCH THE REMAINING CORNER

Power-stretch from the short wall of the starting corner, running the stretcher straight across the room. Attach the carpet to the tack strips, tuck it between the strips and the wall, then work your way across the wall with the knee kicker as shown in Step 13.

13 ANCHOR THE LAST WALL

Attach the carpet along the last wall. Push it into place with the kicker; anchor and tuck it with the stair tool.

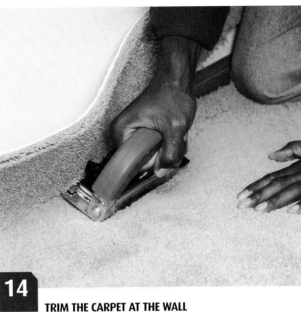

14 TRIM THE CARPET AT THE WALL

Set a wall trimmer to the thickness of the carpet and guide it along the wall to trim the edges of the carpet. Tuck the cut edges into the space between the strips and the wall using a plastic broad knife.

CLOSER LOOK

TYPICAL ROOM INSTALLATION

Carpet layers begin by anchoring carpet first in one corner and then in the other corner of a long wall. The rest of the corners are anchored as the job progresses, but the overall picture looks like this: The installer anchors carpet on a long wall, followed by the adjoining short wall. The remaining long wall is next, followed by the remaining short wall.

The exact order of work is shown here. Short arrows indicate where you push the carpet with the knee kicker. Long arrows show the angle and starting point of the power stretcher. Once you've attached the carpet near either the kicker or the stretcher, reposition the tool and work your way along the wall.

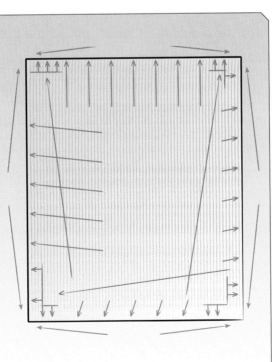

15 INSTALL TRANSITIONS

Install transition moldings wherever the carpet meets other flooring. A binder bar, shown here, is most commonly used. Other options are shown in "Carpet transitions," page 45. Seal the edge of the carpet with latex seam sealer to prevent unraveling. Nail the binder bar to the floor and push with the kicker to fit the carpet over the hooks in the binder bar. When the carpet's in place, hit the bar with a rubber mallet, or put a block of wood over the bar to protect it and hammer the flange closed.

8

CARPET

Installing stretched and seamed carpet

Carpet comes in rolls that are 12, 13½ and 15 feet wide—wide enough to cover most rooms. Occasionally, however, you'll come across a room that requires a seam in the carpet.

If you do, resist the temptation to put the seam in the middle of the room. While it makes planning easier, it also makes the seam more obvious. Put the seam in an out-of-the-way part of the room. Given a choice between putting the seam near a doorway or under a sofa, choose the sofa every time.

An unavoidable problem in seaming is seam peaking. No matter what you do—or no matter what a professional does—the seam will lift slightly off the floor. Peaking occurs as you stretch the carpet during installation. The back of the carpet stretches everywhere except along the seam, where it is backed by tape. The tension tends to lift the seam slightly. The thicker the backing, the greater the problem. In most cases, the seam peaks no more than about 1/16 inch; often you won't be able to feel it with your hand. Because the problem is unavoidable, the seam's location is all the more important.

Not all carpets are candidates for do-it-yourself seaming. Multilevel loops, berbers, and floral patterns are all difficult to seam. In fact, any carpet with a pattern will present a problem. Because carpet is a woven material, it stretches and shrinks. If one side of the seam has stretched while the other piece has shrunk, it takes both skill and experience to bring the patterns into alignment. Stick with level loops and solid colors if you're cutting your first seam. Ask the dealer about possible problems and whether the carpet requires special seams.

You'll cut the seam and join the pieces together before you install the carpet. Once you create the seam, you'll install the carpet as if it were a single piece. For more information, see "Installing one-piece glued carpet" on page 189.

1

CUT THE FIRST PIECE OF CARPET
Put both pieces of carpet in the room, overlapping them by about 4 inches. Make sure you have enough carpet to reach the walls, plus about 3 inches extra on all sides. Snap a chalkline on the back of one piece to mark the location of the seam. Cut along the line with a carpet knife guided by a straightedge.

2 **CUT THE SECOND PIECE**

Overlap the edges again. Double-check that you still have enough carpet at the wall. Guide a row cutter against the edge you cut. The knife in the cutter will cut the other piece of carpet, creating two perfectly matched pieces.

3 **APPLY LATEX SEAM SEALER**

Lay a bead of seam sealer along the carpet backing of one of the cut edges. Apply the sealer carefully to one edge only, without getting any on the carpet pile. The sealer keeps the carpet from unraveling, and failure to use it will cause the seam to pull apart. The sealer must remain wet for the next step.

4 **SEAM THE CARPET WITH SEAMING TAPE**

Put a piece of 3-inch-wide hotmelt seaming tape along the entire length of the seam. Slip a board under the tape at the part of the seam you'll start at, and melt the tape with a seaming iron. Move the iron slowly and pinch the seam together behind the iron, pushing the pieces into the adhesive before it cools. Move the board as you work so you'll have a firm work surface. Some carpets require special seams; check with the manufacturer.

5 **INSTALL THE CARPET**

Once you've created the entire seam, clean up any stray seam sealer with the recommended cleaner. Stretch and install the rug as you normally would.

⌕ **CLOSER LOOK**

"SEAMS" EASY, BUT IT'S NOT

No seam is truly invisible, but some carpets are more difficult than others. If you're working with a patterned carpet, for example, you'll first need to cut the pieces so that the pattern continues across the seam from one piece to another. Because the density of the weave varies, you'll also need to stretch one of the pieces so that the pattern aligns along the seam.

Berber carpets are also difficult. The pile is made from long strands of yarn glued to the backing. They're easy to pull loose, and once you do this, it's like pulling on a loose strand of yarn in your sweater—it just keeps unraveling.

If you're working with berber or a patterned carpet, hire a pro who can give you a good—but not invisible—seam.

Installing glued and seamed carpet

PROJECT DETAILS

SKILLS: Cutting carpet, spreading adhesive
PROJECT: Installing commercial glue-down carpet

TIME TO COMPLETE

EXPERIENCED: 2 hrs.
HANDY: 3 hrs.
NOVICE: 4 hrs.

STUFF YOU'LL NEED

TOOLS: Tape measure, chalkline, carpet knife, steel-wheel seam roller, 75-lb. carpet roller, wall trimmer, row cutter, duckbill napping shears, hammer and nails or pneumatic nailer, screwdriver, notched trowel
MATERIALS: Carpet adhesive, commercial glue-down carpet, seam sealer

1

MARK THE SEAM LOCATION

Snap a chalkline on the floor to mark where the seam will fall. Avoid putting the seam down the middle of the room, where it will be obvious, and make sure neither piece of carpet is less than 4 feet wide.

2

TRIM THE CARPET

Start along the edges to be seamed. Snap a chalkline about 1½ inches from each of the edges that will be seamed, and cut along the line with a knife and straightedge. (The material immediately along the edge makes a poor seam.) Once the edge is cut, snap chalklines and cut two pieces of carpet, each large enough to go over the area they will cover, plus 3 or 4 inches in each direction.

3

LAY OUT THE SEAM EDGE

On the larger piece of carpet, put a screwdriver or ballpoint pen between two rows of tufts about an inch from the seam edge. Drag the pen or screwdriver the entire length of the seam, keeping it between the same two rows of tufts. This creates a valley between the tufts.

4

CUT THE SEAM EDGE IN THE LARGER PIECE

Start the cut in the valley with a carpet knife. Then put a row cutter in the beginning of the valley created by the screwdriver or pen. Angle it about 5 degrees, cutting away slightly more backing than tufted fiber. Guide the cutter along the valley to cut the edge of the seam.

5

OVERLAP THE EDGES

Put the second piece in place, positioning it so the first piece overlaps it by about 2 inches. Make sure the nap runs in the same direction on both pieces, otherwise the pieces will appear to be mismatched when installed. The left edge of one piece, as it came off the roll, should be against the right edge of the other piece that came off the roll. Most carpets have arrows printed on the back to help you align the tuft direction.

6   MAKE THE SECOND CUT

Guide the screwdriver or pen between rows of tufts to create a valley that marks the cut on the second piece of carpet. Align the cut edge of the larger carpet with the valley. Start the cut with a knife, then put the row cutter along the valley, angling it about 5 degrees to cut off more backing than fiber. Guide the cutter along the cut edge of the larger piece to form a perfectly matching edge in the carpet underneath.

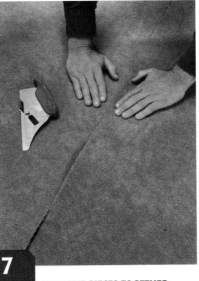

7   BUTT THE PIECES TOGETHER

Check for gaps and slide the pieces back and forth to close them, if necessary. Recut if you must force the edges together to close the gaps.

8   FOLD BACK FOR ADHESIVE

Fold back each piece 3 feet from the chalkline. If necessary, weight down the carpet to hold it in place. Vacuum or damp-mop the floor, if necessary, to remove dust created during cutting.

Seal only one edge of the seam and make sure you don't get sealer on the nap.

9   APPLY CARPET ADHESIVE TO THE BARE SPACE

If you damp-mopped the floor, let it dry before you trowel carpet adhesive onto the exposed section. Use the trowel recommended by the manufacturer. Let the glue dry as directed by the manufacturer.

10   ADHERE THE LARGER PIECE

Put the larger piece of carpet into the adhesive. Have helpers hold the ends of the folded-back edge taut while you hold the middle. Walk slightly ahead of them so you can put down the middle of the carpet and work your way to the edges. This helps avoid wrinkles. In small rooms, you'll have to do this without helpers. Stand in the center, hold the carpet as shown, and walk across the floor with the edges trailing.

11   SEAL THE SEAM

Apply seam sealer to the cut edge of the larger piece of carpet. Squeeze a bead the thickness of the backing onto the backing, without getting any on the nap of the carpet.

CARPET

12 ADHERE THE SECOND PIECE

Immediately fold the edge of the short piece into the adhesive. Work with helpers again, but keep the edge of the carpet in a straight line as you approach the seam. Do not apply seam sealer to this piece of carpet.

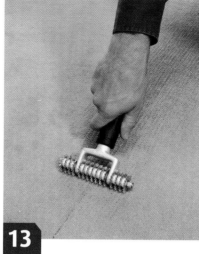

13 PULL THE SEAM EDGES TOGETHER

Work the seam together with a steel-wheel seam roller. The roller helps push the pieces together. Roll along the seam to remove bubbles and push the carpet into the adhesive.

14 ROLL UP THE UNADHERED PIECE

Finish laying the larger piece of carpet. Roll up the unattached section. Apply adhesive to the floor and fold the carpet back into place. Roll with a floor roller across the entire width and length of the longer piece.

15 LAY THE SHORTER PIECE OF CARPET

Roll up the unattached section. Apply adhesive to the floor and fold the carpet back into place. Roll with a floor roller across the entire width and length of the room (see inset).

16 BRUSH AND TRIM THE SEAM

Brush the seam with a broom to raise the nap. Trim off stray fibers with duckbill napping shears.

17 CLEAN OFF GLUE SQUEEZE-OUT

If glue squeezed onto the carpet, remove it using a carpet cleaner recommended by the manufacturer. Glue solvent will dissolve the glue that holds the carpet together. Trim the edges as shown on the opposite page. Avoid walking on the carpet for at least 24 hours.

If the nap doesn't run in the same direction on both pieces, the carpet will appear to change color at the seam.

8

CARPET

Installing one-piece glued carpet

1 CUT THE CARPET TO SIZE
Cut the carpet 3 to 4 inches larger than the room. Measure the room and snap a chalkline on the back of the carpet, laying out a piece 3 to 4 inches longer and wider than measured. Cut along the line with a carpet knife and straightedge. Spread out the carpet in the room where you'll install it and let it rest for at least 24 hours. Make sure the room temperature is between 65 and 95 degrees. Store the cans of adhesive at the same temperature. This makes both carpet and adhesive easier to manage.

2 FOLD BACK THE CARPET
Lift one edge of the carpet and fold it back on itself, exposing half of the floor. If the carpet left a layer of dust on the floor, vacuum it.

3 APPLY ADHESIVE TO THE FLOOR
Use the adhesive and application trowel specified by the carpet manufacturer. The size and spacing of the trowel notches are important because they control the amount of adhesive applied to the floor. Let the adhesive dry for 15 minutes, or as recommended by the manufacturer, until it becomes tacky.

4 UNFOLD THE CARPET
Set the folded section of carpet back on the floor into the adhesive. Fold back the other side of the carpet, apply glue, and set the carpet into the glue. Roll with a 75- to 100-pound carpet roller to remove any bubbles. (Follow the manufacturer's weight recommendations.) Start in the center of the room and roll toward the walls.

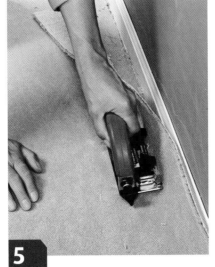

5 TRIM THE CARPET
Cut along the baseboard or wall with a wall trimmer. Set the depth of the knife just deep enough to cut through a piece of scrap. Guide the knife along the edge of the room, leaving a gap of about 1/16 inch between the edge of the carpet and the wall. This allows for expansion of the carpet due to changes in weather.

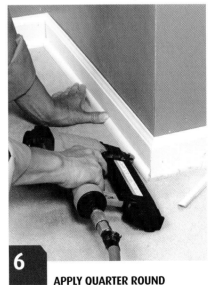

6 APPLY QUARTER ROUND
Cover the gap between the wall and the carpet with quarter-round molding. Apply a finish to the molding before you install it, and let it dry. Avoid crushing the carpet with the molding. Set it gently on top of the carpet and nail the molding to the baseboard, not the floor.

8

CARPET

FLOORING 1-2-3   **189**

Installing indoor/outdoor carpet

PROJECT DETAILS

SKILLS: Cutting carpet, spreading adhesive

PROJECT: Installing indoor/outdoor carpet

TIME TO COMPLETE

EXPERIENCED: 2 hrs.
HANDY: 3 hrs.
NOVICE: 4 hrs.

STUFF YOU'LL NEED

TOOLS: Tape measure, chalkline, carpet knife, straightedge, notched trowel, 75-lb. carpet roller, wall trimmer

MATERIALS: Solvent-based seam sealer, carpet adhesive, indoor/outdoor carpet, metal trim piece

Indoor/outdoor carpets may look like other indoor carpets, but the fiber is very different. Indoor/outdoor carpets are made from olefin, a tough, hard-wearing fiber well-suited to outdoor use. In fact, olefin is a trade name for polypropylene, the material the military uses to make clothing designed for use in extreme weather. As you might expect, olefin is resistant to moisture and mildew. It is also stain-resistant, and the color is part of the fiber rather than a dye. Ultraviolet (UV) stabilizers can make it fade-resistant.

Indoor/outdoor carpet requires a glue-down installation. It comes in 6- and 12-foot widths and can be seamed if necessary. It's available in several grades. The grade you want depends largely on where you'll use it:

- UV-stabilized olefin is required for outdoor use. Buy carpet that has a rubber-based backing known as "marine" backing.
- In a protected outdoor application, such as a porch, UV stabilizers are still recommended. You can buy carpet with either marine backing or polypropylene-based backing.
- Indoors, of course, you can use any carpet fiber, but olefin is well-suited to the basement. If moisture has been a problem, buy a marine backing.

Indoor/outdoor carpet at a glance

- **Concrete surfaces:** Concrete must be clean, dry, and free of alkali. See "Test for moisture," page 82, and "Testing the pH," page 84, for directions. New concrete must cure for 3 to 4 months before you can install glue-down carpet.
- **Wood:** Use either a solvent- or latex-based adhesive over wood that's finished with a clear penetrating finish. Cover silicone-treated surfaces with plywood, and seal with a urethane sealer.
- **Pressure-treated wood:** Pressure-wash and allow to dry thoroughly before applying adhesive.
- **Decks:** Carpet will conform to the spaces between deck boards. Cover with an exterior-grade plywood. Seal with a urethane-based sealer.
- **Painted surfaces:** You can use solvent-based adhesives over wood or concrete that has been painted with an outdoor alkyd (oil) based paint, but the bond will be only as strong as that holding the paint in place. Outdoor carpet adhesives sometimes cause latex paint to blister. Sand surfaces that have been painted with latex. After sanding, seal wood surfaces with a urethane sealer.
- **Asphalt:** Requires a solvent-based adhesive. Adhesive must cure for at least 6 months before carpeting, and it must be clean, dry, and free of grease and oil. Carpet will fail to stick well to rough asphalt surfaces; resurfacing may be necessary.

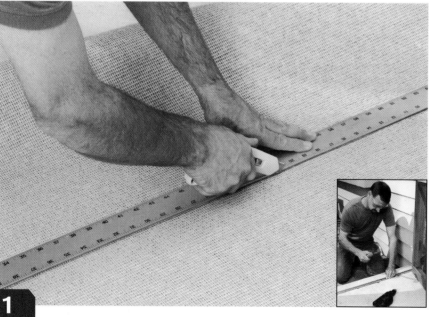

1 **CUT AN OVERSIZE PIECE OF CARPET**

Measure out a piece of carpet that's 6 inches longer and wider than the area you're covering, and snap chalklines on the back. Leave the carpet unrolled over the floor it will cover for at least 24 hours (or as directed by the manufacturer) at a temperature between 65 and 95 degrees, with the humidity between 10 and 65 percent. Nail a carpet gripper across any doorways that will meet the edge of the carpet. (See inset.)

2

FOLD THE CARPET IN HALF

Lift an edge of the carpet and fold it back on itself, exposing half of the floor. If the carpet has left dust on the floor, vacuum it before applying the adhesive.

3

APPLY ADHESIVE TO THE EXPOSED FLOOR

Use the adhesive and application trowel specified by the carpet manufacturer. Either latex- or solvent-based adhesive may be acceptable. (Solvent-based adhesive is stronger.) The size and spacing of the trowel notches control the amount of adhesive that's applied to the floor and vary depending on the carpet backing. Let the adhesive dry for 15 minutes, or as recommended by the manufacturer, until it becomes tacky. Fold the carpet into the adhesive.

4

TRIM THE EDGES

Set the depth of the knife in a wall trimmer so that it's just deep enough to cut through a piece of scrap carpet. Guide the trimmer along the edge of the room, firm against the wall. Trim the carpet against the carpet gripper with a knife, and push the flange over the carpet by hitting it with a rubber mallet.

5

SEAL AND ROLL THE CARPET

Apply a bead of solvent-based seam sealer to all cut edges of the carpet. (See inset. Woven carpets and carpets with ribbed patterns require no sealant.) Apply a bead that's as thick as the backing, without getting sealer on the carpet fibers. Roll with a 75-pound carpet roller to remove bubbles and loose spots. Start rolling in the center of the room and roll toward the edges.

6

REPEAT ON THE OTHER HALF OF THE CARPET

Fold back the other section of carpet. Trowel adhesive onto the newly exposed section of floor and let it dry. Fold the carpet back into the adhesive. Roll the entire carpet with a carpet roller so it bonds well with the glue. Roll no more than once lengthwise and once across the width. Excessive rolling forces the glue to the edges of the carpet.

8

CARPET

Installing carpet tiles

There are two advantages to carpet tiles: First you don't need to master the art of stretch-in installation. Second it goes much faster than a stretch-in installation. The downside: Because the tiles are glued down, there's no pad underneath.

Like vinyl and ceramic tiles, you lay out carpet tiles by finding the center of the room. Once you've found the center, peel-and-stick installation starts by laying a square in it, and then working out toward the walls. Mastic installation also starts in the center, but is done one quadrant at a time because it makes glue application easier. Carpet tile is like other tiles: You can create countless patterns. Take a look at the manufacturer's brochures to see what textures and colors are available.

1 MARK THE CENTER OF THE ROOM

Snap chalklines between midpoints of opposing walls. Like other tiles, carpet tiles are laid out and installed from the center of the room. Find the midpoints of the walls, and snap a line between the midpoints on opposite walls. The lines will cross in the center of the room.

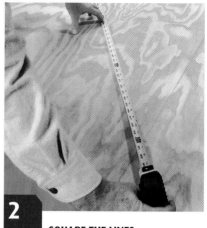

2 SQUARE THE LINES

Make sure the lines are square with each other. Check for square with a 3-4-5 triangle (see page 60). Measure 3 feet from the center point along one line and 4 feet from the center point along the other line. The lines are square if the points are 5 feet apart. Move the end of one line to make any necessary corrections.

3 DISTRIBUTE TILES FOR EQUAL EDGING

Make sure the tiles that meet the wall will be at least half a tile wide. Lay tiles along the layout lines without applying adhesive. Stop laying tiles at the last full tile before the wall. If the space between the tile and the wall is less than half a tile wide, reposition the line parallel to the wall. Move the line by the width of a half tile in either direction, keeping it parallel to the original line. The resulting tiles will be wider at the wall, but will still be equally sized on opposite sides of the room.

4 FIND THE PILE DIRECTION

The pile will lean in a particular direction on each tile, and an arrow on the back tells you which way. Any two tiles with pile facing in different directions will look to be slightly different colors. Depending on the carpet, you will lay the arrows in the same direction, turn every other one 90 degrees, or lay the arrows randomly. Follow the manufacturer's directions. In this case, every other tile is turned 90 degrees to create a checkerboard pattern.

5 LAY THE CENTER TILES

One by one, peel off the backing, and put the corner of a tile in one of the corners formed by the layout lines. Put a tile in the corner of each quadrant, so that the tiles form a square. The next group of tiles will be laid in a square surrounding the one you've just laid.

6 **LAY THE FIRST LARGE SQUARE**

Lay a square surrounding the first square. Work along the layout lines and lay a tile against each edge of the square already in place. Remove the backing one tile at a time. Pay attention to the direction of the arrows, and lay the tile in the pattern recommended by the manufacturer. Always nestle a tile tightly against the corner created by neighboring tiles. Throw out the backing as you go—it's slippery, and there's no point in getting hurt.

7 **LAY THE STARTING CORNERS OF THE SECOND SQUARE**

Lay the corners of the second square. The tiles you have laid so far have left a void in each corner of the square. Lay tiles to fill in the corners, nestling the tile tightly against its neighbors.

8 **LAY THE THIRD SQUARE**

Lay a third square, and work your way to the wall. Lay tiles around the square you just laid to create a stair-step pattern, as seen along the left edge of these tiles. Start at the layout lines and work along the edge of the tiles already laid. Once you've laid the stair-step pattern, fill in each of the steps with a single tile, which creates a second and larger stairway. Continue filling the steps with tiles, working your way to the wall.

9 **TRIM TILES AT THE WALLS**

The tiles next to the walls will probably need to be cut to fit. Measure the space between one of the tiles and the wall at the two corners of the tile nearest the wall. Draw a matching layout line on the back of a new tile. Cut along the line with a utility knife guided by a straightedge. Lay the tile, and repeat the process until you've laid all the tiles.

Not peel and stick

Tiles for commercial installations don't have peel-and-stick backing and require a coat of mastic on the floor instead. Trowel adhesive onto the floor using a trowel with the notch size specified by the manufacturer. (Notch size controls the amount of adhesive you apply.) Spread the adhesive in one of the quadrants created by the layout lines. Start applying mastic at the wall, and work your way back to the center of the room. Let the adhesive dry as recommended by the manufacturer: Tiles set in the adhesive too soon will be impossible to remove if you ever decide to redo the floor. Lay the tile in a stepped pattern used for vinyl tiles. See page 147 for details.

10 **ROLL THE FLOOR**

Once all the tiles are down, roll the floor with a 75-pound floor roller to seat the tiles in the adhesive.

8

CARPET

Framing sleepers for below-grade floors

Although you can install many of today's modern flooring materials—laminate, engineered wood, resilients, and others—directly on a dry concrete slab, a wooden subfloor raised several inches above the concrete will help insulate the flooring from the cold subfloor. It will also provide a little spring in the surface, making it that much more comfortable underfoot.

Before you put down a sleepered floor, you need to cure any moisture problems. If you don't have them, you're ready to go. But you can't assume that a sleeper floor will cure them. Moisture will wick up the 2×4s, through the subfloor, and into the finished flooring. Cure the moisture problem first, then install the floor.

Since headroom in most basements—especially those with finished ceilings—is at a premium, you'll want to conserve vertical space. Use pressure-treated 2×4s to support ³/₄-inch exterior-grade tongue-and-grooved plywood and lay the 2×4s (sleepers) flat.

Prepare the slab by vacuuming it thoroughly, then seal it with an asphalt primer and a layer of asphalt mastic. Lay a moisture barrier (6 mil polyethylene) and mark the plastic sheet with a felt marker so you can position the sleepers on 16-inch centers.

1

PREPARE THE FLOOR

Clean the floor, spread asphalt mastic, and install the poly waterproofing membrane on the mastic. Overlap the seams of the plastic sheet 6 inches and tape the seams with the tape recommended by the manufacturer. Leaving a ¹/₄-inch gap along the walls, mark the sheet with a felt marker at 16-inch intervals, and snap chalklines to help you position the sleepers. Set out the sleepers along the perimeter of the room and in their approximate locations across the rest of the floor, cutting them to length where necessary.

Typical sleeper subfloor installation

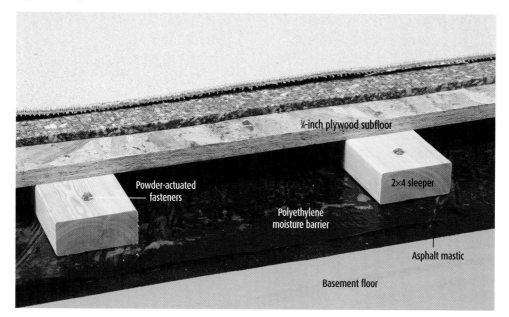

¾-inch plywood subfloor

Powder-actuated fasteners

2×4 sleeper

Polyethylene moisture barrier

Asphalt mastic

Basement floor

2

ANCHOR THE SLEEPERS

To even out irregularities in the floor, use cedar shims to level the sleepers. Then anchor the sleepers (through the shims) with powder-actuated fasteners.

3

SET THE FIRST SHEET

Using the same techniques as you would use to lay plywood underlayment, set the first sheet of plywood (tongue to the wall) with the long side perpendicular to the sleepers and $1/2$ inch from the wall. Fasten the sheet with $2^{1}/_{2}$-inch coated screws—every 6 inches along the walls and every 8 inches in the field of the sheet. Don't drive screws at the grooved edge yet.

4

INSTALL THE REMAINING SHEETS

For each subsequent sheet of plywood, leave a $1/8$-inch gap between the ends. Then, in the second row, start with a half sheet (and the third row with a full sheet) to offset the joints in every other row. Fit the tongue of one sheet in the groove of the other and screw it to the sleepers.

CLOSER LOOK

SETTING SHIMS

Using a 4-foot level (nothing shorter will be accurate), make sure the top edges of the sleepers lie on the same plane. Insert a pair of cedar shims at low spots, crossing them as shown.

Using a powder-actuated nailer

A powder-actuated nailer makes driving nails into concrete faster and easier—and with less chipping. (It can also make the room an ear-busting area, so it's wise to wear ear protection, especially in a small room.)

You can buy a powder-actuated "gun" at most home centers or rent one from rental outlets. It's handy for anchoring both wood or metal framing to masonry. An explosive charge drives a hardened nail into the concrete with ease. Concrete nails (which break or bend if not hit squarely) and hardened screws (which can seem to take forever to install) are slower and less secure than powder-driven nails.

Wear ear and eye protection when using a powder-actuated nailer and plant it firmly against the wood before pulling the trigger or striking the firing pin.

WORK SMARTER

WHERE TO PUT THE FIRST SHEET
Because walls are seldom perfectly straight, you'll want to locate your first sheet of plywood by measuring out 49 inches from the wall and snapping a chalkline at this point.

This will give you enough clearance along the length of the room so you can line up the inside edges (the grooved edges) of the plywood sheets. In some places you will have more than a $1/4$-inch gap along the wall, but you can cover that with baseboard and shoe molding.

8

CARPET

Installing a carpet runner

Installing a carpet runner is a good way to learn about carpet installation. You'll use the same materials, tools, and techniques, but a runner is smaller and easier to manage.

Runners are held in place by both tack strips and staples. The tack strips hold the runner against the back of the step. Staples hold it against the riser. Tension between the two holds the runner on the front of the step.

Buy or rent an electric or pneumatic stapler. Hand staplers will fail to drive staples far enough into the steps. Use 9/16-inch narrow crown staples, and work the gun into the runner before pulling the trigger. Staple the runner directly to the stairs, not through the padding.

When you buy a runner, buy a piece of carpet that's specifically made to be a runner. The unbound edges of scraps or pieces that have been cut off a roll of carpeting will unravel. Runners have bound edges, but you'll have to apply a seam sealer at the top and bottom to prevent unraveling. Buy padding recommended for the runner.

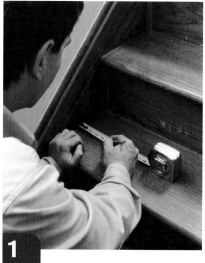

1 LAY OUT THE RUNNER

Subtract the width of the runner from the width of the stair. Divide by two to find out how much space you'll have between the edge of the runner and the edge of the steps. Lightly mark the edge of the runner on each stair tread.

2 CUT AND INSTALL TACK STRIPS

Cut tack strips 2 inches shorter than the width of the runner. Put a scrap piece of carpet against the riser, and put the tack strip against the scrap. Nail the strip in place, positioning it so the tack points angle toward the riser.

3 CUT AND INSTALL PAD

Cut a piece of pad the same length as the tack strip and about 3 inches wider than the stair. Staple the pad to the tread with one edge flush against the tack strip. Wrap the pad around the nose of the tread and staple it to the riser. (Trim with a knife so the pad is just long enough to wrap around the nose.)

4 CUT THE END OF THE RUNNER

The runner end must be square and sealed with latex seam sealer to prevent unraveling. Cut it by guiding a carpet knife against a framing square that's placed across the back of the runner. Following the directions on the container, seal with latex seam sealer.

5 ROLL THE RUNNER UP THE STAIRS

Place the cut end of the runner at the bottom of the stairs, and roll the runner up two or three stairs. Adjust as necessary so the runner falls within the layout lines you drew earlier.

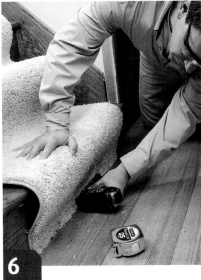

6

STAPLE THE BOTTOM OF THE RUNNER IN PLACE

Make sure the runner is aligned with the layout lines. Put an electric or pneumatic staple gun against the runner at the bottom of the riser. Push it firmly against the carpet, then drive the staples.

7

STRETCH THE RUNNER OVER THE FIRST TACK STRIP

Make sure the runner is still aligned, then stretch it over the tack strip with a knee kicker. Sharp blows against the kicker can cause knee injury; simply push firmly with the portion of your leg above the knee. Start in the center of the step and stretch the runner every 3 inches along the tack strip.

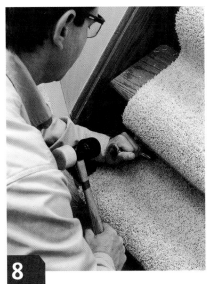

8

TUCK THE RUNNER BETWEEN THE TACK STRIP AND THE RISER

Put a stair tool on the carpet where the tread meets the riser. Strike the tool with a rubber mallet to tuck the carpet between the tack strip and the riser. On each end of the tack strip, staple the runner into the corner formed where the riser meets the tread.

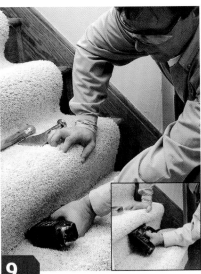

9

STAPLE THE RUNNER TO THE RISER

Pull up on the runner and staple the edges to the riser about 2 inches above the tread. Once you've stapled the runner near the tread, staple it to the underside of the nosing every 3 inches (see inset).

10

CONTINUE UP THE STAIRS

Stretch the runner over the tack strip on the next step. Stretch and install as before, then work your way up the stairs, stretching and stapling as you go. Check frequently to make sure the runner is still aligned with the layout marks.

11

CUT THE UPPER END OF THE RUNNER

If the runner meets another carpet, stop it at the top of the last riser. If the runner meets a wood floor, you can run it along the floor for a couple of feet (see inset). Cut the end so it's square and seal with a seam sealer.

8

CARPET

Carpet care

VACUUM TWICE A WEEK

Yes, vacuum twice a week if two people live in your house. Give the carpet an extra weekly vacuuming for every additional two people in the house. Ground-in dirt is harder to remove than surface dirt, and your goal is to get the dirt before it gets away from you.

Before you vacuum, find the grain of the carpet: Rubbing it with your hand in one direction causes the yarn to stand up; rubbing it in the opposite direction makes the yarn lie flat. When you vacuum, slowly push the vacuum forward in the direction the pile lays flat, then pull it back. Though the trip back across the pile removes more dirt than the initial trip with the pile, make both trips.

The better the vacuum, the better the job. Use a vacuum that has adjustable, rotating brushes and that is strong enough to pull air through the carpet backing. The brushes loosen ground-in soil; the airflow removes it.

Carpet cleaning

Dirt not only takes the luster out of a carpet, it has sharp edges that shorten the carpet's life. To get the most out of your carpet, have it cleaned before it starts to look bad—roughly every 12 to 18 months.

Cleaning the carpet yourself will no doubt save you money, but it may void the manufacturer's warranty. Read the warranty that comes with the carpet and double-check by calling the manufacturer's consumer help line.

If a do-it-yourself cleaning meets with approval, rent a carpet cleaner. Most are steam or hot water cleaners, which pump hot water and cleaner into the rug, then vacuum it back out. Follow directions carefully.

- Vacuum first to remove all the dirt you possibly can.
- Avoid pumping too much water into the carpet; this can cause the backing or seams to separate.
- More soap doesn't result in cleaner carpet. Extra soap can actually stain it.

- Once the carpet is clean, your goal is to have it dry within 4 hours. Use fans, open windows, or turn on the air-conditioner to do the job. Finally, don't walk on the carpet until it is dry.

YOUR NEXT VACUUM

The next time you buy a vacuum, look for one that sports the Carpet and Rug Institute's "green label." A vacuum with this label meets certain standards for removing soil, keeping dust out of the air, and maintaining appearance without damaging the carpet.

- **Soil removal:** An approved vacuum must be able to clean up a given amount of soil in four passes over a test carpet.
- **Dust containment:** Vacuums release some of the dust they collect into the air. A vacuum that has the green label will release no more than 100 micrograms of dust per cubic meter of air, an amount well below National Ambient Air Quality Standards.
- **Maintenance and appearance:** Regular vacuuming will eventually change the appearance of any rug. Approved vacuums cause only minor changes in a rug's appearance after a year's worth of vacuuming.

 WORK SMARTER

REMOVING SPROUTS AND DENTS

If you have carpet, you can't keep it from springing loose a fiber or two every now and then or showing dents where furniture has been. Not even the best carpets boast immunity from these maladies. If your carpet "sprouts," don't pull them—you'll open holes in the fabric. Gently pull the errant fibers up and trim them flush with the others. Use a scissors or duckbill napping shears.

Dents are more difficult to deal with. Once the "temper" in the fibers has been "set" by the weight of furniture, it doesn't want to return to the shape it had at the factory. Start by using the back of a tablespoon to work the fibers up in the area of the dent. If this doesn't work, try wetting the area first or warming it slightly with a hair dryer.

Cleaning carpet with a dry-powdered cleaner

1 SPRINKLE THE POWDER

Check with your retailer before purchasing a carpet cleaning solution. To use a powdered agent, sprinkle the powder evenly across the carpet. Properly applied, it should appear as a thin layer.

2 WORK THE POWDER INTO FIBERS

Using a short-bristled floor brush or rented carpet machine, work the powder into the fibers of the carpet. Do not brush too heavily in any one area. Leave the powder in the fibers for the recommended time.

3 VACUUM THE CARPET

Vacuum the cleaned area thoroughly using a high-quality vacuum with beater bars. Go over each section both with and against the grain in order to ensure removal of all the cleaning powder and soil.

Replacing carpet and cork tile

Use the procedures illustrated below to remove both damaged carpet and cork tiles. You'll find cork tiles more difficult because their reciprocating glue is tough stuff. Always work from the center of the tile outward. Working from the edges will damage them.

1 CUT THE CENTER OF THE TILE

Using a metal straightedge and a sharp utility knife, make several passes in the center of the tile until you have cut through to the subfloor.

2 PRY UP THE TILE HALVES

Insert a 3-inch putty knife under the cut and remove half of the tile by prying and seesawing the putty knife back and forth to break the adhesive bond. Repeat the procedure on the other half of the tile. Replace the adhesive, press in a new tile, and roll it.

8

CARPET

Trim

rim and molding are the finishing touches to any home improvement project. They help hide the gaps that are natural to any flooring installation. They also enhance the style of the room.

By now you've probably decided what style of trim your newly floored room needs and have purchased it. You can go ahead and cut the trim pieces to fit, but you will be better off if you apply the finish to the trim before hanging it. That way the stain or paint meant for the trim will go on the trim and not the wall.

Trim usually comes from the retailer unfinished, so that means its open pores make the wood much more responsive to changes in temperature and humidity than finished wood. Take the trim stock into the room and let it acclimate to the environment 24 hours for each ¼-inch thickness.

One of the most important things to realize about trimwork is that even though this is the stage when you especially want all the miters exactly 45 degrees and all the corners square, you're talking about trying to put perfection into an environment that's

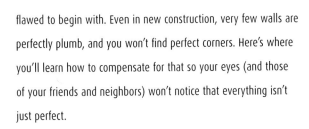

Chapter 9 highlights

202 **INSTALLING DOOR TRIM**
Measuring and miter-cutting door casing is easier with these tips.

204 **INSTALLING BASEBOARD**
Baseboard hides the gap at the corner of the floor and makes a design statement if you want it to.

209 **FINISHING TRIM**
You can paint or varnish door and window trim to enhance your room decor.

flawed to begin with. Even in new construction, very few walls are perfectly plumb, and you won't find perfect corners. Here's where you'll learn how to compensate for that so your eyes (and those of your friends and neighbors) won't notice that everything isn't just perfect.

Installing door trim

⊘ PROJECT DETAILS

SKILLS: Basic carpentry
PROJECT: Installing door trim

🕐 TIME TO COMPLETE

EXPERIENCED: 1.5 hrs.
HANDY: 2 hrs.
NOVICE: 2.5 hrs.

✓ STUFF YOU'LL NEED

TOOLS: Combination square, power mitersaw, clamp, hammer, nail set, safety glasses, ear protection, pencil, stepladder
MATERIALS: Door trim, 6d finishing nails, 8d finishing nails, glazier's compound or wax pencil, wood filler

TOOL TIP

TUNING UP YOUR MITERSAW

If you're having trouble getting accurate cuts on your mitersaw, don't blame yourself. Like all saws, a mitersaw can go out of alignment.

To check the alignment of your saw, cut the widest board it can handle in half. Put the halves back together, end to end, and align the edges on a straight edge. Bring the ends together and look for gaps where they meet. Turn one of the boards over and look for gaps again. A gap that widens from one side of the board to the other indicates the fence is out of square. A gap that forms a uniform valley at the seam indicates the saw is out of square with the table. Check your owner's manual for adjustment directions.

There are as many methods for trimming a door as there are carpenters. But each method has the same goal—the top (called the header) needs to look level, the sides (called legs) need to be straight, the mitered corners need to be tight, and each piece needs to be just the right length. Any mistake along the way will affect the look of the finished job.

The technique shown here is the most methodical way to meet all of these goals. You'll start by mitering one end of the header and a short piece of scrap that you clamp to the place where the top of the leg will go. The scrap serves as a support, a stop, and an alignment tool when you hold the mitered header against it.

Next you miter an end of the leg and put it in place with the miter on the floor. The goal here is not to install the trim upside down but to simplify measuring. While it's difficult to miter a piece to length, it's pretty simple to make a square cut exactly where you want it. With the leg upside down, the header shows you exactly where to cut.

Using this method, you won't need a tape measure because you'll lay out the cuts based on what exists. If everything fits, who needs a tape measure?

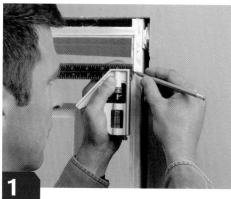

1

MARK THE "REVEAL"

Door molding typically sits back about $1/8$ inch from the edge of the doorjamb. This "reveal" leaves enough room for the hinge barrel, which holds the hinge pin and camouflages any bumps or dips in the doorjamb. Set a combination square to $1/8$ inch, hold a pencil against the end, and guide both all the way around the jamb.

2

LAY OUT THE HEADER

Set a power mitersaw to 45 degrees and miter one end of a header. Clamp mitered scrap as if it were the leg: Align the inside edge of the scrap with the reveal line and the inside of the miter with the corner formed by the reveal line. Put the header into place with the miter against the scrap and the bottom edge along the reveal line. Clamp it in place. Make a mark on the header where the unmitered end crosses the reveal line (see inset).

3 CUT THE HEADER TO SIZE

Start by making the mark on the molding more visible. With a combination square, draw a 45-degree angle across the face of the molding, starting with the mark. Set a power mitersaw to 45 degrees and cut the molding along the line.

4 NAIL THE HEADER

Rest the header on the scrap miter again, and align the bottom edge with the reveal line. Nail the molding into the jamb with 6d finishing nails. Drive 8d finishing nails through the upper part of the molding and into the studs. Leave 1/4 to 1/2 inch of the nails exposed in case you need to remove them to reposition the molding.

5 MITER ONE END OF EACH LEG

Start the legs by mitering an end. (Measure before cutting and make sure the pieces will be longer than needed.) Hold a leg in place but upside down so the miter is on the floor. Mark where the top of the header meets the leg, and cut the leg square at the mark.

If you're going to stain the trim, apply stain and varnish before you install it.

6 FASTEN THE LEGS TO THE FRAME

Start at the top, holding the leg so the miter closes tightly, and drive a 6d finishing nail through it and into the jamb. Leave 1/4 to 1/2 inch of the nails exposed in case you need to reposition the molding. Work your way down the leg, flexing it if necessary, to align it with the reveal line. When you're finished, drive 8d nails through the outer edge of the molding into the framing behind the wall. Repeat on the opposite leg, then set the nails.

7 CINCH THE MITER

Drive a nail through the miter to help prevent the joint from opening up over time. To prevent the nail from splitting the molding, blunt the point by tapping it with the hammer. A blunt tip cuts through the wood instead of pushing the fibers apart the way a pointed tip does.

Miter-free frames

For a Victorian look—and one that involves no miters—install plinth blocks instead of mitering the trim. The blocks are sold in a variety of patterns by lumberyards, home improvement centers, and suppliers that you'll find listed in the back of home renovation magazines. Install the trim much the way you'd install mitered trim. Cut the top trim to length. Position it against a block that's temporarily held in place by a short piece standing in for the leg, and nail the top in place. Once it's in place, cut the legs to fit. Make sure a tight seam forms between the plinth and the trim, then nail the legs in place. Attach the plinth with construction adhesive.

9

TRIM

Installing baseboard

PROJECT DETAILS

SKILLS: Basic carpentry
PROJECT: Installing 8 feet of baseboard

TIME TO COMPLETE

EXPERIENCED: 15 min.
HANDY: 30 min.
NOVICE: 35 min.
VARIABLES: Wide moldings and hardwood moldings will be slower and more difficult to install. Rooms with many doors will also take longer to install.

STUFF YOU'LL NEED

TOOLS: Hammer, drill, power mitersaw, pencil, coping saw, rattail file, combination wood file, sliding T-bevel
MATERIALS: Baseboard, shoe molding, finishing nails

▲ In addition to protecting the wall and dressing up the room, baseboard hides the vertical gap at the bottom of the wall and the horizontal gap between the wall and the floor.

Wood expands and contracts as humidity changes. This expansion and contraction is one reason baseboard exists. Knowing that the floor will expand (in the case of most types of flooring), you leave an expansion gap between the floor and the wall. The baseboard hides this gap. It also protects the wall. In addition, the baseboard itself expands and contracts. As the wood shrinks, mitered corners, should they be used, open up. And if your house settles at all, neighboring pieces no longer align.

Enter the cope joint, in which one side of the trim is cut to the profile of the other piece with a coping saw. Coped joints in corner pieces are cut to fit together like jigsaw puzzle pieces. They expand and contract in unison, leaving no gaps.

Installing coped baseboard usually begins on the wall opposite the door. The first wall is simple enough: The baseboard runs from wall to wall with each end cut square. The pieces that meet the first piece are coped to fit, then cut square on the other end. On the remaining wall (the one with the door in it), the baseboard is coped in the corner and cut square where it meets the door trim.

Finish carpenters cut the molding a bit longer than the wall it goes against, then they nail it flat to the wall. The extra length ensures a tight joint and helps hold the ends of the molding against the wall.

In addition to the usual tool, you'll need an additional saw—the coping saw. It's the woodworker's version of the hacksaw, but it's shorter and deeper with a narrower blade. The narrow blade helps you change directions midcut in order to easily cut an intricate profile.

OLD VS. NEW

IN WITH THE OLD AND OUT WITH THE NEW

Most projects in this book tell you to remove the baseboard before you install the floor. Usually it's because you need to hide the expansion gap around the edge of the floor. You should try to remove the baseboard without breaking it.

If a piece is stubborn, drive the nails completely through it and into the wall. If you break a piece, try to find a new one that matches it so that you'll only need to replace the broken section.

If you live in an old house, keep the moldings. They're part of the house's charm.

If the paint or finish is shot, take the pieces to a stripping shop and have the old stuff removed. Sand once they're dry, and prime or stain before you reattach them.

If you live in a newer house, putting in a new floor creates a good opportunity to replace standard builder materials. Look in old house magazines and in the millwork department of a good home improvement center or lumberyard for molding that adds to the look of your floor and the value of your home.

1 CUT BASEBOARD FOR THE OPPOSITE WALL

Begin on the wall opposite the door. This piece of trim will have two square ends. Avoid gaps at the sidewalls by cutting the piece about 1/16 inch longer than the wall. Put a slip of paper along the floor every few feet to hold the baseboard just above it. Put the baseboard against the corners; it will bow away from the wall slightly because of its length. Push on it to spring it into place.

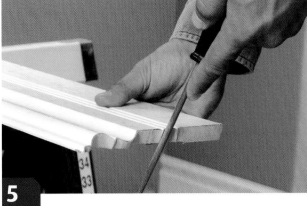

2 FASTEN THE BASEBOARD

Nail the baseboard in place. Drive 6d or 8d finishing nails through the bottom of the baseboard into the 2×4 plate that runs along the floor inside the wall. (The nails chosen need to be long enough to hold the baseboard firmly.) Drive nails through the top of the baseboard into the studs. If the wood splits or is difficult to nail, predrill holes using a nail as a drill bit. Clip off the head of a finishing nail, put it in your drill, and use it as you would a regular bit.

3 COPE THE NEXT SECTION

Cope the next piece of baseboard. Begin with a piece at least a few inches longer than the wall. Use a power mitersaw to miter the end that you'll place against the molding you just installed. Cut the miter as if you were cutting it for a regular inside corner, taking more off the front of the molding than the back. Once it's cut, look at the end grain: You'll see that the cut has revealed the profile of the molding. Trace along the edge of the miter with a pencil to outline the profile.

4 COPE THE JOINT

Cut along the pencil line with a coping saw. This cut creates a razor-thin edge on the end of the molding, one that should nest tightly against the profile of the molding you've already installed. To create this edge, angle the coping saw (use the finest blade you can get) away from the mitered surface at about 90 degrees. Cut along the pencil line, marking the profile, and let the saw do the work. Pushing the saw forward into the wood causes the saw to jam.

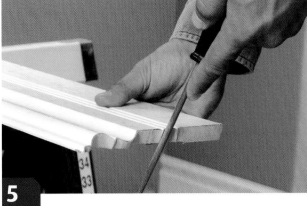

5 SAND FOR A TIGHT FIT

Sand and file to create a tight fit. No coped joint is perfect. Test-fit yours against another piece of molding, and sand and file to make necessary corrections. The tools you use depend on the profile of the molding. A rat-tail file is good for filing inside tight curves. A combination file has a gently curved surface and a flat one, each with two kinds of teeth. It's good for working on flat surfaces and larger curves. Use blades that have finer teeth. Whether you're painting or staining, fill in small mistakes with caulk once the molding is in place. (Use a colored caulk that matches your stain.) If you make a big mistake, cut off the joint and try again.

📖 WORK SMARTER

NO LEG IS THE SAME

The cope joint is so simple that in the days of apprenticeships, 14-year-olds learned how to cut it. But don't expect to pick up the saw and be an instant genius. Buy an 8-foot sample of the baseboard you're going to use and practice, practice, practice. The cost is minimal, and you can cut numerous sample joints out of an 8-foot board. Once you get the hang of it, it's like riding a bicycle: Despite a few bumps and the occasional accident, you'll earn your apprenticeship in no time.

9

TRIM

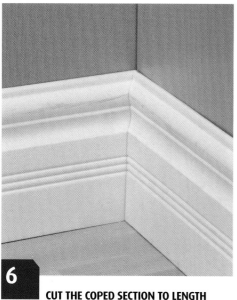

6

CUT THE COPED SECTION TO LENGTH

Add ¹⁄₁₆ inch to the overall length of the wall. Cut the molding to this length by making a square cut on the uncoped edge. Spring the molding into place and nail as before. If the tip of the coped piece is long and thin, you may want to cut it off for a better look.

7

CUT THE REMAINING BASEBOARD

Cut the molding for the opposite wall the same way: Cope, measure, cut, and nail. On the fourth wall—where the door is—cope the molding in the corners and cut butt joints where it meets the door trim.

○ **CLOSER LOOK**

FOR WANT OF A NAIL, THE SHOE MOLD WAS LOST
The way in which you nail in the shoe mold depends largely on who taught you to do it. Three schools of thought exist and all attempt to solve the same problem: Wood expands in humid weather. One theory holds that you nail the shoe mold to the floor to prevent it from moving up and down as the baseboard expands and contracts. Another theory holds that you nail it to the baseboard to prevent it from moving back and forth as the floor expands and contracts. The third theory holds that you drive the nails at a 45-degree angle into the wall plate. The molding will be anchored independently of both the floor and the baseboard and will stay put no matter which moves.

Stain is messy. If you're staining and varnishing the molding, stain it before you put it up to avoid getting stain on your new floor.

8

CUT QUARTER ROUND TO LENGTH

Cut quarter round (also called shoe molding or shoe mold) to fit along the baseboard on the wall opposite the door. Like the piece it sits against, it must be ¹⁄₁₆ inch longer than the wall, and both ends must be butt joints. Nail the quarter round in place.

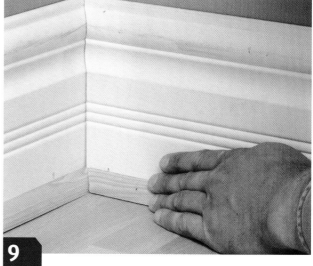

9

INSTALL THE REMAINING QUARTER ROUND

Install the rest of the quarter round just as you installed the baseboard: Once you install the first piece, cope the second and third pieces into it. Cut their uncoped ends square and butt them against the wall. Cut butt joints where the molding meets the door trim; cope the other ends.

9

TRIM

Installing baseboard on outside corners

1 MITER THE OUTSIDE CORNERS
Start by cutting a couple of 45-degree miters in some scrap to see how they meet when you bring them together at the corner. If there is no gap between the pieces anywhere along the joint, cut and install the actual baseboard. If there is a gap in the joint, lay out a custom miter, as explained in Steps 2 and 3.

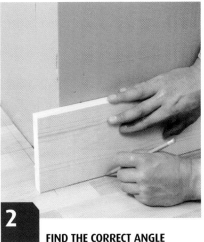

2 FIND THE CORRECT ANGLE
To lay out the proper angle, draw a line parallel to each wall. Many techniques work, but the easiest way is to put one edge of a straight board against the wall and trace along the other edge. Connect the corner that the lines form with the corner on the wall to lay out the angle you'll need to cut.

3 SET A T-BEVEL TO THE ANGLE AT HAND
Set a sliding T-bevel to the angle of the line, and set the saw to this angle. Cut a trial joint, test the fit, and correct as necessary. Cut the miter on both pieces of the actual baseboard and butt the other ends into their corners. Cope the adjoining pieces as described on page 205.

Built-up moldings

1 BUILDING THE BASE
Some baseboards are made up of several moldings. A typical example begins by cutting and nailing 1×4s or 1×6s to the walls. Sometimes you'll need to nail thinner strips to the wall first so the cap molding, installed in the next step, seats properly. Because the board is flat, you won't need to cope or miter. Just butt the boards against each other in the corners.

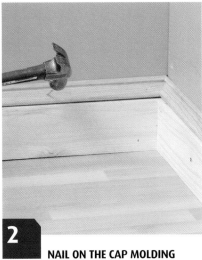

2 NAIL ON THE CAP MOLDING
Lumberyards carry several standard cap moldings, including the one shown here, which was widely used in Victorian houses. You need not use standard cap molding, however. Any profile you find that sits neatly on top of a 1× is a perfect candidate. Cut and cope the cap molding as you would regular baseboard, then nail it to the baseboard.

3 INSTALL THE QUARTER ROUND
Cut shoe molding as you would for any installation. When you're satisfied with the fit, nail it in place.

9

TRIM

Installing no-miter/no-cope baseboard

PROJECT DETAILS

SKILLS: Basic carpentry
PROJECT: Installing an 8-foot section of baseboard

TIME TO COMPLETE

EXPERIENCED: 15 min.
HANDY: 30 min.
NOVICE: 35 min.
VARIABLES: If the inside and outside corners are significantly out of square, making adjustments and scribing the molding may require extra time.

STUFF YOU'LL NEED

TOOLS: Hammer, nail set, stud finder, drill, tape measure, pencil, combination square, power mitersaw, handsaw or circular saw, caulking gun, eye protection
MATERIALS: Baseboard, inside and outside corner pieces, shoe molding (optional), 6d and 8d finishing nails, paintable latex caulk

Cutting miters and coping joints are two jobs that discourage homeowners from installing new molding and trim. If the walls are out of square, as they often are, it's necessary to work around the angle of the miter cut or the position of the molding. However, there's an alternative that eliminates miter and cope joints. Instead of running the molding around the corners, install precut corner blocks that fit the inside and outside corners. Nail the blocks in place and fit the molding in between them. The cuts are square and easily made with a fixed-angle miter box or a power mitersaw.

1 FASTEN THE CORNER PIECES
Predrill and nail the inside and outside corner pieces. The corner pieces are usually longer than you will need. Cut them to a length that is compatible with the molding. Predrill for the 6d finishing nails (see inset). Nail the pieces into place. Use a nail set to drive the heads beneath the surface of the wood. You will fill the holes before you apply the finish.

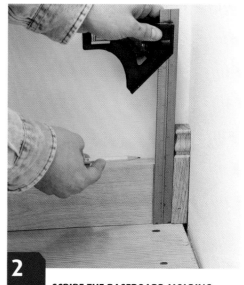

2 SCRIBE THE BASEBOARD MOLDING
Since walls are usually not square, use a combination square to scribe the exact angle of the molding cut on a piece of scrap. Make the cut and transfer it to the piece of molding that will go in between the corners. You must measure carefully and scribe both ends of the molding piece. Cut the molding a little longer than necessary. Test-fit and trim as necessary to get a good fit.

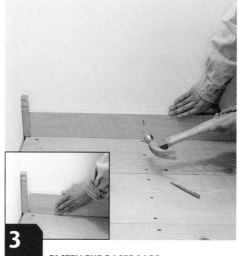

3 FASTEN THE BASEBOARD
Test-fit the baseboard molding (see inset). Find the wall studs with a stud finder. Use 6d or 8d finishing nails to attach the baseboard molding to the studs. Do not nail baseboard into the flooring. This action will inhibit natural expansion and contraction and could cause splitting or warping.

4 CAULK THE GAPS
Caulk any gaps between the wall and the baseboard molding and between the corner pieces and the corners with paintable latex caulk. You can attach shoe molding if you wish. Fill all nail holes, sand, and finish as desired.

9

TRIM

Finishing trim

Whether you finish door trim, window trim, or any other trim, the technique is the same. If you have the sure hand of a professional, pick up a brush and go to work. If you're less sure of your skills, mask the walls thoroughly. Masking goes quickly and lets you concentrate on the job at hand—getting a smooth coat on the trim.

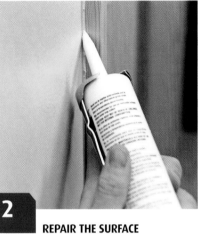

2

REPAIR THE SURFACE

Fill gouges, dings, and dents with wood putty. Caulk to fill gaps between the wall and molding, the wall and ceiling, or two pieces of molding. Smooth the caulk by dipping your finger in a glass of water and running your finger along the caulk. If there are nail holes, fill them with a dab of window glazing. It's easier to apply than wood putty and just as durable. Sand any repairs when they're dry, and wipe the immediate area with a rag dampened in denatured alcohol.

3

MASK AND PAINT

Tape areas with a low-tack tape to avoid getting paint on them. Seal bare wood with an oil-based sealer. If the wood has been painted before, prime it with primer tinted the color of the top coat. When the primer or sealer has dried, sand and wipe down with a rag dipped in denatured alcohol. Apply the paint with a wet brush; then smooth it out in the direction of the grain, using a slightly drier brush. A single top coat applied over primer or sealer is often enough. If you see bare spots, apply a second top coat. Remove the masking tape while the paint is still wet so that any paint you got on the tape won't pull off neighboring trim paint.

1

SAND THE TRIM

Sand the trim to smooth out any chips or drips. Then sand the entire surface to smooth it and to remove any gloss that might prevent the new paint from sticking. When you're done, clean up with a damp cloth dipped in denatured alcohol.

Applying natural finishes

1

PREPARE THE TRIM

Sand and clean the trim as shown above, then apply a conditioner, which helps even the distribution of the stain.

2

APPLY THE STAIN

Brush on the stain, let it soak a bit, and wipe off the excess. Let it dry according to the manufacturer's specifications and if you want it darker, repeat the application.

3

APPLY THE VARNISH

Brush the varnish on a short section of the trim at a time and go back over it to even out the coat. Let it dry and sand according to the manufacturer's instructions.

9

TRIM

Concrete

Many floors and subfloors are made of concrete—basement floors, slabs for patios, pads for tool sheds, and in some parts of the country, where soil conditions and stability make basement construction difficult, concrete slabs are a prevalent on-grade subfloor. An on-grade slab is often the choice for the floor of an addition built on an existing home. Such an addition is less costly because it omits the excavation of a basement.

Pouring concrete for large slabs is hard work and not a chore that anyone should do alone. But large slab construction is not beyond the reach of most homeowners, especially with the assistance of friends and neighbors.

The illustrations on the following pages show a small-scale slab installation, one that would be appropriate for a shed, small utility pad in a dirt basement (for a furnace, water heater, etc.), or pads that support trash cans or recycling containers. But even though the size of the illustrated installation is small, the procedures are essentially the same for a larger slab. Only the scope of the project is different.

Chapter 10 highlights

If you're in need of a new basement floor, or an on-grade base for an addition to your home, and even if you aren't going to pour the floor yourself, it helps to grasp the basics of concrete work.

Concrete work comes with its own lexicon and it will help you become familiar with the language before entering the planning stages of a concrete project.

Concrete is a mixture of portland cement, sand, and stone.

Rebar are metal rods wire-tied in a grid that run through thick pours and tie a pour together in case the ground below it shifts.

Reinforcing mesh, which looks like wire fencing, does the same thing in thinner pads. On small pours, using rebar or mesh is optional.

Expansion strips are made from materials that don't stick to concrete and are installed between two objects to isolate them. It cushions the expansion of concrete between surfaces.

Pouring a concrete slab

PROJECT DETAILS

SKILLS: Making forms, troweling concrete

PROJECT: Placing and finishing 40×72 inches of concrete

TIME TO COMPLETE

EXPERIENCED: 8 hrs.
HANDY: 12 hrs.
NOVICE: 16 hrs.

STUFF YOU'LL NEED

TOOLS: Safety goggles, particulate mask, leather gloves, mason's string, drill, level, hammer, wheelbarrow or mixing bin, hoe, shovel, reciprocating saw, wood or magnesium float, darby, cement jointer, pointing trowel, edging tool, broom

MATERIALS: Ready-mix concrete in bags, flour, batterboards, stakes, metal mesh or rebar, screws, masonry nails or construction adhesive, gravel, plastic or burlap cover, expansion joint, form release agent

P ouring a 40×72-inch slab for a garden shed is a good way to learn the basic techniques necessary to attempt larger projects, such as pouring a slab for an addition or to finish a basement in preparation for a ceramic tile floor.

Concrete is a ratio mixture of sand, gravel, water, and portland cement. A chemical reaction between the water and the mix causes concrete to harden, which means you must keep the slab moist while it cures.

Because concrete is heavy and mixing is hard work, you're probably better off ordering ready-mix if your job requires more than a cubic yard (27 cubic feet), which is the equivalent of 40 to 50 bags of dry mix.

The process is straightforward. You lay out the area for the slab using batterboards, stakes, and mason's lines. Then you excavate to a specified depth, pack the hole with gravel, and build 2× forms to hold the concrete while it cures. The final step is mixing, pouring, and finishing the slab.

WORK SMARTER

BIG CRACKS COULD MEAN BIG PROBLEMS

Shifting and settling can cause a slab to crack, which will damage the flooring installed on it. Take care when you tamp the base; make sure it is compacted firmly to eliminate voids in the base that could later settle. Consider reinforcing the slab (page 214).

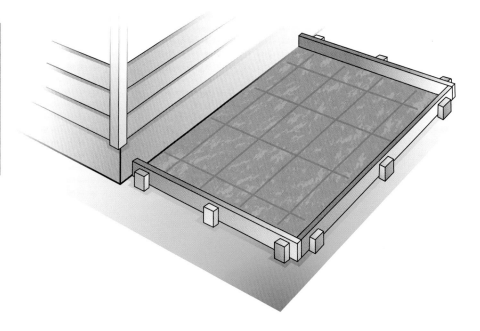

1 LAY OUT THE EXCAVATION

First, lay out the excavation area with 1×3 batterboards and mason's line tied to the crosspieces. Make the area at least 1½ inches wider on each side than the finished slab size to allow for the 2× forms. Check for square and adjust the lines as necessary by sliding them along the crosspiece. Mark the outline with flour and remove the mason's line.

2 EXCAVATE

Following the outline, remove 10 inches of soil (6 inches for gravel and 4 inches for the slab) so the finished height will be approximately level with the surface. (Adjust thicknesses to meet local code specifications as necessary.) Level the bottom of the excavation as much as possible.

3 SET THE FORMS

Position a 2×4 form and drive stakes on the outside of the form. Make the length of the 2×4 equal to the length of the slab, plus 3 inches (so it overlaps the adjacent form pieces). Make 1-foot-long stakes from 1×3 lumber. Drive them about 6 inches from the ends of the form. Retie the mason's string to help position the 2×4, if necessary.

4 LEVEL THE FORMS

Level the form board at the correct height. Attach it to the stakes by driving screws through them into the 2×4.

5 SET THE OPPOSITE-SIDE FORM

Install the opposite 2×4 form board so it is level with the first. This second piece will be the same length as the first. Attach it to stakes parallel to the first form piece. If the distance between form pieces is greater than the length of the level, place the level on a flat piece of lumber.

6 FASTEN THE FORMS

Drive screws through the first two form pieces into the ends of the remaining 2×4 form pieces. The length of these pieces is equal to the width of the pad. Square the form by measuring the diagonals and adjusting as necessary until they are equal. Make sure the form is level. Attach the last two form pieces to stakes driven near the ends. Use a reciprocating saw to remove the top of a stake that is higher than the top edge of the form.

A long level is more accurate than a short one.

7

INSTALL EXPANSION STRIP

Apply an expansion strip to the side of the house with masonry nails or construction adhesive. The expansion strip prevents the concrete from bonding to the structure and cracking as natural shifts occur. If you are pouring a freestanding slab, a 2×4 form will replace the expansion strip.

8

TAMP THE GRAVEL BED

Tamp a 6-inch layer of compactible ³/₄-inch gravel. Make it as level as possible so the correct thickness of concrete can be poured. You can make a tamper, buy a hand tamper, or rent a power tamper, depending on the size of your job. Coat the inside of the form with vegetable oil or a commercial release agent for easy form removal.

Reinforce the concrete with rebar.

 BUYER'S GUIDE

REINFORCING CONCRETE

Concrete expands and contracts with changes in temperature, and it sometimes cracks as a result. Reinforcing the concrete with wire mesh or metal rods, called rebar, helps control the cracks. Rebar not only minimizes the size of the crack, it holds the concrete together when cracks occur.

On a well-tamped surface, rebar is optional. If you use it, it should be in the middle of the slab. Rebar is laid in a grid and the corners are tied together with wire. Rest it on wire supports made especially for the job. You can pour once the rebar is in place. It should be covered with at least 1½ inches of concrete.

9

MIX THE CONCRETE

Mix small batches of concrete in a wheelbarrow. Wear eye protection, a particulate mask, and gloves. Fill the wheelbarrow approximately three-quarters full with premixed concrete or dry ingredients. Dig a crater in the center. Pour water slowly into the crater and mix well with a shovel or hoe. The concrete is the right consistency when it clings to the side of the tool. For larger batches, rent a power mixer.

10

TEST THE CONSISTENCY

Slice the mixed concrete with a shovel. The edges should hold straight without crumbling. If the edges crumble, the mix is too dry and needs more water. If the edges fall, the mix is too wet and needs more dry ingredients.

11

POUR THE CONCRETE

Make a ramp for the wheelbarrow with a 2×8 and a concrete block. The ramp makes pouring easier and prevents the wheelbarrow from damaging the form. Fill the form in sequence, pouring loads next to the previous one to get a seamless mix. When you have filled the form, work the concrete with a shovel or hoe to break up air pockets. Tap the edges of the form with a hammer to help release trapped air.

10

CONCRETE

Finishing a concrete slab

1 SETTLE THE CONCRETE

Plunge a scrap piece of lumber into the concrete in various spots to settle it and to remove air pockets. Don't disturb the reinforcement. Add more concrete until the form is slightly overfilled.

2 SCREED THE SLAB

With a helper, draw a straight 2×4 across the top of the concrete in a zigzag motion to fill in depressions and remove mounds. Repeat to level the slab. Add more concrete if necessary.

3 SMOOTH THE SLAB

Sweep the surface with a darby, pressing down slightly to remove mounds and fill in depressions. Sweep in arcs until water begins to rise to the surface. Let the concrete rest until the water evaporates. When the water is gone, slide a small pointing trowel along the forms to separate them from the slab. Then shape the edges using an edging tool with a $\frac{1}{2}$-inch radius. You want the edges of the slab to be smooth and rounded to prevent chipping when the forms are removed.

4 CUT CONTROL JOINTS

Control joints help prevent the slab from cracking. Cut a control joint in the center of the slab (3 feet in this case) using a jointer with a blade that is one-quarter the thickness of the slab (1 inch in this case). Draw the jointer across the slab using a straight 2×4 as a guide. As soon as the water sheen is gone, smooth and compact the surface with a wood or magnesium float.

5 BROOM THE SURFACE

To create a nonskid surface, drag a concrete broom at right angles to the flow of traffic. The longer you wait to broom, the smoother the surface will be. For best results, buy a mason's concrete finishing brush.

DESIGN TIP

ROCK SOLID

For a different look, sow stones the size of large gravel. Use clean, damp stones, and spread them the way you would sow seeds. Press the stones into the concrete with a screed or darby. Brush any excess concrete off the top of the stones by sweeping with a push broom. Clean the surface by spraying with a fine mist of water until you've washed the concrete film off the stones. Let the concrete cure as you would with a broomed finish.

6 CURE THE CONCRETE

Concrete needs to cure slowly and retain moisture for about 5 days to prevent cracking. With a sprinkler or hose, run water onto the surface every few hours. Cover the slab with water whenever it appears dry. You also can cover the slab with plastic or burlap, which you can dampen with a hose or sprinkler. Don't let the plastic touch the surface, however, because it can create a mottled appearance. Also, try to prevent water from puddling on the cover. Remove the forms when the concrete has fully cured.

Pouring an overlay floor

🎯 PROJECT DETAILS

SKILLS: Applying leveler.
PROJECT: Pouring an overlay.

🕐 TIME TO COMPLETE

EXPERIENCED: Varies w/floor size.
HANDY: Varies w/floor size.
NOVICE: Varies w/floor size.

✓ STUFF YOU'LL NEED

TOOLS: Hammers, chisel, screw gun, roofing rake, shovel, stapler, utility knife, aviation snips, ½" drill, mixing paddle, squeegee, gauge rake, putty knife, 5 gal. buckets, paint brushes, trowel, sprayer, paint roller

MATERIALS: #30 felt paper, metal lath, 1.5" galvanized finish staples, self-leveling compound, concrete thin-finish, colorant, acid stain, clear sealer, ammonia, painter's tape and masking paper

A polymer cement poured to thicknesses from ¹⁄₁₆ to ³⁄₈ inch can emulate much more costly flooring, such as stone, slate, marble, wood plank, quarry tile, and more. They are permanent flooring systems that can outperform many other flooring products. They go on seamlessly, and when protected by industrial-grade sealers, can provide high-traffic wearability on a very low-maintenance floor.

The overlay gives you the beauty of the flooring design you've created without any worry that tiles will crack or grout lines will get dirty. Overlays may be finished to extremely smooth or moderately textured finishes in virtually limitless color and design combinations.

Begin your flooring renovation by removing all of the existing floor covering (tile, vinyl, engineered wood, laminate, etc). Next, remove the underlayment (including backerboard for any tile that was on the floor) and dispose of it. Repair the subfloor as necessary and stabilize it with bracing if required.

1

STAPLE FELT PAPER TO FLOOR
Roll out and staple 30-pound asphalt felt paper to the floor to act as a moisture barrier. Initially it protects the subfloor from moisture in the concrete. In the long run it keeps moisture from coming through the subfloor into the concrete.

2

INSTALL METAL LATH
Working perpendicular to the direction of the felt paper, staple metal lath to floor, overlapping the rows by 2 inches and flattening the overlaps with a hammer to create a uniform surface. Cut the lath where necessary with aviation snips.

3

POUR SELF-LEVELING COMPOUND
Mix up the first batch of the self-leveling compound (to provide a solid concrete base coat) and pour it one bucket at a time onto the metal lath. Spread each bucket before pouring the next one.

4

SPREAD THE COMPOUND

Set a gauge rake to a depth of $1/4$ inch and drag it across the top of the metal lath to give the self leveler a consistent depth. Use a squeegee to get the self-leveling compound into the corners of the room. Let the surface dry for 20 hours.

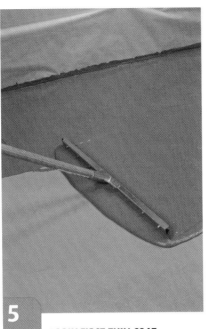

5

APPLY FIRST THIN COAT

When the self-leveling base coat has dried, apply the first coat of thin-finish (which will strengthen the floor and act as a base for the second thin-finish coat). Color this compound to the desired tint while mixing and use the same proportion of coloring agent from bucket to bucket. Pour out this coat and smooth it with a squeegee.

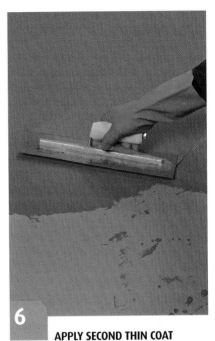

6

APPLY SECOND THIN COAT

Let the first coat of thin-finish dry, then mix and apply the second coat, smoothing it to a depth of $1/8$ inch with a trowel. Let this coat dry overnight.

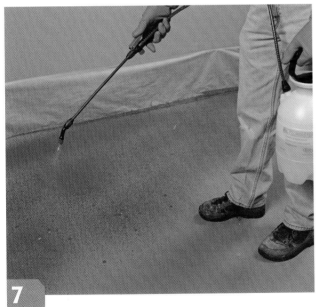

7

APPLY FIRST COAT OF ACID STAIN

Before acid staining the floor, protect the bottom 12 inches of all the walls with masking paper. Cover all the walls and bottom of the cabinets. Mix the stain outdoors with plenty of ventilation, protective glasses, and gloves, and pour it into a plastic-bodied sprayer. Keeping the spray wand about 18 inches off the floor, stain the floor, starting in a corner away from a door and working your way toward the door.

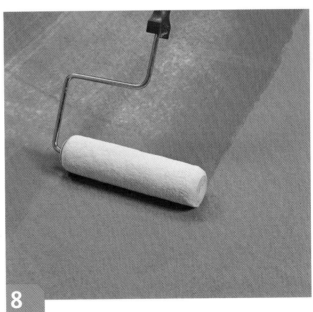

8

APPLY SECOND COAT AND SEAL

Let the first stain coat dry completely, then apply a second coat. Let this coat dry, then neutralize the acid with a mixture of water and ammonia. Let the stain dry completely, then seal the floor.

10

CONCRETE

RESOURCES

T=Top, C=Center, B=Bottom,
L=Left, R=Right

Armstrong World Industries
2500 Columbia Avenue
Lancaster, PA 17603
www.armstrong.com
18T, 24L, 24R, 25T, 27TL, 27B

Daltile
800-933-8453
www.daltileproducts.com
26TR, 28R, 32BL

DuPont
877-438-6824
www.flooring.dupont.com
22TR, 23B

Mohawk
Mohawk makes the room
Carpet • Hardwood • Ceramic • Laminate • Rugs
800-2-MOHAWK
www.mohawkflooring.com
38CR

Nourison USA
800-223-1110
www.nourison.com
39T

Shaw Industries, Inc.
800-441-7429
www.shawfloors.com
37B, 38TL, 39BR

INDEX

INDEX

Timothy Dunkowski
Clarence, NY

John S. Joyce
Canton, MA

Cathy Rogers
Atlanta, GA

Denyse M. Ferguson
Atlanta, GA

Michael Kennedy
Warwick, RI

Robert R. TerVeen
Phoenix, AZ

Many thanks to
the employees of
The Home Depot® whose
"wisdom of the aisles"
has made *Flooring 1-2-3*™
the most useful
book of its kind.

Sandy Golay
Mesa, AZ

Calvin Vande Kolk
Grand Chute, WI

Bill H. Grimm
Mesa, AZ

Rob Laplante
Mesa, AZ

Michael Wasserman
Canton, MA

Robert Guth
Fairfield, CT

Mark E. Nichols
Concord, NH

Ilana Wollin
Atlanta, GA

John Lee Johnson
Phoenix, AZ

Jerry Pederson
Mesa, AZ

Tom Sattler
Atlanta, GA

DPT0140_0406